Judy Colbert

FUN PLACES
to Go with
Children in

Washington, D.C.
COMPLETELY REVISED AND EXPANDED

CHRONICLE BOOKS
SAN FRANCISCO

Printed in the United States of America.

Library of Congress Cataloging-in-Publication Data available.

ISBN 0-8118-1940-X

Cover design: Anne Galperin
Book design and illustration: Karen Smidth
Composition: Words & Deeds
Maps on pages 22, 108, and 132: Ellen McElhinny
Map on page 12: courtesy of the Washington Metropolitan Area Transit Authority
Cover photograph: © Everett C. Johnson

Distributed in Canada by Raincoast Books,
8680 Cambie Street, Vancouver, B.C. V6P 6M9

10 9 8 7 6 5 4 3 2 1

Chronicle Books
85 Second Street
San Francisco, CA 94105

Web Site: www.chroniclebooks.com

Contents

Dedicated, with love and joy, to Arlene and Jazzlyn.

Introduction

WELCOME TO THE THIRD EDITION of *Fun Places to Go with Children in Washington, D.C.* You are joining some 20 million people who come to discover the beauty and history of this area every year. *Fun Places to Go with Children in Washington, D.C.* will help you select those sights that widen the eyes, quicken the pulse, stimulate the senses, inspire the imagination, stir the heart, raise goose bumps, fire up patriotism, and gladden the soul. Everything is here, from airplanes to zoos.

This edition adds new sites in Washington, updates old familiar sites, and, where possible, includes Web sites for the places you'll want to visit. Previous editions mentioned age groups most appropriate for each place or activity, and this information is now highlighted in bold type so you can easily determine how suitable a destination is for your children. Emphasis is placed on details of interest to specific age groups, from pre-school to high school, and (shh . . .) what's educational about them. A dollhouse collection is a dollhouse collection, but it's also a lesson in architecture. If you and your child learn something, how serendipitous. I love to see noses pressed up against the display case, eyes wide in amaze-ment, a passion growing to find out more about something, whether it's science, history, art, or geography.

Entries also provide answers to some of the tricky little questions children expect you to know. Why are those columns in the middle of the arboretum? Why can you hear whispers in Statuary Hall at the Capitol? If I can see the top of the Washington Monument from the gallery at the Washington National Cathedral, is the cathedral taller than the monument?

As one local bank used to advertise, this is the most important city in the world. It may well be, but it also is a living city, populated by people going about their everyday lives. What differentiates you from them is your perspective and the city's design. The layout may perplex you at first, but you will soon realize that the city's large and small parks were designed to keep confusion at bay. Look at the Mall, with its wall of museums and galleries and rows of trees, that keeps Washington, the city, outside the perimeters of Washington, the tourist attraction. These barriers create a quiet sanctuary from the city's noise and protect you from the bustle of the outside world—at least, once you've found a parking place. (You'll be wise to use public transportation, such as the subway system, as much as possible.) That same serenity can be found in Rock Creek Park, the National Arboretum, Kenilworth Aquatic Gardens, and many regional parks in Virginia and Maryland.

Another advantage to Washington's spaces is that, theoretically, alcoholic beverages are not permitted at Lafayette, Farragut, or McPherson squares, the Mall, or at Hains Point, Dupont Circle, and Logan Circle. You should be able to plan a picnic lunch at these public places and not expose your children to others consuming such liquids.

There is so much to see and do, and your energy, attention span, and time are so finite, that it's important to plan your own design of what you want to do. Create your own barrier: inside that wall, decide what you and your children want to do. Let the children help, making sure you're not planning too many activities. Lines will be longer than you expected. You'll want to spend more time than you allocated at some place. It will rain the day you schedule the zoo visit. It will be hotter, or you'll have to walk farther than you anticipated. A carefully detailed, hourly agenda will go down the tubes. Besides that, tempers will flare, and your trip memories will not be pleasant. Be flexible. If you end up with an extra half day, use that time to relax in one of the parks, or have a standby place to visit.

An ideal sightseeing trip considers the geography of the places you'll visit. Save energy by seeing all of the Capitol Hill buildings together, then the buildings on the Mall, in sequence. Don't go from the Library of Congress to the National Zoo, back to the National Air and Space Museum, to Arlington National Cemetery, and then to the National Cathedral. You'll spend too much time in transit.

Be aware that complications are possible. If you want to play with the tarantulas at the Museum of Natural History or watch the sharks being fed at the National Aquarium, you have to bend to their schedule, even if the perfect plan says you should be at the National Archives at that moment. And if you want to save two hours of waiting time, you have to be at the Bureau of Printing and Engraving first thing in the morning. The secret is good planning to avoid disappointment.

My touring philosophy comes from years of sightseeing with children and my first visit to France. I have two very vivid memories of that trip.

The first is of the tour guide pushing, pushing, pushing, telling us we were in France for only a short time and had much to see, for who knew when we would return? Also, the guide said we would not remember our fatigue. Baloney. I may not feel the exhaustion any more, but I remember it. I do not recall much of what we saw because things started blurring together. My second distinct mental keepsake is of schoolchildren sitting at the feet of a docent in the Hall of Mirrors in the Palace at Versailles. They were learning about their history, in French, of course, and I thought how wonderful and amazing that they can do this—speak French at that age and be able to visit this historic place in their backyard, a place that people come to see from all over the world. It then occurred to me that everyone who visits Washington is able to do the same. How basic, but how astounding!

That bank advertisement may have overstated the case to say Washington is the most important city in the world, but it certainly is one of the most beautiful, most exciting, and most interesting. Enjoy yourself!

Before You Visit

Now, let's get to the nitty-gritty. First, you should write to the tourism bureau for the area you will be visiting, as much ahead of your visit as possible. Their addresses and phone numbers are at the end of this section. They will send information about hotels, restaurants, shopping, special events, and other timely information.

If you want a VIP tour of the White House, passes into the House or Senate galleries, foreign policy briefings in the Department of State, the FBI tour, the Kennedy Center tour, or if you want to buy a flag flown over the Capitol (which will include a letter from the architect of the Capitol with the date the flag was flown over the building), then write to your congressional representative at his or her specific office building. (The House of Representatives ZIP code is 20515, the Senate ZIP code is 20510.) Call the congressional switchboard at (202) 224-3121 for address and telephone information. Or look on the Web: http://www.house.gov or http://www.senate.gov.

For all these activities, write at least one month in advance (three months is better; and six months is not too early for some passes), and mention when you'll be visiting, how many will be in your party, and what you want to do. Once you arrive, visit your representative and sign the guest book. If there's time, you may be able to have your photo taken with your representative or senator on the Capitol steps.

Once you're in town, stop by the Washington Visitor Information Center (the address is at the end of this section) to pick up additional free brochures, maps, and advice. Many of these materials are available in foreign languages.

There are several "Dial" numbers that will give you current information on a variety of subjects. Most of these places also have Web sites now, so you can find out what will be happening when you're here ahead of time. Among the most popular are: Dial-An-Event (202) 789-7000 for a recording of major events; Sierra Club Activities (202) 547-2326 or http://webmentor.com/mwrop/index.html; Dial-A-Park (202) 619-PARK (619-7275) for National Park Service schedules or http://www.nps.gov/ncro/; Dial-A-Museum (202) 357-2020 (English) or (202) 633-9126 (Spanish), for Smithsonian Institution activities http://www.si.edu/newstart.htm.; and Skywatchers' Report (202) 357-2000 for announcements on the planets, stars, and worldwide celestial occurrences.

There are four telephone exchanges in the Washington area: (202) for Washington, (703) for suburban Virginia, and (301) and (240) for suburban Maryland. To call from one region to another (i.e., from Washington to Virginia), you need to use the area code, but you do not need to precede it with 1. These are toll-free numbers within the Washington suburban area. You must also dial the Maryland area code even if you're calling within the same Maryland suburban area. Other calls, such as from Washington to Baltimore, or from Maryland to some Virginia locations, will need the 1 and there will be a toll charge. The Baltimore, northeastern Maryland, and Eastern Shore of Maryland area codes are (410) and (443). Yes, this sounds confusing, but you'll work it out eventually.

When you look at a map of Washington you'll note it is divided into four sections: Northwest (NW), Northeast (NE), Southeast (SE), and Southwest (SW). The Northwest section is the largest. The dividing lines set out from the Capitol, so north of East Capitol Street is Northeast, and south of it is Southeast. Streets running north and south are numbered, starting at the Capitol. Those running east and west are lettered and run alphabetically with a single letter (I Street often is spelled out "Eye" Street, and there isn't a J Street in the northwest quadrant), followed by two-syllable words, followed by three-syllable words, and so on. Irving Street will be in the second alphabet, Brandywine in the third. The diagonal roadways are avenues and are named for states. They create the circles and the most confusion for visitors.

Many museums and galleries in the Washington area are open all year, except December 25. Some also are closed on Thanksgiving and New Year's Day. Others are closed on major holidays, or, as they're generally known in this area, federal holidays. These are Martin Luther King Day, President's Day, Memorial Day, Fourth of July, Labor Day, Columbus Day, and Veterans Day. This book's listings will note closures on these holidays.

Metrorail and Metrobus are the easiest ways to travel. Most major museums and many galleries are within easy walking distance from Metrorail stops, eliminating the need to drive, look for a parking place, feed the meter, and make sure you're out of the space by rush hour. After a day of sightseeing and walking, it's nice to be able to relax on the subway before tackling the roads. For detailed, door-to-door instructions on which bus or subway to take and when, call the Metro office at (202) 637-7000 daily between 6 A.M. and 11:30 P.M. Subway lines are referred to by their colors (red, blue, orange, yellow, green), which are keyed to destinations. For example, the orange line goes to New Carrollton (Maryland) and Vienna (Virginia). You can transfer from one line to another without extra charge. See the lobby of each station for specific directions, write to the Washington Metropolitan Area Transit Authority (WMATA), 600 Fifth Street, NW, Washington, D.C. 20001, or check the Web site: http://www.wmata.com.

The subway runs from 5:30 A.M. to midnight weekdays, 8 A.M. to midnight Saturday and Sunday, with extended hours for such special events as the Fourth of July fireworks celebration on the Mall. Rush hours are 5:30 to 9:30 A.M. and 3 to 8 P.M., and rates, which are based on distance traveled, are higher during these hours. Each station posts the last-train departure time for that station. A third automobile rush hour is developing downtown during the lunch hour, but this is not reflected in the subway fares.

You need a Farecard to use the Metro (both to enter and exit the system) and these can be purchased at any station. Up to two children (age 4 and under), traveling with a paying passenger, can ride free. Fares range from $1.10 to $3.15, depending on the time of day and length of travel. If you will be traveling extensively on the system during any one day, going from one station to another, then you will benefit from the $5 one-day pass which allows you to travel all day, starting at 9:30 A.M. on weekdays and all day on Saturday, Sunday, and federal holidays, getting on and off at as many stations as you want. Buy these passes at Metro sales offices; most Giant, Safeway, and SuperFresh supermarkets; commuter centers at Ballston, Crystal City, Rosslyn, and White Flint; and in most Metro stations. Parking is free on Saturday in Metro-operated lots.

Farecard machines, located in every station, accept nickels, dimes, quarters, $1, $5, $10, and $20 bills. There are no change machines in the

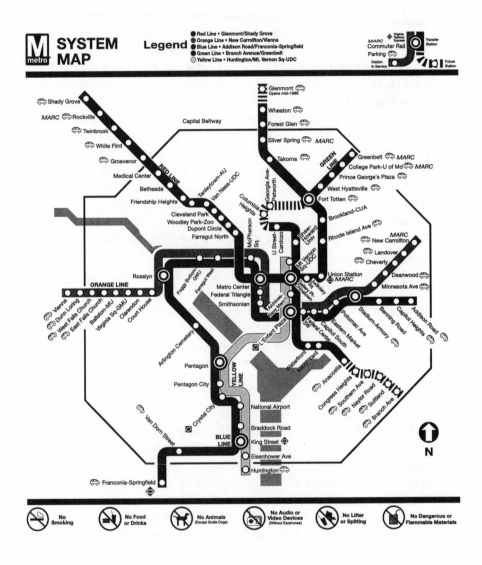

stations (although Farecard machines do give coin change up to $4.95). For convenience, purchase sufficient fare for a round trip. When you buy a Farecard for $10–$19.95, you receive a 5 percent bonus value.

You are not allowed to eat or drink on the bus or the subway. Headphones should be used for portable radios. In April 1994, Metro became the nation's first subway system to enable passengers to use Bell Atlantic cellular phones while in certain underground trains and stations. The service will be expanding.

Every station is accessible by elevator. Floor lights along the tracks flash on and off when a train is entering the station to alert the hearing impaired, and a tone sounds when doors are about to open or close to aid the visually impaired. Incidentally, the bing-bong alerting you to the closing doors is first E above high C, then C. It has been known to bring visiting students to a complete silence, for those are the notes often used to bring classrooms to attention.

Wheelchair space is designated on the train, but remember all space is at a premium during rush hour. Reduced fares are available for handicapped and senior citizens.

Metro has expanded the hours that bikes are allowed on trains. Previously, they were allowed all day on weekends and some holidays, and after 7 P.M. daily. Now, bikers are allowed on subway cars from 10 A.M. to 2 P.M. daily as well. You still need a photo permit, for which you have to take a written test. They cost $15 and are good for three years. Bike lockers are available at some Metro stations for $70 for a year's rent, $45 for six months, plus a key deposit. Call (202) 962-1116 for Bike-on-Rail program information.

Metrorail offers an added bonus: Many children have never been on a train before, so this system can be a good introduction to rail travel. Also, some of the world's longest escalators are in the Wheaton, Forest Glen, and Dupont Circle stations.

To travel on Metrobus ($1.10 in Maryland and Washington; the fare is based on zones in Virginia) you must have exact change. Operators do not carry cash and cannot make change.

Once downtown, you can take the Tourmobile, the Old Town Trolley, or the Lil Red Trolley to get from one sightseeing spot to another. On each, you will hear a narrated tour and be able to disembark at any stop to shop, sightsee, or eat, and reboard later at no extra charge. These services run about every 20 or 30 minutes.

In the summer, the Museum Bus, sponsored by the Cultural Alliance, provides shuttle transportation to 23 of Washington's finest museums and attractions. The bus runs seven days a week, from 10 A.M. to 5 P.M.

Membership at some museums also includes free transportation on the Museum Bus. Otherwise, there's a $5 charge (passes can be purchased at many hotels and participating museums), and the price includes free admission to museums that charge an entrance fee and a 10 percent discount in museum shops and cafes.

The Tourmobile runs from 9 A.M. to 6:30 P.M. June 15 to Labor Day and 9:30 A.M. to 4:30 P.M. the rest of the year. Purchase tickets from the ticket booth at Arlington National Cemetery or from the driver. Fares are $12 for adults and $6 for children ages 3 to 11. A "preview" (also $12/$6) ticket can be purchased after 2 P.M. and is good for sightseeing that afternoon and all the next day. Because the Tourmobile is licensed by the National Park Service, it is by far the most reliable and easiest to use. The stops are well-marked and the vehicles carry more passengers than the other services. For information, call (202) 554-5100 (recording). http://www.tourmobile.com.

There are 18 stops on the 90-minute (or longer) Tourmobile ride, with options for going to Mount Vernon, the FDR Memorial, and the Frederick Douglass home (depending on the season).

Summer trips to Mount Vernon leave from Arlington National Cemetery, and the Lincoln and Washington memorials, at 10 A.M., noon, and 2 P.M. The four-hour tour is $20 for adults and $10 for children. Reservations must be made at least 30 minutes prior to departure.

Summer trips to the Frederick Douglass House leave from Arlington National Cemetery and the Lincoln and Washington memorials at noon. The price is $6 and $3; reservations must be made at least 30 minutes prior to departure.

Tours of Arlington Cemetery are included in the regular trip, or you may purchase a separate tour of the cemetery for $4 and $2, departing every 20 minutes, from 8:30 A.M. to 6:30 P.M. The Tourmobile stops at the Kennedy grave site, the Tomb of the Unknowns, and Arlington House.

The Tourmobile stops at the Washington Monument (Fifteenth Street, NW), Arts and Industries, National Air and Space Museum, Union Station, United States Capitol (First Street and Independence Avenue, SE), National Gallery of Art, Museum of Natural History, National Museum of American History, Bureau of Engraving and Printing, Jefferson Memorial (and Tidal Basin), West Potomac Park, Lincoln Memorial (and Vietnam Veterans Memorial), John F. Kennedy Center for the Performing Arts, the White House (on the south side near Fifteenth and E Streets, NW), and Arlington National Cemetery.

Old Town Trolley Tours offer an enjoyable ride around town in an old-fashioned open-sided orange-and-green trolley car. The two-and-a-half-hour tour makes 18 stops throughout the city, including the Pavilion at the Old Post Office Building; Union Station; Museum of Woman and Arts; Chinatown and the MCI Center; the FBI Building and Ford's Theatre; Freedom Plaza and National Aquarium; White House, Lafayette Square, and Decatur House; National Geographic; the Dupont Circle neighborhood; Kalorama, the Adams Morgan neighborhood, and the National Zoo; National Cathedral; Georgetown; the Lincoln, Vietnam, and Korean memorials; the Air and Space Museum; U.S. Capitol and the Library of Congress.

Trolleys run from 9 A.M. to 4 P.M. Labor Day to Memorial Day and 9 A.M. to 8 P.M. Memorial Day to Labor Day. The price is $20 for adults and $11 for children (ages 4-12). Night tours are available for $24 and $13. Call (202) 832-9800 for information.

The Gold Line/Gray Line sightseeing company has a "Lil Red Trolley," offering a two-hour tour through the city with stops at Union Station, Capitol Hill, National Zoo, Washington National Cathedral, U.S. Navy Memorial, Ford's Theatre, the FBI building, Planet Hollywood, the Old Post Office Pavilion, the Lincoln and Vietnam memorials, the Bureau of Engraving and Printing, the U.S. Holocaust Memorial Museum, the National Air and Space Museum, and Hogate's Restaurant on the southwest waterfront. The Trolley runs from 8:30 A.M. to 6:30 P.M. during the summer. The adult fare is $18 and for children $9 (ages 3 to 11), with all-day on-and-off privileges. Call (202) 289-1995 or (800) 862-1400 for information.

The newest spring-to-fall sightseeing service in Washington is called D.C. Ducks, a group of World War II amphibious carriers that have been converted to sightseeing vehicles. The 90-minute tour covers much the same area as the other services, but you're higher up, giving you a different perspective, over the tops of most vehicles and people. Also, the Duck goes motoring down the Potomac River for about a half hour to the National Airport area. You're allowed to take the wheel, if you wish, even if you're visually impaired and have never held a steering wheel in your life. There are no stops or off-and-on privileges. D.C. Ducks is $23 for adults and $12 for children. Call (202) 832-9800.

Still another way to tour the city is via Bike the Sites Tours, professionally guided tours that lead you on a two-wheeled leisurely visit to Washington's most spectacular and favorite sites. Instead of seeing things from a bus or riding past sites inaccessible by bus, you are right there, able to take pictures (do bring your camera), and get some exercise at the same time. The company provides each rider with a 21-speed Trek Hybrid bike, helmet, handlebar bag, water, a snack, and two guides for a maximum of 15 participants. The basic three-hour, ten-mile tour is mostly flat, with two short hills, on paved and gravel trails. There is an optional residential Georgetown and Embassy Row tour that's another three miles. You should be in relatively good health, but the guides are licensed and trained in CPR and first aid. Reservations (with a list of all individuals and their height) are required. Children ages 9 through 14 must be accompanied by an adult. Children ages 15 and up may ride unaccompanied, but must have a waiver signed by a parent or legal guardian. The three-hour tour is $35.

Bike the Sites also offers an early bird one-hour fun ride, a three-hour ride that's mostly on trails; a Mount Vernon 17-mile ride, day trips to Civil War battlegrounds, and custom rides. Contact Bike the Sites, Inc., 3417 Quesada Street, NW, Washington, D.C. 20015-2508; (202) 966-8662 or send e-mail to bikesites@aol.com.

Still one more way to see the city, this time from a distance, is on a boat cruise. Depending on the season, you might do something as simple as a boat taxi or as elegant as the *Odyssey* cruise. This ride up the Potomac (if the tide is high enough, which is most of the time) takes you past the Awakening statue up to the Kennedy Center area. Brunch, lunch, and dinner cruises are available, each with live music. Catch the boat at the Gangplank Marina in SW Washington. Reservations are suggested. (202) 488-6000. http://www.odyssey-cruises.com.

BECAUSE THERE'S NO ONE WAY to organize a guidebook to sites in and around Washington, I've chosen to assemble this book by geographic areas: Capitol Hill, the National Mall, the Northwest, the Southwest, the Southeast, the Northeast, Maryland, and Virginia. Note, however, that I've included the Tidal Basin, Jefferson Memorial, East Potomac Park (Hains Point), the National Archives, and the Bureau of Engraving and Printing in the Mall section because the continuous green space and memorials go together.

In addition to the book's index, there is a separate A to Z listing that groups destinations by category, from A (as in airplane) to Z (as in zoo). This should be helpful if you just want to visit gardens or are looking for an ice-skating rink.

Almost all museums, galleries, and historic tourist spots in the Washington area close by 5 or 6 P.M. In the summer of 1997, the

Smithsonian started a summer "Art Night on the Mall" and kept the Sackler, Freer, Hirshhorn, and African Art galleries and the Ripley Center open until 8 P.M. Yet there are plenty of things to do in the evening. During the summer, for example, there are free public band concerts every night of the week, weather permitting. The Lincoln and Jefferson memorials and the Washington Monument are open until midnight, so you might do the museums during the day and the memorials at night. In the evening, the memorials are beautifully illuminated, the lines or crowds are smaller, and the temperature is cooler—a definite benefit in the summer.

Many museums, galleries, and other institutions offer memberships. These usually include a regular publication listing upcoming events, discounts in the gift shop, discounts on admissions and programs, and other benefits. If you're visiting and plan to buy a number of items from a particular gift shop, or if you're a local resident and will be visiting one of these institutions frequently, it's probably advantageous to join. Throughout this guidebook, descriptions of institutions will note if a membership is available, but won't detail the benefits.

Virtually all public buildings in the Washington area are wheelchair accessible. Where there is a problem, such as at the galleries around Dupont Circle, call in advance for assistance. Other buildings that are not wheelchair accessible are noted in the descriptive text.

Braille maps of the Capitol and the Mall can be picked up at the Sergeant-at-Arms Special Services Office in the crypt of the Capitol, at the Capitol Guide Service desk at the Rotunda, or from the Capitol Police at all public entrances to congressional office buildings. Free Metrorail maps for the visually impaired are available from the Services Office, Columbia Lighthouse for the Blind, 1421 P Street, NW, Washington, D.C. 20071; (202) 462-2900.

Washington combines the charm of a small southern town with the perils of a major metropolitan area. It is not a hellhole, but you should take normal precautions. Lock your car, secure your belongings (don't bring anything you wouldn't want to lose in the first place), and be careful about where you go, particularly at night. Be cautious traveling alone at night or on bikepaths.

Although the prices given in this book were accurate at press time, they are, of course, subject to change. The price quoted indicates that admission is in the neighborhood of $1 or $5, and any increase should still be within that range. Be sure any students in your group carry student identification cards. Although most places with admission fees have reduced prices for children, some also have lower fees for students with proper credentials.

Also, remember tour times can change. They may vary with the season, the demand, and with the number of personnel or docents available to conduct tours. Call ahead if you want a guided tour, call first to confirm the times. Even then, double check the times with the information desk when you enter a museum or gallery.

● Lost and Found

Unfortunately, in each life at some time, there is a lost item. Should you or your child separate from a beloved stuffed animal, boots, gloves, keys, a ring, scarf, umbrella, wallet, or other possession, there is a chance it has been found and turned into a lost-and-found department. Most places have piles of unclaimed objects. If you think you know where you lost the item, give a call.

MARYLAND
USAirways Arena (301) 350-3400, ext. 1480.

VIRGINIA
National and Dulles airports (703) 417-8034.
Travelers Aid, National Airport (703) 417-3972; Dulles Airport (703) 661-8636.
Patriot Center (703) 993-3000, ext. 0.

WASHINGTON
Amtrak (202) 906-3109.
D.C. Metropolitan Police (202) 727-1010; ask for phone numbers of precincts, to determine if your item is listed in the property book.
D.C. Taxicab Commission (202) 645-6010.
Ford's Theatre (202) 426-6924.
Greyhound (202) 289-5120 or 289-5121; ask for the tracing and claims clerk during business hours.
Kennedy Center (202) 416-7900.
Metro Bus and Rail (202) 962-1195.
National Theatre (202) 628-6161.
National Zoological Park (202) 673-4731.
Smithsonian Institution: Write with a full description to: Lost and Found, 1000 Jefferson Drive SW, B-68 MRC3, Washington, D.C. 20560.
Union Station (202) 289-8355.
U.S. Park Police (202) 426-6849.

ONE MORE WORD OF ADVICE. Public restrooms are scarce in Washington. In museums they are more or less busy according to scheduled events, such as when the crowd exits from the IMAX movie at the Air and Space Museum. There are no public toilets in the White House or in the Washington Monument. You don't want to wait in line for two hours to discover your youngster has a nature call that there's no way to answer. In other words, use the facilities whenever you can and watch the schedules so you'll know when to get in line before the movie ends. When asking for directions, don't always ask for the nearest restroom because it may also be the busiest. A more distant room may have no line at all and be perfectly clean and well-stocked.

● Tourism Bureaus

The following are the addresses and phone numbers for bureaus in the jurisdictions around the Washington area. Some are included even though there are no specific sights mentioned from that region. They will help you locate lodgings and other attractions, such as those in the alphabetical Things to Do from A to Z list.

WASHINGTON, D.C.

Washington Convention and Visitors Association, 1212 New York Avenue, NW 20005. (202) 789-7000. http://www.washington.org.

MARYLAND

For those bureaus below that don't yet have a Web site, check http://www.inform.umd.edu/UMS+State/MD_Resources/Cities/.

Tourism Council of Annapolis and Anne Arundel, 26 West Street, Annapolis 21401. (410) 280-0445, (410) 268-TOUR. http://www.visit-annapolis.org.

Baltimore Area Convention and Visitors Association, U.S.F.& G. Tower, 100 Light Street, 12th Floor, Baltimore 21202. (410) 659-7300, (800) 343-3468. http://www.baltconvstr.com.

Baltimore City Office of Promotion (for special events), 200 West Lombard Street, Baltimore 21202. (410) 752-8632.

Baltimore County Office of Promotion and Tourism, 23 West Chesapeake Avenue, Towson 21204. (410) 887-8000 or (410) 533-7313.

Charles County Tourism, Star Route 1, Box 1144, Port Tobacco 20677. (301) 934-9305.

Calvert County Tourism Director, Department of Economic Development, Courthouse, Prince Frederick 20678. (301) 535-4583, (301) 855-1880. http://www.co.cal.md.us.

Tourism Council of Frederick County, Inc., 19 East Church Street, Frederick 21701. (301) 663-8687. http://www.co.frederick.md.us/tour/tourpage.html.

Howard County Tourism Council, Box 9, Ellicott City 21043. (410) 313-1904.

Conference and Visitors Bureau of Montgomery County, Inc., 12900 Middlebrook Road, Suite 1400, Germantown 20874-2616. (301) 428-9702, (800) 925-0880.

Prince George's Travel Promotion Council, Inc., 9475 Lottsford Road, Suite 130, Landover 20875. (301) 925-8300.

Worcester County Tourism, 105 Pearl Street, Snow Hill 21863. (410) 632-3617. Or Ocean City Visitors and Convention Bureau, Inc., P.O. Box 116, Ocean City 21842. (410) 289-8181. http://www.oceancity.com.

VIRGINIA

Alexandria Convention and Visitors Center (Ramsey House Visitors Center), 221 King Street, Alexandria 22314. (703) 838-4200. http://www.virginia.org.

Arlington Visitors Center, 735 South Eighteenth Street, Arlington 22202. (703) 358-5720. http://www.virginia.org.

Fairfax County Tourism and Convention Bureau, 8300 Boone Boulevard, Suite 450, Tysons Corner, 22182. (703) 790-3329. http://www.visitfairfax.org.

Loudoun County Tourist Information Center, Market Station, Leesburg 22075. (703) 777-0519, (800) 752-6118. http://www.virginia.org.

Prince William County-Manassas Tourist Information Center, 4349 Ridgewood Center Drive, Prince William 22192-5308. (703) 792-6680, (800) 334-9876, (703) 631-1480 (Washington, D.C. line). http://www.co.prince-william.va.us.

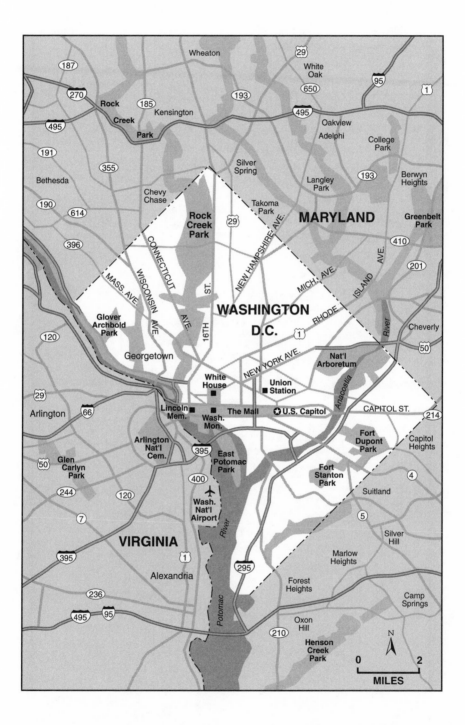

Capitol Hill

● **United States Capitol**

East end of the Mall on Capitol Hill. (202) 224-3121 (Capitol office number). Open daily 9 A.M. to 3:45 P.M. in winter, until 8 P.M. in summer. Closed Thanksgiving, December 25, and New Year's Day. Guided tours are given Monday through Saturday, daily from 9 A.M. to 3:45 P.M.; call (202) 225-6827 for information. Capitol South or Union Station subway station. Tourmobile stop (First Street and Independence Avenue, SE). http://www.house.gov or http://www.senate.gov. Children under age 5 are not permitted in the galleries. **Ages 5 and up.**

Tours, lasting 45 minutes or longer during the off-season, shorter during the peak season, are given about every 15 minutes in the winter and every 5 minutes in the summer. They start in the Rotunda, beneath the white-paint-over-iron Capitol dome, and include Statuary Hall (where whispers can be heard from one side of the room to the other because of the arched ceilings), the restored old Senate and Supreme Court chambers (note that the statue of Blind Justice does not have a blindfold), the crypt area, and the Brumidi corridors in the Senate Wing (Constantino Brumidi spent twenty-five years creating some of the most impressive decorative art in this building).

If you neglected to write in advance to your congressional representative or senator for tickets to the chamber galleries (see Introduction), stop by his or her office to see if any are available. Individual offices of representatives are on the right-hand (south) side of the Capitol as you face it from the Mall. Senate offices are on the left (north). The Senate and House offices are connected to the Capitol by an underground subway system, which you can ride during regular tour hours.

Foreign visitors who want tickets should apply to the office of the sergeant at arms of the Senate or the doorkeeper of the House. Committee meetings, which are listed in the daily newspaper, need no passes if they are described as open hearings.

You can tell when Congress is meeting because a flag flies over the House (when it's in session) and over the Senate (when it's in session), and a light illuminates the Goddess of Freedom statue on top of the Capitol.

The U.S. Army, Navy, Air Force, and Marine Corps bands give free concerts from June through August on the west terrace of the Capitol. They perform weeknights (except Thursday) at 8 P.M. Spectators sit on the steps.

The west lawn of the Capitol is ideal for viewing the entire Mall. Toward the left side (northwest corner) of the lawn is the sunken grotto, which is a good stop on a pleasant day. Hidden among trees and bushes, it has benches and water fountains and a mossy cave with water spraying over the rocks.

Near the statue of Ulysses S. Grant, Central Photos will take a panoramic photograph of your group, with the Capitol in the background, on a Kodak Cirkut camera that is at least 50 years old. Because of the mechanism that operates this camera, someone can stand on one end of the group upon which the lens is first trained, and then, as the shot commences, run quickly to the other end of the group where the panoramic sweep ends. Children particularly enjoy the fact that one person can be in the same picture twice. The cost is $7 for each black-and-white photo and $11 for each color photo. Usually Central Photos requires a minimum of ten people, but they will take your picture if your group is smaller. You must, however, buy a minimum of ten pictures. The photographer is at the statue from 9 A.M. to 3 P.M. Monday through Saturday, from mid-March to mid- or late-June (the busy group season in Washington). It's best to call (202) 544-6065 for an appointment; photos can be taken any time of the year.

The Ulysses S. Grant Memorial, dedicated to the soldiers who fought in the Civil War, is great for climbing.

On the east side of the Capitol you can usually catch a television camera crew doing a "stand-up" report for the evening news.

There is a public cafeteria on the Senate side where you can try the famous bean soup ($1). It's open from 7:30 A.M. to 3 P.M., but the public is restricted between noon and 1:30 P.M.

● Library of Congress

10 First Street, SE (First and East Capitol Streets), (202) 707-5000 (recording about general information). (202) 707-8000 (recording about exhibitions). (202) 707-5458 (tour information). The various libraries and

library reading rooms within the Library of Congress have different hours of operation, but generally are open Monday, Wednesday, and Thursday from 8:30 A.M. to 9:30 P.M.; Tuesday, Friday, and Saturday from 8:30 A.M. to 5 P.M. Closed on Sunday, December 25, and New Year's Day. Request a copy of "Public Services in the Library of Congress" from the National Reference Service, Library of Congress, Washington, D.C. 20540, for a description of the various public services available. Thirty-minute guided tours are given at 11:30 A.M., 1, 2:30, and 4 P.M. Tours are given daily, starting in the Thomas Jefferson Building (101 Independence Avenue, SE). A sign language interpreter is available for the Tuesday 10 A.M. and Thursday 1 P.M. tours. Capitol South subway station. Food service. http://lcweb.loc.gov.
Ages 6 and up.

Also at the Library of Congress is the Children's Literature Center (202) 707-5535, designed for students of children's literature (ages 18 and over), and you can pick up (or have mailed to you) a parents' guide of recommended books and reading lists for children. The Children's Literature Center is open Monday through Friday, from 8:30 A.M. to 4:30 P.M.; closed Saturday and Sunday.

The images of millions of items are being transferred to the Library's Web site, including presidential letters, Walt Whitman's notebooks, pamphlets by Frederick Douglass and Booker T. Washington, and Civil War photographs by Mathew Brady.

The three buildings in this complex—the James Madison, the Thomas Jefferson, and the John Adams—hold the largest library collection in the world. Contrary to popular belief, however, the library does not house a copy of every book that's ever been printed, not even every book that's been printed in English or in the United States. It does contain one of the three remaining copies of the Gutenberg vellum Bibles (1455), 575 miles of bookshelves, and 90,500,000 items in a collection that grows daily. According to library estimates, 26 million books, 10 million prints and photos, and 80,000 films are stored here. For ten years, the Thomas Jefferson building has undergone extensive renovations and improvements. New are a visitor center; a 90-seat theater with a movie about the library; an expanded sales shop; special rooms displaying the collections of Ralph Ellison, Woodrow Wilson, and Oliver Wendell Holmes; a performing arts gallery; and a room honoring the contributions to American music of George and Ira Gerswhin. Special exhibits in the Madison and Jefferson buildings rotate over time, and they can be viewed at http://www.loc.gov/exhibits.

Special Library of Congress tours can be tailored to children if you let guides know you're coming. Children like the atrium with its trees, the Maps Division, and a small fourth-floor exhibit about copyrights that includes some Disney characters and the first Barbie and Ken dolls. The exhibit is open 8:30 A.M. to 5 P.M. weekdays. A 20-minute film on the scope and size of the collection is shown every half hour in Room 139 of the Madison Building.

There are some extraordinary collections in the Library, such as the Music Division with its 1,500 hundred flutes and five Stradivarius violins, the Houdini papers, the Asian Division, and the European Room, which claims the largest library of Russian books in the West. But these are open only to scholars; your older children may qualify if they are doing a research project on one of these subjects. The American Treasures of the Library of Congress is a permanent exhibit displaying 150 of the rarest and most significant items relating to America's past. Free same-day tickets are available in the Jefferson Building, (202) 707-3834.

Free concerts are presented about twice a month, usually on Thursday and Friday nights from October through December and from February through April. These 90-minute chamber music concerts are first-come, first-served and start at 8 P.M. They are performed by the Juilliard String Quartet and the Beaux Arts Trio, both artists-groups in residence. Call (202) 707-5502 (recording) for information.

● Supreme Court of the United States

1 First Street, NE. (202) 479-3000. Open Monday through Friday 9:30 A.M. to 3:30 P.M. Closed weekends and federal holidays. When the Court is not in session, courtroom lectures, covering the history and functions of the Court and defining an oral argument, are presented every hour on the half hour from 9:30 A.M. to 3:30 P.M. Cafeteria hours are 7:15 to 10:30 A.M., 11:30 A.M. to 2 P.M. Snack Bar hours are 10:30 A.M. to 3:30 P.M. Capitol South or Union Station subway station. **Ages 6 and up.**

The highest court in the land is open to the public on a limited basis. Because most people only see the Court as nine robed justices who hand down decisions on the Constitution during television coverage, a personal visit is impressive. The Court hears oral arguments at 10 A.M., 11 A.M., 1 P.M., and 2 P.M. on Monday, Tuesday, and Wednesday for approximately two weeks of each month starting the first Monday in October and continuing through April. During May and June, the Court convenes at 10 A.M. to deliver opinions.

There are no regular guided tours, but you may tour the building on your own. When the Court is in session, there are two lines to enter the courtroom. One line is for people who want to sit through all or part of the entire session. The sessions are open to the public on a first-come, first-served basis. The other queue is for a three-minute visit for those who just want to see the chambers. You can also write to your congressional representative for a special 2 P.M. weekday tour that includes the East and West Conference rooms (if they're not in use for a meeting or reception), plus a glimpse into the capacious and solemn oak-paneled law library.

A 20-minute film that details the activities of the Court is shown continuously. Rotating exhibits downstairs tell a coherent tale of the historical significance of what goes on upstairs. A Supreme Court Historical Society kiosk is on the ground floor. Take a look at the cantilevered marble spiral staircase directly across from the women's room, at the Maryland Avenue basement level. You can't walk on the steps, but you can see them.

● Folger Shakespeare Library

201 East Capitol Street, SE. (202) 544-4600 (library), (202) 544-7077 (concerts). Open Monday through Saturday 10 A.M. to 4 P.M. Closed federal holidays and on Sunday. Guided tours of the Great Hall are given from 11 A.M. to 1 P.M. Union Station or Capitol South subway station. Gift shop.
Ages 11 and up.

This multifaceted operation contains a library, the Great Hall, and the Consort. Henry Clay Folger, a late-nineteenth-century student at Amherst College in Massachusetts and one-time chairman of the board of Standard Oil Company, was the stimulus for this library and the indoor version of an outdoor playhouse. The theater is more properly called the Elizabethan Theatre, in honor of Queen Elizabeth I, who reigned during Shakespeare's lifetime, but almost everyone refers to it as the Folger Theatre.

Free docent-led guided tours of the Great Hall (all of Shakespeare's plays are named around the room) can last 15 or 30 minutes, depending on your interests. Changing exhibits are explained, and there is always a 1632 First Folio of Shakespeare's works on display.

The Folger Shakespeare Library itself is for scholarly research only, and then only for those with previously approved credentials. The Folger's Education Department programs festivals for high-school students in the spring, with sword-fighting demonstrations, slide shows, and other activities. Call to see if you can join them.

From October through May, a music series that features medieval, Renaissance, and Baroque compositions is scheduled on Saturday, Sunday, and Monday evenings, and Sunday afternoon. Many types of early instruments are played, and there's always at least one singer. On occasion, the musicians are dressed in period costumes. The Saturday and Sunday concerts are given in the Great Hall, the Monday night concert in the theater, and the December concerts are given in the Washington National Cathedral. The Sunday night concerts are preceded by a one-hour conversation with the musicians and the audience about the evening's music selections, led by local radio personality Robert Aubry Davis. The experience is accessible to almost every age. Tickets are $22, with a 10 percent discount for children and seniors.

The gift shop is strong on Renaissance souvenirs, including coloring books, children's books, games, note cards, puzzles, unicorn toys, and T-shirts.

The National Mall

THIS SECTION TAKES THE VISITOR from the east (Capitol) end of the National Mall about 1 ½ miles westward to the Lincoln Memorial.

The Mall is the stretch of green parkland that runs between Constitution and Independence Avenues. At one end is the United States Capitol, perched on a rise about 90 feet above sea level (thus the name Capitol Hill). At the other end is the Lincoln Memorial. On either side are galleries and museums and other interesting government buildings. Most, but not all, of these museums belong to the Smithsonian Institution collection. No general admission is charged at these institutions, and only occasionally is there a small fee for a specific exhibit. Periodically, a traveling exhibit will be so popular that timed-entry tickets are required; these arrangements are announced in the local papers.

Five subway stations are very convenient to the Mall, and a couple more are less convenient, depending upon which building you'll be visiting. Do not automatically go to the Smithsonian subway station, particularly if you're visiting the Botanic Gardens (Federal Center SW station is closer) or the Air and Space Museum (L'Enfant Plaza station is closer). The station nearest each sight is included in the description.

Enjoy the Mall. It is an accessible, "please touch" park. Walk on it, play Frisbee, sunbathe, or people-watch. National Park Police patrol the area on horseback and take time to talk with children. Note: alcoholic beverages are not permitted on the Mall. The Mall fills to near-capacity during the all-day festivities on the Fourth of July. Around the end of June and beginning of July, the Smithsonian holds the annual Folk Life Festival celebrating the culture, crafts, and traditions of various communities. The festival usually features one state and one country. It covers several blocks of the Mall, so you can see cooking demonstrations, dancing, native crafts, storytelling, and other activities indigenous to the areas represented.

The Mall is also home to a 1940 Allan Herschell–model carousel with 58 horses and boats. It spins its merry way and its merry tunes, weather permitting, weekdays 11 A.M. to 5 P.M., weekends 10 A.M. to 6 P.M. A three-minute ride costs only $1.25.

Generally, the Smithsonian buildings are open until 5:30 P.M. However, during the summer these times may be extended. The Smithsonian started a Thursday "Art Night on the Mall" program in the summer of 1997, with films, dance, music, and gallery tours, at the Sackler, Freer, Hirshhorn, and African Art galleries, and the Ripley Center. These buildings stayed open until 8 P.M.

Through the Smithsonian Associates programs and the summer camp, activities are scheduled for children from 4 and up, and might include building an aquarium in a two-liter soda bottle, touring the works of the Impressionists, exploring a camera, or creating a miniature ecosystem. For additional information about Smithsonian Associates offerings, call (202) 357-3030. http://www.si.edu/newstart.htm.

With one exception, we'll travel first along Independence Avenue, and then along Constitution Avenue, and we'll begin with our exception, a visit to "The Castle."

● Smithsonian Institution Building (Smithsonian Institution)

Tenth Street and Jefferson Drive. (202) 357-2700. Call daily 9 A.M. to 4 P.M. (TTY 357-1729) for all questions about various Smithsonian operations. Call (202) 786-2942 or (202) 786-2414 (TTY) for the Smithsonian's Accessibility Coordinator. Open daily 9 A.M. to 5:30 P.M. Closed Christmas Day. Walk-in highlights tours are offered on Friday at 10:15 A.M., Saturday at 10:15 and 11 A.M., and Sunday at 11 A.M. Tours are offered in Spanish the first Saturday of the month at 11 A.M. Membership available. Sunday brunch from 11 A.M. to 3 P.M. Smithsonian subway station (Mall exit). http://www.si.edu/newstart.htm. **All ages.**

For your initial or refresher course on what exhibits are in which museum, stop by The Castle, the original Smithsonian Building and now the visitor center for the institution. It opens at 9 A.M., an hour before the museums and galleries, so you have plenty of time to watch a 20-minute film (with captioning and audio loop), explore the touch-screen interactive video monitors, and talk with the information guides. Here's the place to ask what the Hope Diamond is worth, how to get to the National Zoo, or where to find a tobacco hornworm. Information is available in English, Chinese, French, German, Spanish, and Japanese. Not all the buildings along the Mall are part of the Smithsonian (such as the National

Gallery of Art), but the experts (information specialists) here can provide general information on those buildings as well as their own.

Each museum has its own schedule of activities, so ask for a calendar of events or check the *Washington Post* Friday Weekend section for a listing of upcoming adventures. A few wheelchairs and strollers should be available at each museum on a first-come, first-served basis.

Several of the museums, including the Natural History and Air and Space museums, as well as the First Ladies' dresses exhibit at the Museum of American History, offer "iGo," an interactive audio tour featuring a touch-screen computer and headphones. Instead of following a taped description of an exhibit area, you can go where you want, and then punch in a corresponding number to access the information.

The crypt for James Smithson, who left the funding for the Smithsonian, is in the front left lobby. Smithson was an English chemist and mineralogist who died in 1829 and bequeathed money to the United States "to found at Washington, D.C., under the name of Smithsonian Institution, an establishment for the increase and diffusion of knowledge. . . ." The mineral smithsonite is named for him. His body was brought over from England following his death; interestingly, he never visited this country.

In front of the north entrance to the Castle is a statue of Joseph Henry, inventor of the electric motor, father of daily weather forecasts, and the first secretary of the Smithsonian.

Over time the mission and focus of the various Smithsonian Institution museums may change. That means the displays may change. The length and frequency, and even the availability, of guided tours may change. It's wise to confirm that something is on display if that's the only reason you will be visiting a specific building.

Each museum has its own gift shop and its own theme-specific selection of merchandise. If you see something you particularly like in one museum, say Air and Space, buy it there because it most likely will not be sold in another museum.

Now, to start our Mall tour, down the Independence Avenue side.

● United States Botanic Garden

Maryland Avenue, near First Street. (202) 225-8333. Program office (202) 226-4082. Open daily 9 A.M. to 5 P.M. Closed December 25 and New Year's Day. Guided tours with advance notice. Free horticulture classes and lectures September through June. Wheelchair accessible, and a limited number of wheelchairs are available. No admission charge. Federal Center SW subway station. http://www.aoc.gov. **All ages.**

The Botanic Gardens closed for approximately three years for renovations in September 1997. You can see botanic exhibits across the street in the Bartholdi Gardens.

For future reference, though, children who've never left their own climate before will be fascinated by the different biomes represented here. There are subtropical plants (orchids and ficus trees), bromeliads (Spanish moss and the pineapple plant), ferns (the vessel fern, thought to be the oldest plant in the garden), cacti (agave and barrel), more than 300 palms, and even an economics section (citrus and chocolate trees are examples of plants with an economic value) to illustrate that trees provide more than shade and a great place to put a secret clubhouse.

More than 10,000 species and varieties of plants tempt your eyes and your nose, including the bunya bunya tree from Australia, the lychee tree from China, the tapioca plant from Brazil, and the Arabian coffee tree.

Each season has its own show, which might include 90 varieties of azaleas or an extensive orchid collection. The annual Easter exhibit has thousands of spring blooms. The Christmas greenery display features 3,000 poinsettia plants. Surprises abound: one spring exhibit featured the characters from E.B. White's Charlotte's Web, complete with farmer Zuckerman's barn; a county fair; topiary pigs, sheep, rats, and geese; and a Spanish moss Wilbur, the pig.

● National Air and Space Museum (Smithsonian Institution)

Independence Avenue between Fourth and Seventh Streets. (202) 357-2700 (Smithsonian information), (202) 357-1686 (recording about Langley Theater presentations). Open daily 10 A.M. to 5:30 P.M., but there are evening showings of the IMAX films. Closed December 25. Free hour-long highlights tours are given at 10:15 A.M. and 1 P.M. Food service. Membership available. Tourmobile stop. L'Enfant Plaza subway station (Maryland Avenue Exit). http://www.si.edu/newstart.htm. **All ages.**

The museum's two theaters, the Samuel P. Langley IMAX Theater and the Albert Einstein Planetarium, must be mentioned first, because if you plan to visit them you should buy your time-specific tickets as you enter the museum, then tour until your theater time. Tickets are $5 adults and $3.75 for children (12 and under) and senior citizens for daytime films and the planetarium shows. Evening prices are $5.50 for one adult or $7.50 for two, and $4.50 for one child and $6.50 for two. Ask about pre-seating for those with disabilities; captions and hearing enhancement equipment; recorded descriptions of films; and translations in German, French, Spanish, and Japanese.

At the IMAX theater, several large-format films are shown daily. They give viewers the feeling that they are as close to flying or being out in space as they'll ever get without setting a foot in a plane or a spaceship. The screen is five stories high and seven stories wide, or 50 by 75 feet. *To Fly!* takes viewers from one coast of America to the other, swooping down through the Grand Canyon, along cliffs, and over cities and farms. *The Dream Is Alive* is about the astronauts of four space-shuttle missions. Both these films, *Blue Planet,* and the newest presentation, *Destiny in Space* (an examination of how new technologies are changing our concepts of space exploration, with a focus on the dramatic Hubble Servicing Mission, and how living and working in space affects the human body), offer audio descriptions via special headsets to help partially sighted and blind theater patrons comprehend the action of the film. During pauses in the film's regular narration and dialogue, a second narrator describes exactly what is being shown on the screen. This audio description is the work of Metropolitan Washington Ear, Inc., where Cody and Margaret Pfanstiehl are the inspirations behind this worthwhile project.

The Albert Einstein Planetarium show, *Universe of Illusions,* is screened daily, about every 40 minutes. *The Stars Tonight* is shown daily at 3 P.M. and is free. The show is recommended for ages 10 and up; the lectures are suitable for older children.

Air and Space is one of the most visited museums in the world, with as many as 10 million people walking through its doors each year. Although much of the aviation history took place before today's children were born, almost all of it took place during the lifetime of today's grandparents, so this "ancient history" actually is quite current. What are your first memories of flight? How do they compare with today's supersonic planes and intergalactic ships? What are your children's first memories of flight? When it comes to basics, though, children don't seem nearly as interested in that miraculous concept of gravity-defying action as they do in how astronauts eat, sleep, and go to the bathroom.

Among the museum's highlights are the *Voyager* (the flying fuel tank that made the first nonstop, unrefueled flight around the world in 1986, piloted by Dick Rutan and Jena Yeager—talk about tight quarters), the Wright Brothers' original *Kitty Hawk Flyer* (which didn't fly any higher than it's hanging in the museum now), the X-1 (the first aircraft to break the sound barrier, flown by Chuck Yeager), and a *Skylab* orbital workshop that children (even grown-up children) can walk through to examine the astronauts' living and lab quarters (the line for this attraction tends to be very long during peak season). Some of the exhibits are very large, and obviously they weren't brought in through the front door. Instead, there's a glass door at the Seventh Street end of the building that opens to allow these monsters to be brought in and removed.

Future women aviators and astronauts may be interested in several displays, including the bright red *Lockheed Vega* that Amelia Earhart flew across the Atlantic in 1932 (the first woman to fly solo across the Atlantic), and wonder at their innocence. Also on the second floor is a plane flown by Charles and Anne Morrow Lindbergh when she was her husband's navigator and radio operator on preliminary flights they took to survey possible overseas routes. Astronaut Sally Ride's flight suit is here as well. Children's books about Earhart and other women aviators are on sale in the museum shop.

The 800-seat Flight Line cafeteria and the 180-seat Wright Place full-service restaurant (with sandwiches called The Titan I and the Apollo 8) are at the east end of the museum, providing a great view of the Capitol. The gift shop features aviation-themed items, of course, including freeze-dried foods. I'd pass on everything but the Neapolitan ice cream.

Free special-interest lectures, demonstrations, films, and displays on aviation, the skies, and space exploration are scheduled regularly. For a free events calendar write Calendar, Room 3363, NASM, Washington, D.C. 20560. Many events are in the evening, after the museum has closed.

You can see other planes, the work of the Smithsonian restorers, at another Smithsonian Institution property, the Paul E. Garber Facility in Suitland, Maryland. See the Maryland section for a description.

● Hirshhorn Museum and Sculpture Garden (Smithsonian Institution)

Eighth Street and Independence Avenue. (202) 357-2700 (TTY 357-1729). Open daily 10 A.M. to 5:30 P.M. Closed December 25. Guided walk-in tours of about 45 to 60 minutes are given Monday through Saturday at 10:30 A.M., noon, and 1:30 P.M., and on Sunday at 12:30 P.M. A 12-minute slide show that introduces the collection is screened continuously in the orientation room on the lower level from 10 A.M. to 5 P.M. daily. Special tours for children and groups, sculpture tours for the visually impaired, and sign-language tours for the hearing impaired should be arranged a month in advance by calling (202) 357-3235. Outdoor food service, during the summer. L'Enfant Plaza subway station (Maryland Avenue exit). http://www.si.edu/newstart.htm.

All ages.

This doughnut-shaped building is designed to show huge works on the outer, windowless walls, and smaller pieces along the inner circle. The Hirshhorn, the modern gallery in the Smithsonian group, displays paintings and sculptures by Rodin, Calder, Eakins, Matisse, Davis, Stella, and Estes.

Children's films, from cartoons to mainstream, such as a Babar tale and *The Little Mermaid,* to the avant-garde, are screened on Saturdays at 11 A.M. throughout the school year. Program subjects vary and are not necessarily related to the museum exhibits. The films generally are of most interest to 6 to 12 year olds.

The outdoor sculpture garden is a great place for a relaxing break, but remind your children that these sculptures are not for climbing.

● Arts and Industries Building (Smithsonian Institution)

900 Jefferson Drive. (202) 357-2700, (202) 357-1500 (Discovery Theater reservations, voice or TDD). Open daily 10 A.M. to 5:30 P.M. Closed December 25. Walk-in tours are offered on Saturday as announced by the docent. Tourmobile stop. Smithsonian subway station (Mall exit). http://www.si.edu/ newstart.htm. **All ages.**

Arts and Industries is to the United States of a century ago what Epcot and World's Fairs are to our future. In fact, most of the exhibits here came from the 1876 Philadelphia Centennial Exposition, which showed items from the 37 states that were then in the Union, plus goods from several countries. Wings of the museum are dedicated to machinery, furniture, and technology. Displays showcase manufactured goods and machinery of the Victorian age. The objects range from silver services to a beautifully restored locomotive engine and Liberty Bell replicas made from tobacco, sugar, and stone. A central rotunda has a fountain and changing floral displays.

Discovery Theater presents live theatrical performances for young people and their families. The 45- to 60-minute presentations, which may be about Sojourner Truth (a nineteenth-century abolitionist, reformer, and freed slave who traveled widely preaching emancipation and women's rights), West African folktales, Beatrix Potter stories, or dance, are addressed to children from pre-kindergarten to ninth grade. Promotional literature about the programs includes the appropriate age group with the description of each production. Show times are 10 A.M. and 11:30 A.M. Tuesday through Friday and 11:30 A.M. and 1 P.M. on Saturday. Admission is $5 per person. The theater is closed on Thanksgiving and for several days around December 25 and New Year's Day.

● Enid A. Haupt Garden (Smithsonian Institution)

Tenth Street and Independence Avenue. (202) 357-1926. Open daily 7 A.M. to 8 P.M. in summer; 7 A.M. to 5:45 P.M. in winter. Garden tours are offered on Sunday at 2 P.M., weather permitting. Smithsonian subway station (Mall exit). http://www.si.edu/newstart.htm. **All ages.**

Part of the Quadrangle, immediately behind The Castle, this terrific spot for a respite includes a formal Victorian parterre, the Moongate Garden with two nine-foot-tall moongates and pools shaded by weeping cherry trees, and the Fountain Garden with a waterfall and thornless hawthorns. It's also said to be the largest rooftop garden in the country, for underneath its peaceful setting are floors of Smithsonian displays. Check out the animal-shaped topiaries, including some leafy bison.

Three stories beneath the garden are the Arthur M. Sackler Gallery, the National Museum of African Art, and the S. Dillon Ripley Center's International Gallery of the Smithsonian Institution. Enter from three pavilions in and near the garden: The Sackler access adjoins the Moongate Garden, the African art museum is entered from the Fountain Garden, and the International Gallery entrance is via a kiosk-shaped building north of the Castle. The Sackler and African art museums entrances are topped by a large skylight that allows daylight to flood down the wide staircases to the bottom floors some 57 feet below. (Elevators are also available, and are interesting because the floors are labeled 1, 2, and 3, as you descend. The idea of floor numbers increasing as an elevator goes down is an odd concept.) The galleries and museum are connected on level one, so you don't have to return to the surface to go from one to another, although you may want to for a relaxing break between the two distinctly different collections, and whatever special display may be at the Ripley Center.

Consider combining a visit to the Sackler with one to the nearby Freer Gallery for a comprehensive visit to the world of Asian art.

● Arthur M. Sackler Gallery (Smithsonian Institution)

1050 Independence Avenue. (202) 357-2700 (Smithsonian information), (202) 357-3200 (recording, Education Department), (202) 357-4880. Open daily 10 A.M. to 5:30 P.M. Closed December 25. Hour-long guided walk-in tours are given Monday through Friday at 2:30 P.M.; weekends 1:30 P.M. Guided group tours must be arranged several months in advance by calling (202) 357-3200. Smithsonian subway station (Mall exit). http://www.si.edu/newstart.htm. **All ages.**

The Sackler contains a permanent collection of art from China, the ancient Near East, and South Asia and Southeast Asia. Included are objects in bronze, jade, silver, gold, lacquer, and ceramic, as well as paintings and sculpture that span the period between 4000 B.C. and the twentieth century. The museum also houses a major collection of Persian and Indian manuscripts and paintings, and a selection of Japanese works, along with visiting exhibits. Look for the pamphlets that provide brief, illustrated texts for each exhibit.

Regularly scheduled workshops, storytelling events, and activities, some of which may be appropriate for children, are listed in the monthly calendar. The gallery also produces activity guides for children, available at the information desk. Group tours (for classes from kindergarten on up, and scout troops) are scheduled a month ahead of time and are tailored to specific interests and fields of study. They may include a hands-on tour and activity sheets. Call the Education Department to see if one is scheduled and if you may join it.

ImaginAsia is a program for children ages 6 through 12 and their adult companion (at least one adult is required for every three children), who are invited to participate in Saturday morning drop-in programs at 10 A.M. for a small-sized group and at 1:30 P.M. for larger groups (8 to 20 children; these must be reserved three weeks in advance) in the Sackler Gallery's education classroom. Participants use an activity guide to explore and analyze works of art, based on the collections of the Freer and Sackler galleries. A theme might include the examination of the design and decoration of Korean Art in general or the exploration and inspiration of objects from eighteenth-century Korea. Then they create their own masterpieces. Groups of 20 or fewer are invited to register for Saturday afternoon, 2:30 P.M. to 4:30 P.M. activities by calling at least three weeks in advance at (202) 357-4880, ext. 422.

Free, hands-on thematic tours at the Sackler and Freer Galleries, exploring either the depiction of animals in Asian art or the art of China (or your own experience and theme) can be arranged four weeks in advance by completing a tour request form. For information, call (202) 357-4880, ext. 245.

Sign language interpreters, oral interpreters, and cued-speech interpreters are available to students, again at no charge, with one week's notice.

● National Museum of African Art (Smithsonian Institution)

950 Independence Avenue. (202) 357-2700 (Smithsonian information), (202) 357-4860 (Education Department). Open daily 10 A.M. to 5:30 P.M. Closed December 25. Introductory tours (about one hour) are given weekdays at 1:30 P.M.; and weekends at 11 A.M., 1 P.M., and 3 P.M. Group tour requests should be made by mail three months in advance. African folktale storytelling for children takes place on Saturday. Confirm time at the information desk; no

*reservations needed. Smithsonian subway station (Mall exit). http://
www.si.edu/newstart.htm.* **All ages.**

The museum is the only national museum dedicated solely to the
collection, study, and exhibition of the traditional sub-Saharan African
heritage. Its permanent collection of bronze, wood, cast metal, and ceramic objects is an important resource for the study of African art and
culture. These works share gallery space with changing exhibitions. A
nice touch: large color photographs illuminate what purpose masks, statues, and divination boards serve in African culture.

Along with a lot of interesting child-themed books and activity items
in the gift shop, summertime workshops are scheduled for young people.
Topics might include art for children ages 5 to 8 or ways of seeing for
children ages 9 and older.

● International Gallery, S. Dillon Ripley Center, (Smithsonian Institution)

*100 Jefferson Drive, SW. Daily 10 A.M. to 5:30 P.M. (202) 357-2700.
Special exhibits are mounted here, just below the kiosk to the north of the
Castle. Call for details.*

● Freer Gallery of Art (Smithsonian Institution)

*12th Street and Jefferson Drive. (202) 357-2700 (Smithsonian information).
Walk-in highlights tours are offered weekdays at 11:30 A.M. and 2:30 P.M.
and weekends at 11:30 A.M. and 1:30 P.M. Docent training generally is given
on Wednesday, so the tour schedule may be light or nonexistent on that day.
Group tour requests should be made several months in advance by calling the
Education Office; (202) 357-3200 (TTY 786-2374). Smithsonian subway
station (Mall exit). http://www.si.edu/newstart.htm.* **Ages 6 and up.**

Charles Lang Freer donated the collection of Oriental and American
art that fills this gallery. Freer's friend, James McNeill Whistler, created
the Peacock Room, the highlight here for many children because of its
striking dark and gold colors. See if you can find the six peacocks, six
more than you will see at the National Zoo. And yes, probably more than
any room in this gallery—or any room anywhere—people tend to whisper
when they're here.

Ask at the information desk for the children's activity guide for the
Peacock Room. Other treasures include Buddhist sculpture, early Biblical
manuscripts, Chinese jades and bronzes, paintings, Japanese screens, and
Indian miniatures. The vast collection has regularly changing displays,
but Freer's will stipulated that items in the collection may not leave the
gallery, nor may other objects be displayed here.

● Bureau of Engraving and Printing

Fourteenth and C Streets, SW. (202) 874-3019 or (202) 874-3188. Open Monday through Friday 9 A.M. to 2 P.M. Tickets, available at the ticket booth on the Fifteenth Street side of the building from 7:45 A.M. to 2 P.M., are required during the summer. Additional 5 P.M. to 7:30 P.M. tours during the summer. Closed weekends, federal holidays, and December 24 through January 2. Twenty-minute self-guided tours begin at the Fourteenth Street entrance. Forty-minute guided tours are offered from early June through late August. Tourmobile stop. Smithsonian subway station (Independence Avenue exit). http://www.bep.treas.gov or http://www.moneyfactory.com. A children's Web site was under construction at the time of publication. **Ages 2 and up.**

This is one of the most popular sights in the area, so arrive early (particularly March through September) to avoid long lines and major disappointment. The daily supply of tickets is usually gone by 11 A.M.

All of the nation's paper money (the paper is produced by the Crane Paper Company) is designed, engraved, and printed here, along with bonds, 30 billion postage stamps a year, White House invitations, and several hundred other items you'll learn about in the introductory film. Some 22 million bills are printed daily and about $60 trillion are printed every year in $1, $5, and $10 denominations. Larger bills—$20, $50, $100—are printed less frequently. The largest bills—$500, $1,000, $5,000, $10,000—have not been printed for many years. This is the only bureau that prints paper money; coins are minted in Denver and Philadelphia.

You'll walk past exhibits about counterfeit money, printing methods, and outdated currency, and you'll see presses working, machines cutting and stacking the bills, and money being checked. You are separated from the actual printing process by thick glass windows. The beginning of this tour can be a little dull, but there's no denying that seeing all that money being printed, examined, cut, and packaged is fascinating. After the tour, enter the visitor center and a gift shop where you can purchase shredded currency and uncut blocks of currency. Several signs and recorded announcements respond to the inevitable question about free samples.

● United States Holocaust Memorial Museum

100 Raoul Wallenberg Place. (202) 488-0400. Open daily from 10 A.M. to 5:30 P.M. Box Office is open from 10 A.M. to 4 P.M. Closed Yom Kippur and December 25. There is no admission charge, but you do need a timed ticket to visit the permanent exhibit, representing about 80 percent of the museum. You can get a ticket the day you arrive, but you should be in line about 8 A.M., then return at your scheduled time. Advance passes (no more than 10) also are

*available for a service charge through ProTix (800) 400-9373 (or 703-
218-6400 or 410-481-5400) from 10 A.M. to 9 P.M. Without a ticket to
the permanent exhibition, you can still see the temporary displays. No flash or
video photography allowed. Group tour reservations should be made at least
four weeks in advance by calling the schedule coordinator. Museum shop. Food
services available at the Annex across the plaza on Fifteenth Street. Membership available. Tourmobile and Lil Red Trolley stop. Smithsonian subway
station (Independence Avenue exit). Gift shop. http://www.ushmm.org.
Daniel's Story:* **Ages 8 and up.** *Other areas:* **Ages 11 and up.**

The United States Holocaust Memorial Museum is dedicated to presenting the history of the persecution and murder of millions of Jews and
other victims of Nazi tyranny from 1933 to 1945. Its primary mission is
to inform Americans about this unprecedented tragedy, to remember
those who suffered, and to inspire visitors to contemplate the moral impli-
cations of their choices and responsibilities as citizens in an interdepen-
dent world. The museum is divided into permanent and temporary
exhibition areas.

The permanent exhibition, a comprehensive history of the Holocaust
shown through artifacts, photographs, film, and eyewitness testimonies, is
not recommended for children under 11. As you enter the three-story
permanent exhibit, pick up an identity card (on your left before entering
the elevator) and check the computer for more information about your
"companion" before you leave.

Other parts of the museum, including the Wexner Learning Center
(with a multimedia Holocaust Encyclopedia), the Resource Center, and
the Wall of Remembrance exhibit of expressions on tiles by children, are
open without a ticket. "Daniel's Story: Remember the Children," is specifically designed for visitors ages 8 and up and their families. It tells the
story of the Holocaust through a child's narrative in ways that are easily
understood. This exhibit is labeled as temporary, but is due to stay
through about 1998. You should allow several hours to completely tour
this museum.

Now, on the other side of the Mall, along Constitution Avenue, again
starting from the Capitol end, you'll find the following buildings.

● National Gallery of Art

*Sixth Street at Constitution Avenue. (202) 737-4215 (TTY 842-6176).
Open Monday through Saturday 10 A.M. to 5 P.M.; Sunday 11 A.M. to 6 P.M.
Closed December 25 and New Year's Day. West Building walk-in introductory tours are given Monday through Saturday at 10:30 A.M., 12:30 P.M.,
and 2:30 P.M.; Sunday 11:30 A.M., 1:30 P.M., and 3:30 P.M. Each tour
lasts about one hour. Terrific gift shops. Handicapped entrance for the West*

Building is located at Sixth Street and Constitution Avenue. The East Building access is at Fourth Street and Constitution Avenue. Wheelchairs and strollers are available at entrances. For information about listening devices and sign language interpreters, inquire at the Art Information Desk, or call (202) 737-4215 or TDD (202) 842-6176. Food service. Tourmobile stop. Archives subway station. http://www.nga.gov. **All ages.**

The gallery, which is not part of the Smithsonian, is comprised of two buildings, the West (or Main) Building and the East Building. The West Building houses pre-twentieth century art. Across the National Gallery Plaza in the East Building are twentieth-century artworks.

When your children start talking about those Teenage Mutant Ninja Turtles, you can show them two of the artists, Raphael and Leonardo. The gallery has a Donatello drawing in its print collection, and you can set up an appointment to see it. There's no help for Michelangelo, though.

Major European and American artists are represented in the West Building, including Raphael (Gallery 8) and Leonardo da Vinci (Gallery 6; the only da Vinci in the western hemisphere).

There are a number of special programs for children and families. You can take the free self-guided tour; a book is available in the gift shop that helps explain the paintings, or you can pick up a free brochure. Special exhibitions are usually accompanied by special tours and activities for children ages 6 to 10. Call the Education Department for the schedule (202) 842-6249, or ask to be put on the mailing list by writing to the National Gallery of Art, Washington, D.C. 20565.

Tours also are available for children ages 3 or 4 to teenagers. Many of these organized tours are scout or classroom groups, but you "qualify" as a group even if it's a birthday party. In fact, the staff will happily organize a special tour for those with specific interests. If your group wants to study, say, the depiction of weather in the artworks, then the staff will create that tour for you. These are all conversational tours and can include items from the permanent or touring exhibits, from either the West Building or the East Building.

Many children seem to have fun just walking by the cascade in the passageway connecting the two buildings.

The Gallery gift shop has a nice selection of art supplies, books, videos, creative kits, toys, and games specifically tailored to the young, budding artist.

● National Gallery Sculpture Garden

Between the West Building of the National Gallery of Art and the National Museum of Natural History is an outdoor sculpture garden, complete with a fountain in the summer and an ice rink in the winter. Among the trees, curvy lanes, shrubbery, open lawns, benches, and upscale cafe are a selection of primarily twentieth-century sculptures. As of this writing, sculpture selection hadn't been made yet, nor was it decided if the statuary would be permanent or feature traveling exhibits, or a mixture of both.

● National Museum of Natural History (Smithsonian Institution)

Tenth Street between Constitution Avenue and Madison Drive. (202) 357-2700 (Smithsonian information). Open daily 10 A.M. to 5:30 P.M. Closed December 25. Guided tours (about one hour) are offered daily at 10:30 A.M. and 1:30 P.M. The Insect Zoo's tarantula feedings are weekdays at 10:30 A.M. and 1:30 P.M. and weekends and holidays at 1:30 P.M. During peak season and on many weekends, free timed tickets are sometimes issued for the Discovery Room and the Insect Zoo; check at the information desk. See also the Naturalist Center, Leesburg, Virginia. Food service. Tourmobile stop. Federal Triangle or Archives subway station. http://www.si.edu/newstart.htm. **All ages.**

Greeting you as you enter from the Madison Drive entrance is a large African bush elephant. He stands in the three-story-high rotunda. He is 13 feet tall and when alive weighed 12 tons and had 24-inch foot tracks. At the Constitution Avenue entrance, two huge (30 feet and 40 feet) totem poles carved by the Haida Indians, and one pole carved by the Tsimshian Indians, tribes native to the Pacific Northwest, guard the east stairwell of the building. From there you can venture into any corner and find everything in the natural sciences, all the way down to the tiniest insects.

And it's the Insect Zoo that particularly excites children. Want to watch tarantulas being fed? How about petting a live Madagascar hissing cockroach or stroking a fat green tobacco hornworm? Would you find a one-foot-long centipede slightly intimidating? Well, this is the place to become friendly with the little critters. Children love it. Fortunately, for adults, children under 12 must be accompanied by an adult.

Other exhibits include animals from all parts of the world in realistic settings. Among the skillfully executed displays is one of birds in flight and another of special-interest birds, such as the Antarctic penguin, the pheasant with its enormous colored plumes, and the ostrich, complete with just-hatched babies.

Dinosaurs used to roam this land, and you can see reconstructed dinosaur skeletons here. Dioramas show these animals in their natural habitats, and flying reptile reconstructions hang on the nearby walls.

In the Naturalist Center, it's time for hands-on learning, with drawers full of minerals and arrowheads, and ready-to-use microscopes.

About halfway through the Gem and Mineral Hall, you'll see the Hope Diamond, the largest blue diamond in the world. Then there's the 330-carat sapphire known as the Star of India. And there are hundreds, if not thousands, of other mineral examples in virtually every hue and size.

The Gem and Mineral Hall was renovated as of September 1997 and is now called the Janet Annenberg Hooker Hall of Geology, Gems, and Minerals. This exhibit covers aspects of earth science, including volcanology, plate tectonics, and the importance of mining. A team of more than 100 experts planned the 20,000-square-foot project, and the new hall features natural and reconstructed environmental surroundings. You'll also find interactive computers, animated graphics, film and video presentations, and hands-on specimens. A special highlight of the new hall is the Whole Earth Theatre, a short, multimedia presentation providing a "big picture" story of the earth on a 40-foot screen.

In addition to the big gift shop, which offers books on nature, stuffed animals, and nature souvenirs, there's a Dinostore that carries dinosaur-related items only, including cookie cutters, decorated apparel, models, and puzzles, and a recently renovated Gem Shop selling gems, rocks, fossils, and arrowheads.

● National Museum of American History (Smithsonian Institution)

Fourteenth Street between Constitution Avenue and Madison Drive. (202) 357-2700 (Smithsonian information). Open daily 10 A.M. to 5:30 P.M. Closed December 25. Hour-long walk-in highlights tours are scheduled Monday through Saturday at 10 A.M. and 1 P.M.; Sunday at 10:30 A.M. Check at the information desk for tour times of the "First Ladies: Political Role, Public Image" exhibition and for other displays. Times and topics of regular tours, concerts, lectures, films, and other activities are posted at the information desks, staffed daily 10 A.M. to 4 P.M. Tourmobile stop. Food service. Smithsonian subway station (Mall exit). http://www.si.edu/ newstart.htm. **All ages.**

This 10-acre collection devoted to the exhibition, care, and study of artifacts that reflect the experience of the American people can be daunting and easily take a day or more to explore, so here are some highlights. The first thing you see when you come in from the Mall entrance is the crowd of people surrounding a circular railing. This overlook affords a view of the large Foucault pendulum, which demonstrates the rotation of the earth.

Among the national treasures on view is the original Star-Spangled Banner, the flag that Francis Scott Key saw the night he wrote the national anthem, displayed every hour on the half hour during a short sound-and-light show. The inaugural gowns of recent first ladies are on exhibit. Some presidential memorabilia, White House china, and decorative art objects also are on display in the Ceremonial Court, a place where children can view a collection of toys from the 1830s forward. They belonged to White House children and grandchildren, and include a wooden chest of travel games that once belonged to Thomas "Tad" Lincoln, and a gathering of ragtag well-loved Teddy bears named after Theodore Roosevelt, who once shied at shooting a bear cub.

A new exhibit, part of the fiftieth anniversary commemorating Jackie Robinson's first game with the Brooklyn Dodgers, opened in 1977. This area explores his career and his historical significance in American sports.

Other treasures, perhaps not national in scope but of historic interest, are a nineteenth-century post office, Archie Bunker's chair, Judy Garland's ruby slippers from the *Wizard of Oz,* and Howdy Doody.

Other interesting exhibits are display cases filled with hidden and trick cameras concealed in lighters, opera glasses, shoe heels, and even a lacy black garter.

The five-storied Doll House, which reflects life at the turn of the century, is always a favorite with children. Its twenty-two rooms, including parlors, bedrooms, and guest rooms, are outfitted with all sorts of grown-up furnishings in miniature, such as a fish tank in the living room and a typewriter in the study.

One hands-on exhibit that lives up to its name is "Hands-on History." It gives young carpenters the opportunity to assemble a Chippendale chair or a wooden barrel. This room is so popular that free timed passes are sometimes issued to control the crowds.

Transformers are not a phenomenon of the 1980s; we've been "transforming" things throughout our history, although not in quite the same manner. "A Material World" shows how we have transformed such everyday natural resources as wood into functional tools or clay into earthenware coffee cups. One of the stars for children in this exhibit is the low-slung Swamp Rat 30A. It was the first dragster to exceed 270 miles per hour in the quarter mile (1986), and has perhaps 60 different and distinct materials in its construction. Another interesting stop is a hands-on display of a 10-foot, 17-ton section of a main cable from the George Washington Bridge that has 26,474 individual steel strands.

You can see all kinds of money in Money and Metals. The exhibit tells the whole story, from primitive bartering with beads and shells to our present complex monetary system. There is a lumpy-looking Lydian coin from 65 B.C. and a $100,000 bill bearing the likeness of President Wilson.

Transportation takes up space, too, and features enormous train engines (take note of the photographs by Jack Bittner that show how the engine was moved into the building). Other rail-related objects are Southern Railway's Pacific-type passenger engine; the Seattle cable car of 1888; the 1836 eight-wheel passenger car, the oldest in existence; a diorama of New York's Third Avenue El as it looked in 1880; and a collection of scale models showing the development of rail transportation.

Automobile enthusiasts will want to pause at the first Duryea (1893), an 1894 Haynes, a 1903 Oldsmobile, and a 1913 Ford Model T. (Note: cars rotate and may not always be on display.) Computer buffs will like the adding and calculating machines and the various data-processing devices in the Information Age exhibit.

Demonstrations of how laser and maser beams work are among the displays illustrating the development and application of electricity theories. Scientists of tomorrow can observe and study the contributions to science made by Benjamin Franklin, Michael Faraday, and others.

The importance of petroleum and the role of the petrochemical industry in modern society are presented through a description of the methods and equipment used to discover, drill, recover, refine, and transport petroleum.

The list of exhibits continues, with navigational equipment, musical instruments from the eighteenth and nineteenth centuries, and the combination country store and post office that operated in Headsville, West Virginia, from 1861 to 1914. It still serves as a post office and your mail deposited here will have a cancellation stamp that reads "Smithsonian Station."

A new "Science in American Life" installation opened in April 1994. The exhibition starts with the 1870s when the first research laboratories in the universities of the United States opened. From there you will see how Americans looked toward science as the solution to a finer future. Various intersections of science and society explore the effect of World War II as it drove scientists to develop radar and produce penicillin. Further steps explore biotechnology and its impact on tomorrow's environment and disease.

A Hand-On Science Center features 25 activities, including water-sample testing, DNA fingerprinting, and detecting radioactivity in common household objects.

● Washington Monument

The Mall between Fifteenth and Seventeenth Streets. (202) 426-6839. Open daily 8 A.M. to 12 midnight April through Labor Day, 9 A.M. to 5 P.M. the day after Labor Day through March. Free timed tickets are issued so you know *when to enter. There is no limit to the time you may spend there, once inside. The ticket kiosk is on Fifteenth Street, between Constitution and Independence Avenues. For advance tickets (which cost $1.50 per ticket handling fee plus $.50 per order) call TicketMaster (800) 505-5040, 9 A.M. to 10 P.M. daily, up to about two months in advance of your visit. Tourmobile stop. Smithsonian subway station (Mall exit). http://www.nps.gov/ncro/.* **All ages.**

At 555.5 feet (169 meters) tall (the tallest building in the city), the Washington Monument is pretty tall, but note that the Metro subway stations are 600 feet long, so the Washington Monument, tipped on its side, would fit inside of these stations. Fifty flags, one for each state, surround the base of the monument. Between 1998 and 2000, the Monument will undergo a $5 million facelift, the most comprehensive since it was completed in 1884. The aging elevator and air-conditioning system will be replaced. The entire edifice will be covered with scaffolding so workers can check all the mortar joints and clean the surface.

Take the elevator up to the observation deck at the 500-foot level for the four-way view of the city. From the two north windows you can see the Ellipse and the White House; from the east the Mall Area and the Capitol; from the south the Tidal Basin and Jefferson Memorial; and from the west the Reflecting Pool and Lincoln Memorial. For nighttime viewing, note that the lights at the White House go out at 11 P.M., and the Jefferson and Lincoln memorials are illuminated until midnight.

The elevator takes 70 seconds to ascend, 60 seconds to descend (it will be faster when the new elevator is installed), and the last elevator departure is 15 minutes before closing (11:45 P.M. in the summer and 4:45 P.M. in the winter). The line may be closed off as much as an hour before actual closing time.

On weekends, if a staff member is available to lead, you can walk down the 897 steps from the top with a guided tour. During the 45-minute descent, you will hear tales about the wonderful walls, which include 193 ornately inscribed blocks of marble dedicated to President Washington. They came from various cities, states, fire companies (showing firefighters in action), train companies (an entire train carved into the stone), and countries, such as Japan, Turkey, Siam (now Thailand), Greece, and Switzerland. There are 50 landings, no windows, and the upper portion of the monument is a little narrow. If you can't take this tour, you can see some of the stones through the elevator window (next to the elevator operator) as the ride goes up and down the monument. You are not allowed to walk up the 897 steps.

Many activities are scheduled at the Sylvan Theater on the southeast corner of the Washington Monument grounds at Independence Avenue and Fifteenth Street. As with any outdoor venue, performance schedules are subject to the weather. Listen to the radio stations for notice of cancellation.

Prime summertime activities at the theater are concerts performed by military bands, big bands, and other music groups, usually on Tuesday, Wednesday, Friday, and Sunday at 7:30 P.M. The evening may feature such local singing stars as Karen Henderson with the Trux Baldwin Orchestra. Bring a picnic and a blanket or lawn chairs and celebrate a summer evening with music and dance.

A boomerang competition is held on the monument grounds every spring, preceded by instructions in making and throwing the object. There is a moderate charge for instructions, but no entry fee for the competition.

The Fourth of July concert that used to feature the Beach Boys is held here, and crowds along the Mall on that day can number half a million without too much of a problem (except when everyone tries to leave via the Smithsonian subway station at the end of the festivities).

Another annual event is a kite-flying competition held in late March or early April, when as many as 5,000 kites fill the air. Started by Paul Garber (see the Paul E. Garber Facility under Maryland listings), it's a celebration of spring and childhood. Many of the contestants have long outgrown their childhood clothing, though. From box kites and newspaper kites to multilayered Mylar structures, the event is a great day to be a kid again. All competition kites must be made from scratch and fly at a minimum altitude of 100 feet for at least one minute. Awards are divided into several age groups. You can write to Margo Brown, 6636 Kirkley Avenue, McLean, Virginia 22101, for instructions on how to make some basic kites. Enclose a self-addressed, stamped envelope with two first-class stamps on it.

Jousting, Maryland's state sport, takes place on the monument grounds usually during October.

● Lincoln Memorial

Memorial Circle between Constitution and Independence Avenues. (202) 426-6841. Open daily 24 hours, with guides on duty from 8 A.M. to midnight in the summer and 9 A.M. until 5 P.M. from Labor Day to Memorial Day. Closed December 25. Tourmobile stop. Smithsonian subway station (Mall exit). http://www.nps.gov/ncro/. **All ages.**

The Lincoln Memorial (the memorial on the back of the $5 bill) is another special treat at nighttime. Looking from Lincoln's seat, you'll see the Reflecting Pool with the Washington Monument reflected in its waters. Only from Lincoln's eyes, it is said, can you see the entire Washington Monument reflected in the pool. There are 36 columns along the perimeter of the memorial, representing the 36 states that comprised the Union when Lincoln was president. Also, there are 56 steps, representing the number of years Lincoln lived.

Because the memorial was built on swamp land, huge supporting pillars were set deep into the ground. The area between the pillars was not filled in and, in the brief 55 years of the memorial's existence, stalagmites and stalactites have formed. Underground tours used to be given in the spring and fall, but when authorities found asbestos, the tours were canceled.

● Vietnam Veterans Memorial

Constitution Avenue between Henry Balm Drive and Twenty-first Street. (202) 619-7222. Open daily 24 hours. Tourmobile stop (Lincoln Memorial). Smithsonian subway station (Mall exit). http://www.nps.gov/ncro/. **All ages.**

Two polished black granite walls set in a wide V form the surface on which 58,203 names of dead and missing Vietnam veterans are inscribed, carved alphabetically, and grouped by the year each died. A book, one at each end of the V, tells you on which panel each name can be found. Regardless of your feelings about the Vietnam War, this memorial, designed by Maya Ying Lin, is very moving. It is the most-visited memorial in Washington, D.C., and is particularly poignant during a rainfall, when the very granite seems to cry. People leave flowers, war medals, notes, pictures, and other items by the names of loved ones. These mementos are gathered regularly and catalogued in a collection and some of the letters, flags, and other memorabilia left by visitors are on display in the National Museum of American History, East Wing, third floor. The rest of the collection is not open to the public at this time.

A large selection of photographs and books that will help you explain and help your youngster understand the Vietnam conflict is available in the Lincoln Memorial gift shop.

● Reflecting Pool

Between the Washington Monument and the Lincoln Memorial. http:// www.nps.gov/ncro/. **All ages.**

The Reflecting Pool is home to ducks in the summer and ice skaters in the winter. Because the pool is fairly shallow, solid ice forms with just a few days of subfreezing weather. National Park Service people will tell you if it's safe to skate.

● Constitution Gardens

Between the Washington Monument and the Lincoln Memorial. (202) 426-6841. Open daily dawn to dusk. http://www.nps.gov/ncro/. **All ages.**

Commonly referred to as the Duck Pond, this 42-acre park contains a six-acre lake, gardens, and an information center. A wooden bridge leads to a one-acre island dedicated to the 56 signers of the Declaration of Independence. On the island stands a semicircle of knee-high granite stones that double as benches, and on each stone the name, signature, hometown, and occupation of a signing father is inscribed.

If you're planning to sit for a spell, go for one of the lesser-known names such as Josiah Bartlett (New Hampshire) or William Ellery (Rhode Island), rather than Hancock, Franklin, Adams, or Rodney. If you go for the biggies, you'll have to keep getting up because people always want to see the replicas of the most famous signatures.

The island and gardens are a nice place for sunbathing, biking, hiking, and for feeding the ducks and seagulls.

● Korean War Veterans Memorial

West Potomac Park, between the Washington Monument and the Lincoln Memorial, on the other side of the Reflecting Pool from the Vietnam Veterans Memorial. **All ages.** *http://www.nps.gov/ncro/.*

This memorial to the Korean conflict includes statues of 19 larger-than-life-size ground troops as they move toward the goal of victory and freedom. Recognition is given to the Republic of Korea and the 20 other countries that sent men and women to participate in the United Nations' force.

● Tidal Basin

Fifteenth Street and Ohio Drive (East Potomac Park). (202) 619-7222. Open daily dawn to dusk. Tourmobile stop. Via Metro, go to the Smithsonian station (Independence Avenue exit), walk west two blocks on Independence Avenue, then south on Raoul Wallenberg Place (Fifteenth Street) to the Tidal Basin and the trees. http://www.nps.gov/nacc/cherry. **All ages.**

So named because it helps dissipate the incoming Potomac River tide, the Tidal Basin is the perfect place for looking at cherry blossoms and renting pedal boats. The Cherry Blossom Festival is held in late March or early April. In addition to the 1,233 Yoshing cherry trees growing around the Tidal Basin (which may or may not be in bloom during the festival) and the well-known parade, the festival is celebrated with a treasure hunt at the Constitution Gardens, band concerts, a pedal-boat regatta, and a 10-kilometer run. Even in the cherry blossoms there is a lesson for children to learn, for the Japanese compare the fleeting loveliness of the cherry blossoms (they may stay on the trees for as long as two weeks, but they may also last only three days) to the brevity of human life when compared to eternity, although both life and blossoms are wonderful and worthwhile. The Japanese have a saying for it: "Life is short, like the three-day glory of the cherry blossom."

Pedal boats can be rented at the Tidal Basin boathouse, Fifteenth Street and Maine Avenue, SW, generally from the end of March through the end of October, seven days a week 10 A.M. to 7 P.M. (202) 479-2426.

● The Floral Library

Near the Tidal Basin, between the Washington Monument and Jefferson Memorial. http://www.nps.gov/ncro/. **All ages.**

Created by the National Park Service in 1969, the living library opens its season in April with an incredible fanfare of tulips, and continues through the warm months with other flowering arrangements. Please feel free to walk between the beds, but don't pick the flowers and don't stand in the beds. Call (202) 619-7222 for more information about seasonal floral displays in the Washington area.

● Jefferson Memorial

South bank of Tidal Basin (Fourteenth Street and East Basin Drive, SW, East Potomac Park). (202) 426-6822. Open daily, with guides on duty from 9 A.M. to midnight in the summer and until 5 P.M. from Labor Day to Memorial Day. Closed December 25. Tourmobile stop. http://www.nps.gov/ ncro/. **All ages.**

This famous site is perhaps best seen at dusk or nighttime, when it is bathed in floodlights, but it can't be beat at any time for views of Washington over the Tidal Basin, and of the floral extravaganza known as Cherry Blossom time. Dedicated to our third president, the memorial is programmed with short interpretive speeches, presented every half hour upon request. Children love to stand in front of the 19-foot (6 meter) statue of Jefferson, so have your camera ready to shoot the disparity.

● Franklin Delano Roosevelt Memorial

West Potomac Park, across the Tidal Basin from the Jefferson Memorial. (202) 376-6704. http://www.nps.gov/ncro/. **All ages.**

This new 7½-acre memorial, open 24 hours, consists of four outdoor gallery rooms featuring 10 bronze sculptures of President Franklin Delano Roosevelt (the only president to be elected to four terms of office), Eleanor Roosevelt, and events from the Great Depression and World War II. The park setting includes waterfalls, quiet pools, and granite upon which President Roosevelt's inspiring words are carved. The monument is totally wheelchair accessible. Although you may get away with sticking your toes into the pools, all-out swimming is prohibited. There is a visitor center, and a gift shop that sells two books about Fala, the president's dog—a White House pet long before Socks, the current occupant.

The closest Metro stops are the Smithsonian and Foggy Bottom, each about a mile's walk. Parking is available, but limited.

● Hains Point

Hains Point, or East Potomac Park, is the peninsula created by the Washington Channel. http://www.nps.gov/ncro/. **All ages.**

Recreational activities abound here, as do beautiful views of the city. Automobile traffic sometimes is restricted, closely directed, or otherwise diverted because of congestion.

The Awakening, however, is the main reason to visit Hains Point. Created by artist Seward Johnson, the sculpture is a half-buried body of a giant man emerging from the ground. Children particularly love to play with this big fellow, making a stop here another one of those terrific photo opportunities everyone raves about in Washington. There's talk of removing the statue and replacing it with a garden, so if you may not be back this way for another 10 years, this is the time to visit.

The Tidal Basin is not the only place to view blooming trees when it's cherry blossom time. East Potomac Park boasts more than 1,200 cherry trees, including Yoshing, Kawnzan, and weeping varieties. In all, there are some 3,000 cherry trees on the grounds of the Tidal Basin.

Northwest Washington (including Downtown)

IN THIS SECTION, PLACES of interest are organized by subway station, and those not near a station are listed under the heading "Elsewhere in the Northwest." Special sections are dedicated to the Georgetown and Dupont Circle areas; the latter is covered under the subway station of the same name.

ARCHIVES SUBWAY STATION

● National Archives

Constitution Avenue between Seventh and Ninth Streets. (202) 501-5000 (recorded information about special programs), (202) 501-5205. Open daily 10 A.M. to 9 P.M. April 1 through Labor Day, 10 A.M. to 5:30 P.M. the rest of the year. Closed December 25. Guided tours are given Monday through Friday by appointment only; call (202) 501-5205 for reservations. The Pennsylvania Avenue entrance provides access to the Central Research and Microfilm Research rooms. Call for hours. Closed Sunday and federal holidays. Call (202) 501-5400 for research information. Archives subway station. http://www.nara.gov. **Ages 6 and up.** *Children under 16 are not allowed in the research rooms.*

America's most revered documents are stored here, including all four pages of the Declaration of Independence, the Constitution, and the Bill of Rights. They are kept in sealed glass-and-bronze cases filled with protective helium. During the day, two pages of the Declaration of Independence, the Constitution, and the Bill of Rights are on display. At night the cases are lowered into a bomb- and fireproof vault 20 feet below floor level. On September 17, Constitution Day (the anniversary of the presentation of the Constitution), all four pages of the Declaration of Independence are on view. There's also a copy of the Magna Carta (1297) on display.

Among the many other documents in the collection are 3.2 billion textual documents, 1.6 million cartographic items, 5.2 million still photographs, 9.7 million aerial photographs, 110,000 reels of motion picture film, and 173,000 video and sound recordings.

Summertime children's programs include a film series, lectures, special activities, and exhibits. Call (202) 523-3347 for information.

Serious genealogy research is done here, plus students also may research term papers on such diverse subjects as the Civil War photographs of Mathew Brady, Tokyo Rose's World War II radio propaganda tapes, land claims by Indian tribes, passenger ship manifests, documents from the Civil Rights March on Washington, and the Watergate tapes.

Next to the National Archives, on the Pennsylvania Avenue side, is a small white marble block dedicated to President Franklin D. Roosevelt, who supposedly said he did not want a monument built to him that was larger than his desk. Of course, a much larger tribute to President and Mrs. Roosevelt, the new FDR Memorial, sits across the Tidal Basin from the Jefferson Memorial.

● United States Navy Memorial Visitors Center

Pennsylvania Avenue at Eighth Street. (202) 737-2300. Open Monday through Saturday, 9:30 A.M. to 5 P.M.; Sunday from 12 noon to 4 P.M. Closed federal holidays. Tours are available for groups of 20 or more, with advance reservations. Admission to the museum is free; there is a charge for the film. A self-guided, laminated walk-around brochure is provided for individuals and smaller groups. Gift shop. Archives subway station. http:// www.lonesailor.org. **Ages 6 and up.**

The center includes an outdoor amphitheater where service bands and other performers appear (free concerts are performed by the various components of the U.S. Navy Band on Thursday evening at 8 P.M. during the summer), a commemorative area for official navy ceremonies, a world grid map (reportedly, the largest map in the world, and great for geography lessons) surrounded by bronze bas-relief sculptures depicting historical naval events, and a 7-foot-tall statue of the Lone Sailor gazing toward the far horizon. According to the Navy legend, the Lone Sailor is the U.S. Navy bluejacket: young, maturing fast, enchanted by the seas and their beauty and strength. He's confident and believes in himself, his ship, his leaders, and his navy.

Inside the center, a wide-screen theater shows films depicting the role the sea has played in United States history. During the summer, the 36-minute movie *At Sea,* about life aboard an aircraft carrier, is shown at 10 A.M., noon, 2 and 4 P.M., Monday through Saturday; and 1 and 3 P.M.

on Sunday. The winter schedule varies, and there are no showings on Saturday and Sunday. Note, this is a very noisy film, with jets taking off and landing on the carrier. If your children don't like loud sounds, this is not the place for them, no matter how much they like boats. Admission is $3.75 for adults and $2.50 for children. The center also houses exhibits, a reception area with a diorama, and Navy artworks. Of interest here is the Navy Memorial Log, a computerized roster of present and former Navy members. It lists name, rank, date and place of birth, and dates of service alongside those of such naval heroes as John Paul Jones, Stephen Decatur, Chester Nimitz, and William Halsey. Visitors can display on a giant video screen the individual names of family members, friends, or shipmates who are entered in the log. You can add a name and record for a $25 tax-deductible donation to the memorial.

A bookstore features gifts and commemorative items.

● Washington Project for the Arts

400 Seventh Street. (202) 347-8304. Open Tuesday through Saturday 10 A.M. to 6 P.M.; Thursday 10 A.M. to 7 P.M. Closed Monday. Free guided tours are available by appointment. Membership available. Bookstore. Archives subway station. **Ages 6 and up.**

Elevated to hero status when it housed the controversial Robert Mapplethorpe photography exhibit after the Corcoran Gallery canceled it, this gallery specializes in showcasing Washington-area artists. Other attractions include performance works and videos. To buy works from up-and-coming artists, attend the annual fall auction.

CLEVELAND PARK SUBWAY STATION

● National Zoological Park (Smithsonian Institution)

3000 block of Connecticut Avenue. (202) 357-2700 (Smithsonian information), (202) 673-4717 (direct line to zoo), (202) 357-1729 (TDD), (202) 357-4800 (voice recording). Buildings are open daily 9 A.M. to 4:30 P.M.; grounds are open daily 8 A.M. to 8 P.M. April 15 through October 15 and 8 A.M. to 6 P.M. October 16 through April 14. When going to the zoo, use the Cleveland Park subway station; it's downhill from the station to the zoo. When departing the zoo, use the Woodley Park/Zoo station; it's downhill from the zoo to the station. If you drive to the zoo and park in the lot, there is a fee. Food service at the Panda Cafe, Mane restaurant, and Express Grill. http://www.si.edu/natzoo. **All ages.**

Thousands of animals, birds, reptiles, and many rare species, some of them gifts from foreign governments, fill this wonderful zoo. The Bird

House has a free-flight room equipped with special temperature and humidity controls for its large collection of tropical birds, including fairy bluebirds, cock-of-the-rocks, and Rothschild's starlings.

The zoo's most famous resident is its giant male panda bear, Hsing-Hsing, a gift to the children of America from the People's Republic of China. There are also red panda bears, white tigers, and many other marvelous creatures.

The lions, tigers, and pandas are fed at 11 A.M. and 3 P.M.; the elephant care demonstrations are at 11:30 A.M. Seal and sea lion training are at 11:30 A.M. most days. The Herplab, open Wednesday through Sunday from 12 noon to 3 P.M., allows you to check out a box containing a live snake or frog and examine the reptile up close, put together a tortoiseshell puzzle, or see a movie about the zoo's lizards.

One of the zoo's newest exhibits is Amazonia, a 15,000-square-foot exhibit complex with a 55,000 gallon aquarium for Amazon River fishes; a living rainforest with 358 species of plants, including 50-foot-tall trees; and dozens of animals indigenous to the Amazon basin. This unique exhibit is maintained within a specially designed building with a translucent, domed roof. Amazonia gives zoo goers the chance to experience the rainforest by walking among spectacular plants and animals and to see firsthand the diversity of life in this replication of the oldest tropical forest ecosystem on earth.

One of the innovative approaches to learning at Amazonia takes place at Dr. Brasil's field station. Here, with the help of Dr. Brasil's lab assistants, visitors are encouraged to look around a simulated riverside rainforest research laboratory and to read the natural history notes scribbled by the elusive Brazilian biologist, Dr. Brasil.

Consider visiting Amazonia early to avoid waiting in line later in the day. It opens at 10 A.M. and the last visitor is admitted at 4 P.M.

Another new component is the Amazonia Science Gallery, opened in December 1996. The gallery, adjacent to the zoo's Amazonia habitat, showcases scientific research on the complex interdependency of species and their environments as well as lets visitors see how scientists work. Children, starting with those who are old enough to color, will find a variety of activities here, such as computer programs to learn about the earth, labs to inspect, a scientist or two to talk with (this is a working laboratory), a nutrition lab to understand the analysis of animal feed, and a demonstration of the separation of DNA.

Another exhibit of interest is the Reptile House, which centers around Komodo dragons (yes, the ones from the old Bob and Ray comedy routine about the slow-talkers of America). Friendty (male) and Sobat (female) have been living here since 1990. They've been prolific breeders since then, producing 45 offspring, several of which have found their way to other zoos across the country including Atlanta, New Orleans, Honolulu, Albuquerque, Fort Worth, and St. Louis. These dragons will grow as long as 10 feet and are true eating machines.

Two new one-horned Asian rhinoceroses appeared at the zoo in 1996, a male and a female. The world population of rhinoceroses is only about 2,000, so these rare zoo births are key to rhinos' survival.

Incidentally, during the warm, humid summer months, you may find the zoo is open earlier than the posted time. You can beat the crowds and see the animals when they're waking. Often, they come to the edges of their cages when you walk by because they think you're bringing their food.

Sunset serenade concerts are presented from 6:30 to 8 P.M. every Thursday night from about late June through early August on Lion/Tiger Hill. The repertoire ranges from jazz to reggae. No admission is charged; bring a picnic and a blanket. Call (202) 673-4717 for program information. Or, if you prefer, call the Friends of the National Zoo (FONZ) at (202) 637-4978 at least a day before the concert to order a picnic basket (from $7.50 for adults; $4 for children) with sandwich, salad, beverage, and dessert.

FONZ volunteers conduct two-hour walking tours for groups of five or more from mid-March to May. To make reservations, call (202) 673-4955.

A huge wooden sculpture, "Volunteers," carved from a single tree and dedicated to the workers of FONZ, is in front of the education building. About 25 feet tall, the sculpture is adorned with humans and animals, and it's a puzzle trying to figure out where and what everything is.

A late-1994 addition to the zoo is Uncle Beazley, a fiberglass triceratops that used to sit in front of the Museum of Natural History. Due to some injuries, he was moved and now is located in the male rhino yard, to the left of the elephant house (as you're facing it).

DUPONT CIRCLE SUBWAY STATION

Named for Civil War Rear Admiral Samuel Francis Dupont, Dupont Circle is an environment unto itself. This is where the avant-gardist, the gay, the blue collar worker, and the executive merge to create one of Washington's most intriguing neighborhoods. On balmy summer nights, you'll find people virtually attached to the 10 concrete chess tables on the south side of the circle until the wee hours of the morning. If you and your child have different chess abilities, each of you can find a suitable level or challenging partners. At anytime there may be wandering minstrels. On Saturdays look for Joel Berg, who will write a poem for you for a couple of dollars.

Centered around Dupont Circle are seven museums and galleries, all members of the Dupont Kalorama Museums Consortium, which can be reached at (202) 387-2151. These include the Phillips Collection, the Textile Museum, the Woodrow Wilson House, the Anderson House, the Historical Society of Washington, the Meridian International Center, and the Fondo del Sol Visual Arts Center. All but the Meridian International Center are within a few blocks of the Dupont Circle subway station and of each other. The museums are located in elegantly restored mansions that have been homes to presidents and embassies. Call ahead for wheelchair accessibility.

Of the seven institutions, the Meridian International Center and the Phillips Collection are probably the most tuned into what interests younger children. The Textile Museum is suited to children who are at least 10 years old. Other museums are aimed at junior-high or senior-high students.

The consortium presents a series of activities and tours throughout the year, including Walk Day (first Saturday in June with free admission), special art exhibits, music programs, demonstrations, and hands-on activities for all ages and interests. The first Thursday evening after Thanksgiving is Museum Shop Night, for those looking for unusual gifts. Free refreshments and transportation between the museums are provided.

● Anderson House Museum

2118 Massachusetts Avenue. (202) 785-2040. Open Tuesday through Saturday 1 to 4 P.M. Closed Sunday, Monday, and federal holidays. Self-guided or hour-long guided tours by appointment only. Dupont Circle subway station. **Ages 11 and up.**

This is the headquarters, library, and museum of the Society of the Cincinnati, which was founded by General George Washington and the officers of the Continental Army in 1783. Exhibits pertain to the American Revolution and display such relics as the swords, firearms, and uniforms of the French regiments and the naval units that fought in the war. Military miniatures ready for battle and European and Oriental decorative arts are on view. Most appropriate for older children or for any child who has studied the Revolutionary War.

● Columbia Historical Society Heurich House Museum

1307 New Hampshire Avenue. (202) 785-2068. Mansion is open Wednesday through Saturday from noon to 4 P.M. Closed Sunday, Monday, Tuesday, *and federal holidays. Hour-long docent-led tours of the mansion are conducted throughout the day, with the last tour beginning at 3:15 P.M.; all visitors to the house must join the tour. Adults, $3; senior citizens, $1.50; children, free. Library is open 10 A.M. to 4 P.M. Wednesday, Friday, and Saturday. Washingtonian Bookstore and Victorian Garden are open Tuesday through Saturday 10 A.M. to 4 P.M. Membership available. Dupont Circle subway station.* **Ages 11 and up.**

Whatever it is you want to know about Washington—history, regional and local trends, movements and personalities—you can find it at the Columbia Historical Society, located in the Christian Heurich Mansion. The library houses 12,000 books, maps, and manuscripts, and more than 70,000 photographs, 3,000 glass-plate negatives and lantern slides, 1,500 etchings, many sketches and watercolors, and a complete set of City Directories and major reference books related to the city.

The society offers museum tours designed for children, by appointment only, although it's best if they already know something about the city's history. Technology, Victorian architecture, decorative arts, and Washington's domestic life since 1790 are among the subjects covered on the tour through this 31-room late-Victorian mansion.

● Fondo del Sol Visual Arts Center

2112 R Street. (202) 483-2777. Open Tuesday through Saturday 1 P.M. to 5:30 P.M. Closed Sunday, Monday, and federal holidays. Admission is $2. Students are free. Self-guided tours, or guided tours by appointment only. Dupont Circle subway station. **Ages 11 and up.**

The center mounts changing exhibits of works by contemporary artists who reflect the multicultural makeup of the Americas. There are permanent collections of pre-Columbian art, santos (carved, wooden saints), folk art, and contemporary art. Concerts, lectures, poetry readings, performance art programs, touring exhibits, and education programs are scheduled throughout the year.

An annual Caribbean Festival, held in late summer, features outdoor performances of salsa and reggae music.

● Meridian International Center

1624 and 1630 Crescent Place. (202) 939-5568. Open Tuesday through Friday and Sunday 2 to 5 P.M. Closed Monday, Saturday, and federal holidays. Dupont Circle subway station. **Ages 6 and up.**

Intercultural understanding is promoted here through changing exhibits, lectures, and concerts. The two historic mansions housing the Meridian International Center were designed by John Russell Pope, one in classic eighteenth-century French style, the other in Georgian style. This is a nonprofit educational and cultural institution that promotes international understanding through a variety of conferences, services, and programs. A lively program of children's activities is available to acquaint youngsters with the multilingual, multiethnic community of Washington. The surrounding gardens offer a pleasant place to rest and reflect, and the view of Washington, from this perch on 16th Street at Crescent Place, is breathtaking.

● The Phillips Collection

1600 21st Street. (202) 387-0961 (recording), (202) 387-2151. Closed Monday. Open Tuesday through Saturday 10 A.M. to 5 P.M.; to 8:30 P.M. on Thursday. Sunday noon to 5 P.M. Closed federal holidays. Weekday admission is free with contributions accepted. Weekend admission fee is $6.50 for adults and $3.25 for seniors and college students. Ages 17 and under are free. Introductory tours are given Tuesday through Saturday at 10 A.M., 11 A.M., 2 P.M., and 3 P.M. Tours are not given on Sunday. Tour fees, including admission to the museum, are $7 for adults and $4.50 for senior citizens. Tours are given on Wednesday and Saturday at 2 P.M.; lectures are given on the first and third Thursday of the month at 12:30 P.M. Tours for kindergarten through twelfth grade by appointment only. Museum shop is open Tuesday through Saturday 10 A.M. to 4:30 P.M.; Sunday 2 to 6:30 P.M. Cafe hours are Tuesday through Saturday 10 A.M. to 4:15 P.M.; Sunday 2 to 6:15 P.M. Sunday concerts and song recitals at 5 P.M. from September through May, except Easter; no reservations, so arrive early. Membership available. Dupont Circle (Q Street exit) subway station. Gift shop. **Ages 6 and up.**

The Phillips Collection is the nation's oldest museum of modern art, featuring El Greco, Chardin, Manet, Bonnard, Braque, Cezanne, Klee, Monet, Rothko, O'Keeffe, and others. The collection is frequently rearranged, and special exhibits, concerts, lectures, and family programs are regularly scheduled.

As an example, during a special exhibition called "Americans in Paris," students in grades one through five were "transported" to the fascinating, fantastic world of acrobats, dancers, matadors, and musicians. Through a make-believe circus, creative pantomime, role play, and other interactive gallery activities, children learned how artists suggested performers' gestures, expressions, and emotions. Students "saw" a circus with Calder, a sideshow with Daumier, a ballet rehearsal with Degas, and a bullfight with Picasso.

The museum has an extensive children's program, and a quarterly publication about parent-child workshops is available. Ask to be placed on the mailing list.

"A Parent-Child Guide: A Child's Adventure into the Artists' World of Color" is a workbook for children ages 6 through 12 (available for a voluntary contribution of 50 cents). It is designed for adults and children to use together, with sections for drawing and looking activities. A worksheet for high-school students called "Conversations with Art" involves a three-part critique, with each student choosing a painting and then writing about the way the artist used color, line, and subject matter to convey cultural history.

● Woodrow Wilson House

2340 S Street. (202) 387-4062. Open Tuesday through Sunday 10 A.M. to 4 P.M. Closed Monday and federal holidays. Adults, $5; senior citizens (over 65), $4; students, $2.50; children under 12, free. Guided tours are given throughout the day. Dupont Circle subway station. http://www.wwh.nthp.org. **Ages 8 and up.**

Local schoolchildren often take field trips to visit this, the only presidential museum in the nation's capital. You may join them, which probably will give your children a more interesting perspective than the regularly available tour. Standard 45-minute tours follow a 30-minute film newsreel about Wilson's life and his fight for the League of Nations. President Wilson lived here after his presidency, until his death in 1924.

The tour also covers Mrs. Wilson's life as first lady and as private citizen. Children are particularly interested in objects from a life gone by, such as the Victrola with a wooden needle. Students who have studied this period of history are the most appropriate age group for a visit.

● Textile Museum

2320 S Street. (202) 667-0441. Museum and museum shop are open Monday through Saturday 10 A.M. to 5 P.M.; Sunday 1 to 5 P.M. Closed federal holidays. Free admission, but a $5 contribution is suggested. Walk-in highlights tours are given Wednesday, Saturday, and Sunday at 2 P.M. September through June. Library hours Wednesday through Friday 10 A.M. to 5 P.M., Saturday 10 A.M. to 2 P.M. Membership available. Gift shop. Dupont Circle subway station. **Ages 7 and up.**

Serious textiles studies take place here, but some exhibitions, such as those including Navajo rugs, can be interesting to children. Call about joining a school group for a specially tailored tour.

This is the place to learn everything you ever wanted to know about textiles, weaving, and related subjects. More than 14,000 textiles from around the world and 1,300 Oriental carpets are housed here, and the collection continues to grow. A library contains literature on all facets of textile art. Special exhibits, lectures, workshops, craft demonstrations, and seminars are given, and the gift shop is a treasure trove of hand-crafted weavings, rugs, blankets, scarves, and other items.

The new Activity Gallery of the Textile Learning Center shows diagrams representing a variety of textiles, from a pile rug to beaten bark cloth. You'll learn about the dynamics of creating textiles, including color, fiber, structure, and pattern. Four hands-on stations emphasize these components and each asks the viewer a question that helps explain the ways textiles can be produced. Videos and photographs tell the stories of people who make and use textiles.

● National Museum of American Jewish Military History

1811 R Street. (202) 265-6280. Open Monday through Friday from 9 A.M. to 5 P.M.; Sunday, 1 to 5 P.M. Open Memorial Day and Veterans Day, 1 to 5 P.M. Closed Saturday, Jewish holidays, and some federal holidays. Admission is free, contributions are accepted. Dupont Circle subway station. Membership available. http://www.penfed.org.jwv/museum.htm. **All ages.**

Under the auspices of the Jewish War Veterans of the USA, this museum documents and preserves the contributions of Jewish Americans to United States peace and freedom.

● Kramerbooks & Afterwords Cafe

1517 Connecticut Avenue. (202) 387-1400. Open Monday through Thursday 7 A.M. to 1 A.M.; Friday, Saturday, and Sunday 24 hours. Dupont Circle subway station. http://www.kramers.com.

Kramerbooks is an institution around Dupont Circle; plus it's the obvious place to go when you want to buy a book in the middle of the night.

You can bring your older children to the cafe (in back of the bookstore) for an enjoyable evening of live music, from folk to jazz to blues. Try for a table upstairs or in the back (you can't hear the music in the atrium).

FARRAGUT NORTH SUBWAY STATION

● Explorer's Hall, National Geographic Society

17th and M Streets. (202) 857-7588 (recording). Open Monday through Saturday and holidays 9 A.M. to 5 P.M.; Sunday 10 A.M. to 5 P.M. Closed December 25. Admission is free. Farragut North subway station. Gift shop. http://www.nationalgeographic.com. **All ages.**

Virtually everyone reads the *National Geographic,* and most children these days know *National Geographic World,* the little sibling of the yellow magazine. At the Explorer's Hall, they can live the discoveries and excitement of geography.

The south wing houses a number of exhibits throughout the year, but the north wing is home to a permanent display, "Geographica: A New Look at the World," that thrills youngsters. They can touch a tornado, walk beneath a flying dinosaur, and play with interactive-computer displays that teach them about the earth. They can meet the world's peoples and study their customs; examine jungles, lonely mountain peaks, and the world beneath the sea; and look out to the moon, the planets, and the stars beyond. At the heart of Geographica is a 72-seat interactive amphitheater that allows visitors to explore a giant globe (11 feet in diameter and weighing 1,100 pounds). At their seats, "travelers" push electronic buttons to answer questions from a "pilot" narrator. Responses are analyzed by computer and displayed on twin video walls. It's all about the geography of the earth and the fragile balance that exists among its inhabitants.

● B'nai B'rith Klutznick National Jewish Museum and Exhibit Hall

1640 Rhode Island Avenue. (202) 857-6583. Open Sunday through Friday 10 A.M. to 5 P.M. Closed Saturday and Jewish and federal holidays. Guided tours by appointment only. Farragut North subway station. **Ages 8 and up.**

Ancient and modern Jewish ceremonial art objects, items of Jewish daily life, and a historic letter George Washington wrote to the Newport, Rhode Island, Hebrew congregation following a visit are in the permanent collection. There are also changing exhibits of contemporary painting and sculpture organized along Judaic themes. An extensive library of Jewish Americana is available for research.

FARRAGUT WEST SUBWAY STATION

● Museum of Modern Art of Latin America

201 Eighteenth Street. (202) 458-6019. Open Tuesday through Saturday 10 A.M. to 5 P.M. Hour-long tours are given on request, or by appointment. Farragut West subway station. **Ages 8 and up.**

Rising behind the Pan American Union Building that houses the Organization of American States, this structure was built by Andrew Carnegie in 1912. Blue tile and a terra-cotta fresco adorn the rear portico, which overlooks the lily pond in the Aztec Garden. The art here is diverse, collected from different Latin American countries, cultures, and traditions. This museum is most appropriate for older children.

● Daughters of the American Revolution (DAR) Museum and Constitution Hall

1776 D Street. (202) 879-3241, (202) 879-3239 (children's tour and children's program information), (202) 638-2661 (concert information), (202) 879-3254 (gift shop), (202) 879-3229 (library). Open Monday through Friday 8:30 A.M. to 4 P.M.; Sunday 1 to 5 P.M. Hour-long tours are given Monday through Friday 10 A.M. to 3 P.M. (last tour starts at 2:15). Children's tours (for ages 7 and up) are given Monday through Friday at 10:30 A.M. Farragut West subway station (five long blocks). **Ages 7 and up.**

The property and headquarters of the Daughters of the American Revolution, the museum consists of 33 period rooms featuring decorative arts—furniture, ceramics, glass, paintings, silver, costumes, and textiles. The displays illustrate the artistry and craftsmanship of American artisans prior to the Industrial Revolution. Changing exhibits are presented in the museum gallery.

In the famed dollhouse exhibit, exceptional artisans decorated rooms to represent 28 states, revealing interesting tidbits about regional America. The doll collections and the schoolbooks used by pioneer children also are favorite displays.

A docent-led tour enables you to visit the New Hampshire attic where dolls, toys, and children's furniture from the eighteenth and nineteenth centuries are displayed. The "Touch of Independence" is the museum's hands-on gallery, where children can explore the discovery boxes and cubbies or sit down in reproduction chairs for a make-believe tea party. On two Sundays most months, children 5 to 7 years old can partake in a special "Colonial Adventure" program. "The Colonial Child" is a similar program for fourth through sixth grade school groups. Reservations are necessary for both programs.

Constitution Hall, a 3,746-seat auditorium, presents concerts, lectures, and meetings, but the acoustics have been known to be terrible, so try for a seat on the floor near the front.

The DAR library, a genealogical research facility in the museum, is open Monday through Friday 9 A.M. to 4 P.M., Sunday 1 to 5 P.M. (closed to nonmembers in April). Nonmembers' fee to use the library is $5 Monday through Friday, $2 between 11:30 A.M. and 1:30 P.M., and $3 on Sunday.

● Old Executive Office Building

17th Street and Pennsylvania Avenue. (202) 395-5895. Tours by advance reservation Saturday from 9 A.M. to noon. Call for reservations Tuesday through Friday 9 A.M. to noon. Security approval required; you must supply your social security number and birth date when making a reservation. Farragut West subway station. **Ages 12 and up.**

This marvelous gingerbread house, with people for gargoyles, has interesting decorative items everywhere, even on the doorknobs (shield, anchor, and eagle reflect the original history of this building, which once housed the Departments of War, Navy, and State). The East Rotunda is a favorite area with its centerpiece (designed by Richard von Ezdorf), an oval skylight in blue, white, and salmon glass supported in the corners by sirens. This site is most appropriate for older children.

● Department of the Interior Museum

Eighteenth and C Streets. (202) 208-4743. Open Monday through Friday 8 A.M. to 5 P.M. Closed federal holidays. Adults are required to show photo identification at the entrance. An Indian arts-and-crafts shop is open daily 8:30 A.M. to 4:30 P.M. (not affiliated with the department). Self-guided tours, or one-hour guided tours by appointment arranged at least two weeks in advance. Many school groups visit during the academic year, so call to see if you can join one of them. Farragut West subway station. Bring photo ID to facilitate entering the building. **Ages 12 and up.**

The Department of the Interior and the Bureau of Indian Affairs are the subjects of this museum. Children particularly like the dioramas showing historical vignettes, information about the westward expansion, and the displays of Indian objects, such as pottery, kachina dolls, stuffed eagles, and Indian headdresses. Perhaps the most unusual thing about the exhibits is that they show the warts as well as the beauty marks of the department. Another highlight is the display of murals created during the New Deal years.

FARRAGUT WEST OR FARRAGUT NORTH SUBWAY STATIONS

● Corcoran Gallery of Art

500 17th Street, NW and between New York Avenue and E Street. (202) 639-1700 (recording). Open daily except Tuesday, 10 A.M. to 5 P.M., Thursday until 9 P.M. Closed Tuesday, December 25, and New Year's Day. Admission is free, with a suggested contribution of $3 for adults, $1 for senior citizens and students, and $5 for family groups. Admission is charged for *selected special exhibitions only. A 45-minute tour is offered daily at noon and on Saturday and Sunday at 10:30 A.M., noon, and 2:30 P.M. Half-hour tours of the permanent collection are offered daily, except Tuesday, at 12:30 P.M. and Thursday at 7:30 P.M. Gift shop. Farragut West or Farragut North subway station.* **All ages.**

The Corcoran, the oldest gallery in the capital, has an extensive collection of American paintings, drawings, prints, and sculpture from the eighteenth century to the present. Its permanent displays include the William A. Clark Collection of European paintings and sculpture, tapestries, and pottery. The gallery also offers changing exhibits of prints by fine-arts photographers and regularly features the works of Washington-area artists. Lectures, films, exhibition-related workshops, and special events are regularly offered.

The Musical Evening Series presents free chamber music concerts on Friday at 8:30 P.M., about once a month, between October and May. The renowned Tokyo String Quartet and Cleveland Quartet participate regularly in the series, performing on matched sets of Amati and Stradivarius stringed instruments owned by the gallery.

To frame your refrigerator art in style, stop by the Art Shop, 500 17th Street, NW, to purchase magnetized "gilt" frames that come in four styles and two sizes, from about $4.95.

● Octagon Museum

1799 New York Avenue. (202) 638-3221. Open Tuesday through Sunday, 10 A.M. to 4 P.M. Admission is $3 for adults, $1.50 for students and senior citizens. Membership available. **Ages 9 and up.**

The Octagon Museum is the oldest museum in America dedicated to architecture, and appropriately offers exhibits and tours relating to that field. Some events include a "behind the scenes" walking tour of the museums in close proximity to the White House with a focus on the architects and design history at each site, a "Haunting Historic Houses" tour around Halloween with ghost stories and legends, and the "Architectural Details of the Federal Triangle." A most unusual tour is "Architecture Afloat," which is a 2½-hour kayak tour on the Potomac River with a focus on the architecture and history of Washington from the unique perspective of the Potomac. No kayaking experience is necessary. Children ages 10 and up are welcome. Other programs and exhibits are designed for children and families.

● Renwick Gallery (Smithsonian Institution)

17th Street and Pennsylvania Avenue. (202) 357-2700 (general Smithsonian Institution information phone number). Open daily 10 A.M. to

*5:30 P.M. Closed December 25. Guided highlights tours are given daily
10 A.M. to 1 P.M. Group tours should be arranged several weeks in advance by
calling (202) 357-2531. No admission fee. Farragut West subway station
(17th Street exit). http://www.si.edu/newstart.htm.* **All ages.**

Part of the Smithsonian Institution complex but not located on the
Mall, the Renwick showcases contemporary American crafts ranging from
the chairs of Frank Lloyd Wright to the clocks of Wendell Castle. The
building's Second Empire architecture and the Victorian-era paintings
hanging in the elaborate Grand Salon belie the contemporary feel of most
of the exhibitions. Comfortable sofas encourage a leisurely pace. The gallery is most appropriate for older children.

FEDERAL TRIANGLE SUBWAY STATION

● National Theatre
*1321 Pennsylvania Avenue. (202) 628-6161 (ticket information), (202)
783-3372 (schedule for Saturday morning and Monday night children's
programs). Federal Triangle subway station.* **All ages.**

Pre-Broadway and touring companies fill the National's stage with
top-notch entertainment. Children's programs featuring puppets, live
music, dance, magic, vaudeville, and plays are presented from fall through
spring Saturday morning at 9:30 A.M. on a first-come, first-seated basis.
Doors open at 9:15 A.M. Activities for older children are scheduled for
Monday night at 7 P.M. and at 8:30 P.M. also on a first-come, first-seated
basis. Doors open at 6:45 P.M. Write to the theater's Outreach Program
for a schedule; enclose a self-addressed, stamped envelope.

Older, theatrically minded students can stop by the theater's
fourth-floor archives to do research Monday through Friday 9:30 A.M.
to 3:30 P.M. The archives collection, which was begun in 1976, houses
5,000 books, including reference works, biographies, and scholarly studies, plus scripts and sheet music. There is also a complete collection of
National Theatre playbills dating to 1900, an architectural history of the
National, and a poster from each production, signed by the performers,
in the archives.

● Freedom Plaza
Across the Street from the National Theatre. **All ages.**

The large letters and map carved into this granite park, between the
National Theatre and the District Building, feature a paving design based
on L'Enfant's 1791 plan for the downtown portion of the city. Find Pennsylvania Avenue on the map and retrace the route you've traveled while
sightseeing.

On mild Sundays—and maybe even some other days during high tourist season—you're apt to find an impromptu circus on the Plaza as talented people (and novices) perform on Rollerblades, skateboards, bicycles, and even a unicycle, or maybe a combination of bike and skates. There may also be a juggler and who knows what else to entertain you. Your verbal approval and applause are welcomed by these exhibitionists.

● Shops at National Place

Between Thirteenth and Fourteenth Streets and E and F Streets. Federal Triangle subway station.

You'll find a variety of eateries and boutiques here. Within the block are the J.W. Marriott Hotel, the National Theatre, The National Press Club, and the Washington bureaus of many distant papers and magazines.

● Old Ebbitt Grill

675 Fifteenth Street, NW. (202) 347-4801. Open Monday through Thursday, 7:30 A.M. to 2 A.M.; Friday, 7:30 A.M. to 3 A.M.; Saturday 8 A.M. to 3 A.M.; Sunday 9:30 A.M. to 2 A.M.

The Grill has been frequented by National Theatre goers since 1856 and is still a popular spot. Children's selections are available.

● Pavilion at the Old Post Office

1100 Pennsylvania Avenue. (202) 289-4224, (202) 523-5691 (bell tower). Boutiques are open Monday through Saturday 10 A.M. to 8 P.M., eateries until 9:30 P.M.; Sunday 10 A.M. to 6 P.M. for stores and noon to 6 P.M. for eateries. Tours of the bell tower are given daily 8 A.M. to 10:30 P.M. in summer, 10 A.M. to 5:30 P.M. in winter. The tower is closed July 4, Thanksgiving, December 25, and New Year's Day. Federal Triangle subway station. http://www.oldpostofficedc.com. **All ages.**

The Old Post Office ain't what she used to be. Now there's a football-field-sized skylight over stores and boutiques, a food court, an entertainment stage, and a bell tower. Entertainment is provided just about every day at lunch time, and "after work" in the early evening hours.

Tours of the bell tower are given by the National Park Service. The ten bells (which weigh more than $6\frac{1}{2}$ tons) were presented to the U.S. Congress by the British in honor of the bicentennial. The 20-minute tours start at the glass elevator and are conducted every 5 minutes for 10 people (the elevator's capacity), but you may stay up in the belfry longer to take pictures. And this is a marvelous place for picture taking. You can see everything here that you can see from the Washington Monument, except for two things. You cannot see the shape of the Pentagon, and, of course, you cannot see the bell tower in the Old Post Office. The tower windows are large, wide, and extremely accessible. The tour explains change ringing, the art of ringing bells of various tones in various orderly progressions.

The carillon is played on Thursday from 7 to 9 P.M., when the Washington Ringing Society practices. Concerts are performed, usually around noon, on holidays and for special events (no definitive schedule).

There are no tours of the bell tower when the ringers are practicing or performing, and the tower may also be closed due to weather conditions. Because Washington skies get yucky sometimes, it's best to go early in the morning, or when you can see the sky is crystal clear, particularly if you're planning to take pictures.

The National Park Service gives walking tours from the beginning of June through mid-October of the historic preservation project known as Pennsylvania Avenue. The one- to two-hour tour covers the avenue from the White House and the Treasury Building to the Capitol.

● TICKETplace

Pavilion at the Old Post Office, ground floor. (202) TIC-KETS or 842-5387 (recording). Open Tuesday through Saturday from 11 A.M. to 6 P.M. It is closed Sunday and Monday. Federal Triangle subway station. http:// www.cultural-alliance.org/tickets.

This is the place to go for half-price, day-of-performance tickets for dance, music, and theater at more than 60 well-known Washington-area venues including Arena Stage; Kennedy Center; Lisner Auditorium; Washington Project for the Arts; Dance Place; the Folger, Ford's, Hartke, National, and Warner theaters, and a variety of dinner and alternative theaters. This is a cash-only operation. The staff also handles advance-purchase full-price tickets. A service charge of 10 percent of the full-price value is levied on each half-price ticket. Advance, full-price tickets can be charged; full-price tickets carry a $1 service charge. Performance availability is posted on a board outside TICKETplace, or you can tune to WGMS (103.5 FM) Saturday at 10:05 A.M. for a listing. The service is sponsored as a joint project of the Kennedy Center for the Performing Arts and the Cultural Alliance of Greater Washington.

● Department of Commerce

Fourteenth Street and Constitution Avenue. (202) 482-2825 (recording), (202) 482-2826. Open daily 9 A.M. to 5 P.M. Closed December 25. Aquarium admission; Adults, $2; children 2 to 12 and senior citizens, $.75. Federal Triangle subway station. **All ages.**

There are three attractions of interest in this building. The first is the huge census clock in the lobby that ticks off the births, deaths, immigration, and emigration of everyone in the United States. It gives an approximate total population count, second by second.

Although we most often hear about earthquakes in other parts of the country, the Washington area has been known to have a tremor or two, including several in Maryland in 1993. The second attraction, again in the lobby, is the seismograph machine that registers the vibrations of earthquakes.

The oldest aquarium in the country, the National Aquarium, is located on the lower level of the building. This institution can't hold a fishstick to the National Aquarium in Baltimore, but if you can't visit Charm City or if the tanks at the National Museum of Natural History only whet your appetite, then try this option. Three nurse sharks and three lemon sharks, octopuses, eyeless cave fish, lookdown fish, snapping turtles, sea anemones, baby alligators, and other strange and exotic species live here. There are no guided tours past the 70 tanks, but exhibits are well documented and the helpful staff is always nearby (Room B-037) to answer questions. Piranha feeding is scheduled on Tuesday, Thursday, and Sunday at 2 P.M. Shark feeding is Monday, Wednesday, and Saturday at 2 P.M.

Spunky, the green sea turtle that began living here in 1969, moved in 1990 to the Clearwater Marine Science Center in Florida. At 46 pounds he outgrew his 3,000-gallon tank. He has been replaced by Dundee, a smaller Australian turtle.

FOGGY BOTTOM/GWU SUBWAY STATION

● Albert Einstein Statue

2201 C Street. (202) 334-2000. Building is open Monday through Friday 8:30 A.M. to 5 P.M. Foggy Bottom/GWU subway station. **All ages.**

Children love to climb on Einstein's friendly lap, so this statue, located near the entrance to the National Academy of Sciences, is a perfect picture-taking spot. Good for picnics as well. Inside the academy are occasional art, photography, and scientific displays. There's also a Foucault pendulum. Top high-school students from across the country are selected by the Westinghouse Science Talent Search program and are honored in Washington every year. Their science projects are displayed here during the weekend they're in town, usually late February or early March.

● Department of State

2201 C Street. (202) 647-3241. Free one-hour tours of the eighth-floor diplomatic reception rooms are offered Monday through Friday at 9:30 A.M.,

10:30 A.M., and 2:45 P.M.; reservations are required. This fine-arts tour is recommended for children 12 and up. No strollers are allowed, and there is no storage space for strollers. Foggy Bottom/GWU subway station. **Ages 12 and up.**

Part of the executive branch, this agency is responsible for formulating and implementing U.S. foreign policy. The building also houses the International Development Cooperative Agency, the Agency for International Development, and the Arms Control and Disarmament Agency.

Eighteenth-century English cut-glass chandeliers cast a warm glow on the reception rooms that house eighteenth- and nineteenth-century decorative arts, period furniture, and paintings. Corporations and private citizens have donated most of the furnishings, with pieces by and in the style of Chippendale, Hepplewhite, Queen Anne, Sheraton, and Early American.

The secretary of state meets the press in the International Conference Room, while foreign dignitaries are received in the Diplomatic Reception Rooms. A short, twice-weekly briefing is open to the public, and is of particular interest to students studying government. Call (202) 632-2406 for information or ask your congressional representative to make arrangements.

● John F. Kennedy Center for the Performing Arts

New Hampshire Avenue at Rock Creek Parkway. (202) 467-4600, (800) 444-1324 (recording about shows and ticket purchase), (202) 416-8341 (tours). Free tours, about 45 minutes long, are conducted daily from 10 A.M. to 1 P.M. starting at the Motor Lobby on parking level A. Congressional tours begin at 9:30 A.M., with a 9:45 tour added during the summer. Half-price tickets to Kennedy Center produced and presented attractions are available to students, persons with permanent disabilities, senior citizens, military personnel in grades E-1 through E-4, and others on fixed low incomes. Gift shop. Tourmobile stop. Foggy Bottom/GWU subway station. Restaurants. http:// www.kennedy-center.org/. **All ages.**

Tours, given by the Friends of the Kennedy Center, include the theaters, lounges, and displays of gifts from various countries. The 7-foot-high Kennedy bust is in the Grand Foyer. The Hall of Nations (between the Concert Hall and the Opera House) displays flags from every country recognized by the United States, and the Hall of States (between the Eisenhower Theatre and the Opera House) has a flag from each state. Children like finding their home state flag or other flags they recognize.

The Kennedy Center houses six theaters: the Eisenhower (usually reserved for plays and comedies), the Opera House (musicals), the Concert Hall (concerts), the Terrace Theater (small, intimate productions), the

Theater Lab (for children's and experimental theater productions), and the American Film Institute Theater (224-seat auditorium for classic and new films). The Opera House and the Eisenhower have audio loops for the hearing impaired. The Metropolitan Washington Ear provides an audio description for the visually impaired during selected performances. For these audio-described performances, the company provides door-to-door transportation for the visually impaired who live in Prince George's, Montgomery, Arlington, Alexandria, and Fairfax counties, or within the District of Columbia. Call (301) 681-6636 for additional information.

The Millennium Stage, in the foyer, is the location for a daily free concert at 6 P.M. Performances range from professional jazz artists to college choirs, from Gnawan music and dance of Morocco to storyteller Namu Lwanga telling Ugandan tales. No tickets are required. (All ages.)

Theater for Young People stages music and theater of America and other countries for children from preschool and up. The show may present a fairy tale such as "The Billy Goat's Gruff," the art of Kabuki, the music videos of Frank Cappelli, a kazoo band, a Trinidad and Tobago steel band, or the masks, costumes, music, and dances of a traditional Mexican-American festival. If you're a resident, or will be visiting frequently enough to order a season subscription, you can join the First Nighters' Club, which entitles you to three specific shows and a chance to talk with the actors and designers at the after-the-show parties. Shows are staged in the Theater Lab or the Terrace Theater.

A free Open House Arts Festival is held each year in late September from noon to 6 P.M. More than 50 Washington-area artists present dance, music, and theater performances (including blues, classical, country, and gospel music; ballet, jazz, tap, ethnic, and modern dance; and puppets), with an emphasis on audience participation. Activities are held inside and outdoors.

Young people who will be in the area during July and August can apply to the Kennedy Center Theater for Young People, a component of the center's Education Department. An intensive four-week theater-training program is offered to 40 students, grades 5 through 12. They study performance and ensemble acting techniques, improvisation, character development, voice, and movement for the stage.

During the last three weeks of December, many free events are presented by local performers in the Grand Foyer. Weekend performances are every hour from 11 A.M. to 7 P.M. and weekday performances are held one hour prior to ticketed hall events.

One other place you should visit is the terrace that overlooks the Potomac and is in the flight path for planes landing at or departing from

Washington National Airport. It can be a little noisy, but is very pretty in the springtime.

When you enjoy the all-you-can-eat Sunday morning brunch at the Kennedy Center Roof Terrace Restaurant (about $9 for children under 12, $18.95 for adults), you go through the main kitchen for the buffet line. Then, the children (even toddlers) are allowed to go through the second kitchen (even adults aren't allowed), and if that's not enough, the children are invited into the pastry room. Executive Chef Max Philippe Knoepfel and assistants will give each child a toque, and they can watch the start of those mouth-watering cookie creations (12 different varieties) as 50-pound bags of flour are thrown into the mixing machines.

FRIENDSHIP HEIGHTS SUBWAY STATION

● Washington Dolls' House and Toy Museum

5236 44th Street. (202) 244-0024. Open Tuesday through Saturday 10 A.M. to 5 P.M.; Sunday noon to 5 P.M. Closed Thanksgiving, December 25, and New Year's Day. Adults, $4; children under 14, $2; seniors $3. No admission charge to the gift shops. Friendship Heights subway station. **All ages.**

Grandparents will delight at the sight of toys and games they used to play with as children. Doll and dollhouse lovers will treasure this collection of antiques assembled by Flora Gill Jacobs, who started writing about and collecting the pieces in 1945. Under all this Victorian loveliness you will find that Mrs. Jacobs dedicated the museum to the proposition that antique dollhouses comprise a study of architecture and the decorative arts in miniature, and that toys of the past reflect social history.

Items displayed are but a small part of the collection, and special exhibits salute such annual occurrences as the baseball season, Easter, and Halloween. Among other recent exhibits was one that included miniature zoos, arks, and games of a zoological nature, which was lent to the National Zoological Park in 1978-9.

Children particularly like to ring the bell in the Ohio Schoolhouse belfry and to turn the handle on the W.S. Reed Capitol to see 1884 views of the Capitol and the White House roll past.

The Edwardian Tea Room with ice cream parlor tables and chairs is available for birthday parties. Two popular gift shops provide items for dollhouse collectors. One shop stocks miniature furniture, accessories, and dolls in what is considered to be one of the most complete inventories of its kind in the United States. The other shop is directed toward dollhouse builders, with a wide assortment of building and wiring supplies, kits, and books.

GALLERY PLACE SUBWAY STATION

● National Portrait Gallery and National Museum of American Art (Smithsonian Institution)

Eighth Street between F and G Streets. (202) 357-2700 (Smithsonian information). Open daily 10 A.M. to 5:30 P.M. Closed December 25. These two galleries share one building. They also share a cafeteria open weekdays 10 to 11 A.M. for breakfast, and every day 11 A.M. to 3 P.M. for lunch. Walk-in tours (lasting about 45 minutes) for the National Portrait Gallery are offered by request on weekdays between 10 A.M. and 3 P.M. and weekends at 11:15 A.M. and on request at other times. National Museum of American Art walk-in tours (lasting about one hour) are given weekdays at noon and weekends at 2 P.M. Tours with sign language and oral interpreters (lasting about one hour) are available upon request (preferably with advance notice). School groups wishing to visit the Museum of American Art should call (202) 357-3095. Gallery Place subway station (Ninth Street exit). http:// www.si.edu/newstart.htm. **All ages.**

The National Museum of American Art is often referred to as the "unknown" museum, because its more frequently visited sisters in the Smithsonian family are all along the Mall and this one is a few blocks away. That generally means the crowds are smaller here so you'll have more time to enjoy the displays.

The collection encompasses the full range of America's artistic ancestry, from colonial to contemporary, from masters to less-than-masters, including Gilbert Stuart, Mary Cassatt, John Singer Sargent, James McNeill Whistler, Winslow Homer, Robert Henri, and Helen Frankenthaler.

Occasionally, workbooks are created and family workshops are held to accompany a special exhibit.

A special collection in the museum consists of more than 1,400 diverse and dynamic works by black American artists: Henry Ossawa Tanner, William H. Johnson, Palmer Hayden, Sargent Claude Johnson, William Edmondson, Eldzier Cortor, James Hampton, Jacob Lawrence, Bob Thompson, George W. White, Jr., Alma Thomas, and Sam Gilliam.

Another special collection showcases the huge family of Hispanic-American artists. The works range from the traditional religious painting and sculpture of Jose Benito Ortega and Pedro Antonio Fresquis (also known as the Truchas Master), the primitive carving of Patrocinio Barela, the folk sculpture of Felipe Archuleta, the painting of the self-taught artist Alexander Maldonado, and the drawings of the schizophrenic Martin Ramirez, to the more sophisticated modern work of Pedro Cervantez and Luis Jimenez.

One item in the permanent collection that simply fascinates people is James Hampton's *The Throne of the Third Heaven of the Nations' Millennium General Assembly.* The 177 glittering articles that make up the work are constructed of such ordinary objects as bottles, old furniture, cardboard, kraft paper, desk blotters, transparent plastic, and light bulbs, all covered with aluminum and gold foil. A throne sits in the center, flanked by the Old Testament on the right and the New Testament on the left. Crowning the chair are the words "Fear Not," and tacked to Hampton's bulletin board is the inscription, "Where There Is No Vision the People Perish." Although the work is religious in intention, most people tend to focus on the radiance, symmetry, decorative patterns, and eccentric improvisation of the throne. This is guaranteed to be one exhibit you'll never forget.

A CD-ROM about the NMAA is available in the American Art museum shop. It explains such things as how the colorful fiberglass statue of a Mexican cowboy came to stand on the steps of the museum, and other interesting facts about 762 NMAA artworks. You can video tour the museum with Director Elizabeth Broun, or find a timeline that groups art by period from 1727 to 1995. You also can locate artists from a particular geographic area and other artworks associated with that state. Sound bites and media clips (62 of them) include an interview with Luis Jimenez, the creator of *Vaquero,* the statue on the NMAA steps.

On the opposite side of the building are the National Portrait Gallery and the Archives of American Art. Together they house an extensive collection, including 250,000 paintings executed before 1914, 127,000 photographic negatives documenting works by more than 11,000 artists, and much, much more. An active program of lectures and seminars ensures that continuing research in American art is presented to a broad public.

● MCI Center

7th and F Streets. (202) 628-3200. For information about accessible seating, call (202) 661-5065. The TTY number is (202) 661-5066. Tours (202) 661-5061. http://www.mcicenter.com. Gallery Place subway station. **All ages.**

This new 20,000-seat sports and entertainment arena provides entertainment for you, even while you're home. Go to the Web page and you can view a Quicktime movie of the arena being constructed. Click again, and you can view a live shot from the center. A Kids Corner features a puzzle page and trivia questions.

The MCI Center is home to the professional basketball team the Washington Wizards, and hockey team the Washington Capitals; and the Georgetown University men's college basketball team. However, even when the teams aren't playing, there are things to see and do. The 25,000-square-foot MCI Sports Gallery commemorates the finest players of American sports, and has a huge memorabilia collection. Technology-driven and participatory sports-themed exhibits make this much more interesting than your old sports halls of fame. You can play a technology age of basketball against an NBA superstar, throw a game-winning pitch in the World Series, or make an amazing save against hockey's top players, all in a virtual world.

The American Sportscasters Association Hall of Fame is also here. At each display, the voices synonymous with the great moments of sports—Curt Gowdy, Red Barber, Jim McKay, Harry Caray, and others—narrate the memories.

Discovery Communications (Discovery Channel's parent company) launched its Discovery Channel Destination store, which features an interactive environment and plenty of sports-related items to buy.

The Velocity Grill, an upscale restaurant, offers a place to eat before or after the game, or a prime spot to watch the Wizards working out on their practice court. An in-house video set-up shows arena events. (202) 347-7780.

● Hard Rock Cafe

999 E Street. (202) 737-7625. Restaurant and gift shop open daily 11 A.M. to 2 A.M.; after 9 P.M. gift shop can be entered only from inside the restaurant. Gallery Place subway station. **All ages.**

This cafe, as with others in the chain, is filled with memorabilia that children love (and enough memories from our generation that we can be appreciative as well). Chubby Checker's checkered boots, the trumpet from Sergeant Pepper's Lonely Hearts Club Band, Elvis's hat and microphone, Al Jolson's Uncle Sam costume, and other items from or about Michael and Janet Jackson, Grace Jones, Bo Diddley, Dion, Dave Edmonds, Wilt Chamberlain, and local celebrity Donna Rice.

The gift shop carries T-shirts, hats, watches, badge and guitar pins, key rings, towels, fanny packs, jackets, and other goods that are indispensable for HRC collections.

● Chinatown Friendship Archway

Seventh and H Streets. Lit for an evening visit. Gallery Place metro.
All ages.

This marvelously colorful arch marks the entrance to the eight-block Chinatown neighborhood, bounded by H, I, Sixth, and Eleventh Streets. Said to be the largest Chinese-motif archway in the world, the intricate red, blue, green, and gold foil structure has 7,000 tiles, 272 painted dragons in the styles of the Ming and Qing dynasties, and numerous other animals. The annual Chinese New Year's Parade of dancers, floats, and dragons passes under the arch. Several Chinese restaurants are located in the area.

JUDICIARY SQUARE SUBWAY STATION

● National Building Museum

Judiciary Square, F Street between Fourth and Fifth Streets. (202) 272-2448. Open Monday through Saturday 10 A.M. to 5 P.M., Sunday 12 noon to 5 P.M. Closed Thanksgiving, December 25, and New Year's Day. Guided tours are given daily at 12:30 P.M. and also at 1:30 P.M. on weekends, and federal holidays at 1 P.M.; reservations are required. Some exhibits are more interesting to children than others; call for a schedule. Gift shop. Coffee bar. Membership available. Judiciary Square (F Street exit) subway station. http://www.nbm.org. **Ages 5 and up.**

One permanent highlight of this monument to the building arts in America is an exterior terra-cotta frieze (1,200 feet long, 3 feet high) that encircles the building and depicts a processional of veterans returning from the nation's wars. It is dedicated to all who gave their lives for an ideal. The building features the world's tallest Corinthian columns.

This museum is devoted to the study of architecture and how it reflects and affects our lives. At one time this structure was the Pension Building, and one of the permanent exhibits, which includes an audiovisual program, is about the building's history. Another exhibit looks at the Brooklyn Bridge, with seven full-scale, three-dimensional models explaining the unique construction. Try doing that with an Erector Set.

It has been said that the steps in this 1880s building were constructed with unusually short risers so horses could more easily walk up them to their quarters on the top floor, where plenty of air circulated through the windows. Museum officials denounce this tale as rumor and hearsay. But who are you going to believe? A group of experts or a good story about horses?

Family Programs include constructing a gingerbread house, designing and building a miniature model city, or assembling an 8-foot-by-11-foot house. Demonstrations, hands-on experiences, films, music, and folklore are used to familiarize children with the skills and traditions of builders. On Saturday, 20-minute explorations are offered via demonstration carts covering basic structural principles, building tools, and materials. Activity booklets on such topics as architectural style and engineering are available at $3 a set.

School programs are offered for grades kindergarten through 12 and highlight critical thinking, creative problem solving, and visual literacy.

● National Law Enforcement Officers Memorial

Between Fourth and Fifth, E and F Streets. (202) 737-3400. The memorial is open 24 hours a day. The visitor center is two blocks away at 605 E Street and is open Monday through Friday from 9 A.M. to 5 P.M.; Saturday from 10 A.M. to 5 P.M.; Sunday from 12 noon to 5 P.M. Call for a tour of the memorial. **All ages.**

The gray marble walls of this memorial are engraved with the names of more than 14,000 federal, state, and local law enforcement officers who have died in the line of duty.

MCPHERSON SQUARE SUBWAY STATION

● White House

1600 Pennsylvania Avenue. (202) 208-1631 or (202) 456-7041. TTY (202) 208-1636 or (202) 456-2121. Open Tuesday through Saturday 10 A.M. to noon; Saturday, during June, July, and August, until 2 P.M. Closed federal holidays and during special events. Guided tours are available. Tourmobile stop. McPherson Square subway station. Note: as of this writing, security barriers prohibit vehicular traffic in front of the White House. The District of Columbia government is trying to have Pennsylvania Avenue re-opened, but that possibility has not been resolved at this time. http:// www.whitehouse.gov. **Ages 8 and up.**

Every president since John Adams has called the White House home. There are two ways you can arrange to visit select parts of their home. The first (and less desirable) way is to stop by the White House Visitor Center, 1450 Pennsylvania Avenue, NW, between 7:30 A.M. and 4 P.M. to pick up free timed tour tickets. People line up as early as 5:30 A.M. for these passes, and scalpers have been known to charge late-comers as much as $50 for these free passes. Sometimes, these passes are forgeries or outdated. Be careful if you buy a White House pass.

If you are visiting during the tourist season and do not have an early tour, you will have plenty of time to do some other sightseeing and then return a little before your appointed time. This is not a narrated tour, but guides will answer questions. You'll see seven of the mansion's 132 rooms, including the Green Room (look for the Monet painting), the Blue Room (with portraits of the first seven presidents), the Red Room (with Gilbert Stuart's portrait of Dolley Madison), the great gold-and-white East Room (featuring Gilbert Stuart's portrait of George Washington), and the State

Dining Room (look for John Adams's blessing carved into the mantel-piece). The tour may last as few as 10 minutes.

The second, and much better, way is to write to your congressional representative (write early; there are relatively few tickets available) and ask for a VIP tour. This will allow you to enter the White House for an 8:30 A.M. tour with real guides. You'll see the above-mentioned rooms, plus the lobby and three smaller rooms, the China Room, the Diplomatic Reception Room, and the Vermeil Room. Another advantage to this tour is that you're out early enough to do an entire day's sightseeing, or even make the early line at the Bureau of Engraving and Printing or at the FBI Building.

A number of special events are held at the White House, such as the egg roll on Easter Monday morning for children ages 8 and under. It takes place on the White House lawn and the eggs are provided. Children must be accompanied by an adult. The mid- to late-April Spring Garden Tours show off the beautiful gardens, including the Jacqueline Kennedy Rose Garden and the west lawn.

When the President leaves the city, he usually flies via helicopter to Andrews Air Force Base in nearby Prince George's County. The helicopters take off from the south lawn of the White House, so if you know this is scheduled (check the *Washington Post*), you can watch from the E Street area.

Stand on the Pennsylvania Avenue, or north side, of the White House around six o'clock on a busy news day, and you're likely to see network television crews and White House reporters do segments for that evening's broadcasts. Also across the street, in Lafayette Square, are chess tables.

The White House Christmas Candlelight Tour is available each season on two evenings only. This free tour, which begins at 6 P.M., is an opportunity to view the lovely White House Christmas decorations aglow with candlelight. Call (202) 456-2200 for information.

● **Ellipse**
During the last two weeks of December, the Ellipse grounds behind the White House are the site of the National Christmas Tree and nightly caroling, a Nativity scene, a burning yule log to warm chilled hands, and a glorious display of decorated Christmas trees, representing each state and territory in the United States. McPherson Square subway station. Call (202) 628-3400 for information. **All ages.**

A Twilight Tattoo is presented on the Ellipse by the U.S. Army Drill Team, the U.S. Army Band, and the Third U.S. Infantry (The Old Guard) with their Fife and Drum Corps every Wednesday at 7:30 P.M. from mid-July to mid-August. The concerts are free, and no tickets are required. Call (202) 475-0856 for information.

Behind the White House, on the Ellipse, is the zero mile marker. All mileage distances to Washington are measured from this spot.

● Bethune Museum and Archives

1318 Vermont Avenue. (202) 332-1233. Open Monday through Friday 10 A.M. to 4 P.M. Saturday and Sunday by appointment. Hour-long tours are available by appointment. Free admission. Membership available. McPherson Square subway station. **All ages.**

This Logan Circle Victorian townhouse was the former home of civil rights leader and educator Mary McLeod Bethune. Born in 1878, Bethune believed in the education of black Americans. As a child, she walked 10 miles a day to attend school, and was then given money to go to college by a white dressmaker. In 1904 she opened her own school in Dayton Beach, Florida, with $1.50. She begged strangers, hunted the city's dump and trash piles to get what she needed, and mended and cleaned everything. In 1923, the school became Bethune-Cookman College, and she was its first president.

When President Franklin Roosevelt named her in charge of Negro Affairs of the National Youth Administration in 1936, she became the first black woman to be a presidential advisor. She died in 1955 and is buried on the grounds of Bethune-Cookman College. Today this home provides a backdrop for changing and permanent art and history exhibits that focus on African-American women's issues.

● *Washington Post*

1150 Fifteenth Street. (202) 334-7969. Guided one-hour tours are given Monday and Thursday at 10 A.M., 11 A.M., 1 P.M., and 2 P.M.; reservations are required and children must be at least 11 or in the fifth grade. McPherson Square subway station. **Ages 11 and up.**

Children watch newspaper operations so much on television, from the old mom-and-pop paper to the big-city newsroom, that you'd think there's nothing new to see. A visit to the *Post* changes that opinion, because there's no way to appreciate how many people are involved and how much activity goes into the paper's production until you see it in person.

The tour takes you to the newsroom, production area, and the press room, although the presses are not running during the visit (the *Post*, a morning paper, is printed at night).

METRO CENTER SUBWAY STATION

● National Museum of Women in the Arts

1250 New York Avenue. (202) 783-5000. Open Monday through Saturday 10 A.M. to 5 P.M., Sunday noon to 5 P.M. Gift shop. (202) 783-7994. Mezzanine Cafe (202) 628-1068, reservations accepted. Membership available. No admission fee; suggested donation of $3. Metro Center (Thirteenth Street exit) subway station. http://www.nmwa.org. **All ages.**

This is the only museum in the United States dedicated to women's historical contributions to art, including the fields of visual and performing arts, and writing. Special tours for families with children usually are conducted on Sunday afternoon, and reservations are requested. Guided walk-in tours usually are given twice a day, depending on docent availability. Guided reserved tours ($5 per person) need advance request notice. The museum offers a variety of education programs for children, teens, adults, and teachers, designed around three themes—"Discovering Women Artists," "Women in Performance," and "Women and Creativity." Lectures by and about women artists, symposia, gallery talks, readings and book signings, concerts, theater and dance performances, film, trips and workshops are regularly scheduled. Some of these complement exhibits, but others are offered independently.

Although most children tend to prefer the contemporary art in this collection, they all seem to love the building, starting from when they walk in and see the huge, lovely open-space lobby with winding marble staircases on either side of the Great Hall.

There are numerous changing and permanent exhibits, and the Education Department is working toward a family activities guide for the permanent collection and for the major temporary exhibits.

The NMWA has a partnership with the Girl Scouts of the U.S.A., which produces special materials that teach girls about the world of art and women artists. With all purchases, troops receive a troop membership to the museum. (202) 783-7369 or (800) 222-7270.

● Federal Bureau of Investigation

Ninth Street and Pennsylvania Avenue. (202) 324-3447. Open Monday through Friday 9 A.M. to 4:15 P.M. Closed federal holidays. Cameras are not allowed. Metro Center subway station. http://www.fbi.gov. **Ages 8 and up.**

Also known as the J. Edgar Hoover Building, this stop offers one of the more popular tours in town. Everyone knows you get to see all kinds of guns, an agent practicing in the basement firing range, posters of the

10 most wanted criminals, mini spy cameras, hollowed-out coins that hide microdots, a walking cane that is actually a shotgun, and other representations of the "bad guys" of drugs, terrorism, organized crime, bank robbery, and white-collar crime versus the "good guys."

Arrive early to avoid the up-to-two-hour lines (in peak tourist season) or write to your congressional representative for FBI tour passes that are scheduled for a specific time. This tour is not recommended for children under 7, because younger children normally aren't tall enough to see through the glass windows.

The hour-long tour starts every 15 or 20 minutes. It takes visitors past laboratories (serology, ballistics and microscopic analysis, fingerprint files), a collection of 5,000-plus guns (80 percent of which were confiscated or donated—mostly from criminals), and the room where the FBI displays $1.5 million worth of jewelry and furs confiscated from drug dealers. Along the way, you'll see G-Man toys from the 1930s and 1940s, and a safety film made by Bill Cosby. You will end up at the range for target practice, a stop that may include a few dozen hollow-tip .38-caliber, 9 mm, and machine-gun slugs fired at the heart of a paper-target bad guy. A question-and-answer session follows with the agent from the firing demonstration.

A noontime Courtyard Concert Series is scheduled periodically from May to September, usually featuring military bands.

● Ford's Theatre/Lincoln Museum

511 Tenth Street. (202) 638-2941 (ticket information), (202) 426-6924 (museum). Open daily 9 A.M. to 5 P.M. Closed December 25. Theater is closed to sightseers during matinees and rehearsals. No guided tours. Bookstore. Metro Center subway station (Eleventh Street exit). **Ages 6 and up.**

Restored in 1968, Ford's Theatre, where President Abraham Lincoln was fatally shot on April 14, 1865, has been restored once again. The presidential box, where Lincoln was sitting during a performance of *Our American Cousin,* is as it was. The basement houses a museum of objects used by Lincoln in his personal and public life, as well as exhibits about the assassination plot. Clothing, the assassin's gun, photographs, editorial cartoons, and other memorabilia almost give life to this tall man. And if you want to see how tall he was, compare yourself with the "Measure of Lincoln."

The restoration of the theater as a museum and a performing-arts venue can be attributed to the hard work and dedication of such people as executive producer Frankie Hewitt and Ford's Theatre Board of Trustees member Roger Mudd (whose relative was accused of being part of the plot because he set Booth's broken ankle, and then was later exonerated).

Regular theatrical productions are presented here, almost all of which are suitable for family audiences.

● Petersen House

526 Tenth Street. (202) 426-6830. Open daily from 9 A.M. to 5 P.M. Closed December 25. No guided tours. The house is not wheelchair accessible. Metro Center subway station (Eleventh Street exit). **Ages 6 and up.**

Across the street from Ford's Theatre is the home where the dying President Lincoln was carried. Mary Todd Lincoln and their son Robert spent the night of April 14 in the front parlor, the first room to the left. Through the double doors is the back parlor, and in the rear of the house at the end of the hall is where Lincoln died. The rooms are decorated much as they were on the night of the assassination. The furnishings are not original, but they are either good reproductions or pieces from the same period. Look at the bed and realize that Lincoln was much taller than it was long.

● Treasury Building

Pennsylvania Avenue and Fifteenth Street. (202) 622-0896 (recording of open tour dates). Tours are given Saturdays at 10, 10:20, and 10:40 A.M.; reservations are required at least three days in advance, and you must provide the name, birth date, and social security number of everyone who will attend. Adults need a photo identification upon arrival. Video cameras are not allowed. Enter on the lower level (marked Employees Entrance) on the Fifteenth Street side. Metro Center or McPherson Square subway station. **Ages 12 and up.**

Blocking the view from the White House to the Capitol, this building is noted for its balconied marble hall (72 by 32 feet and $27\frac{1}{2}$ feet high), an 1864 burglarproof vault, and the suite of rooms that once served Andrew Johnson as a temporary White House. Wear flat shoes, for there are lots of steps.

ELSEWHERE IN THE NORTHWEST

● Hillwood

4155 Linnean Avenue. (202) 686-5807. Two-hour guided tours are given daily, except Sunday and Monday, at 9 A.M., noon, 1:30 P.M., and 3 P.M.; reservations are required. Spring and fall are extraordinarily busy times and reservations for these seasons must be made months in advance; March and

November tours are much easier to arrange. Admission is $10 to the house and grounds, $2 to the American Indian exhibit and gardens only (11 A.M. to 3 P.M.). Children under 12 are not admitted into the house. Reservations also are needed for tea. Closed January and February. Some of the house is not wheelchair accessible. Gift shop. Hillwood has been closed since November 1997 for a two-year renovation and restoration. **Ages 12 and up.**

During her four marriages and for the rest of her life, Marjorie Merriweather Post compulsively accumulated things, especially Russian and French decorative art pieces, and particularly when her second husband, Joseph E. Davies, was ambassador to the Soviet Union. Although she lived in this huge house with 40 rooms (but only three bedrooms), Post designed Hillwood to be a museum for her extraordinary gatherings.

The collections are fascinating and mind-numbing at the same time, and even 12-year-olds, the minimum age permitted entrance, may be too young to enjoy the experience, except for the exceptional child who's fascinated by collections of "things." It's almost too much for adults, and after hearing about the dozens of china place settings and the multitudes of this and that, most people on the tour start asking questions about Post's daughter, Dina Merrill. The value of the collection probably is in the quantity gathered rather than in the quality, although the Russian imperial Easter eggs and other items by Fabergé are nothing to sneeze at.

The grounds, including rose gardens, a formal French garden, a Japanese garden, and the Friendship Walk dedicated to more than one hundred of Mrs. Post's friends, are gorgeous. A peak time is when the azaleas, rhododendrons, and dogwoods are in bloom. From the south portico and the south lawn you can see across Rock Creek Park into downtown Washington.

Nearly 200 American Indian artifacts are displayed in the Indian Building. They include basketry, beadwork, leather moccasins, Navajo blankets, and pottery from the Hopi, Acoma, and Santa Clara tribes. The collection was moved here from Topridge, Mrs. Post's summer home in the Adirondacks. The building replicates the rough country nature of the camps constructed in upstate New York early in this century. Children seem particularly fascinated with the playing cards dating from the early 1900s, made of tanned and painted hide. The suits are clubs, coins, cups, and swords, rather than the clubs, diamonds, hearts, and spades of today's cards. The display shows an Apache playing with the cards.

● United States Naval Observatory

Massachusetts Avenue at 34th Street. (202) 762-1467 (recording) or (202) 762-1438. Monday night celestial tours, with a look through the telescope, are at 8:30 P.M. except on holidays. Valid photo identification is required. Passes are issued to the first 90 people in line. http://aa.usno.navy.mil/aa/. **Ages 12 and up.**

One of the most famous observatories in the world, this is also the Navy's oldest scientific institution. Established in 1844, it originally occupied a small office where chronometers, charts, and other navigational equipment were kept. It now encompasses a complex of 50 buildings on 72 acres.

This is the place that keeps our time, and the time for dozens of other countries, and helps make sure that clocks on ships at sea and in the air are absolutely accurate; if a plane is a second off, that's the equivalent of about a fifth of a mile—as good as a miss when it's headed for an airport landing.

Tours here include a movie explaining the Observatory's mission, taking you into two areas of the Observatory, including an area about the history of telling time with a myriad of clocks and timepieces from old to modern. You'll learn a little about planets, comets, and eclipses, as well. Then you'll go into the 12-inch telescope dome. (At times, the tour includes the 36-inch telescope. Either one affords an incredible view.) If this is your first look through a telescope, it's going to be a wow. You're sure to feel that you're the first person ever to witness such a miraculous sight.

One of the best souvenirs of the city can be purchased here, for about $10: a glow-in-the-dark sky T-shirt. Expose it to the light, and then reflect upon where you've been.

● Rock Creek Park

Tilden Street and Beach Drive. (202) 426-6832. Sections of Beach Drive are restricted to bicycle riders and other non-motorized traffic from 7 A.M. Saturday morning until 7 P.M. Sunday evening, extended through 7 P.M. Monday if the day is a federal holiday. **All ages.**

Whatever you might wish to do in a park, you probably can do here. There's hiking, biking, horseback riding, police canine demonstrations, an art barn, an old mill, a golf course, an orienteering course, tennis courts, picnic areas (some need reservations), a planetarium, a nature center, and more. Of course, the National Zoological Park is located in the park as well. Information on some of these attractions follows.

● Art Barn Gallery

Rock Creek Park, 2401 Tilden Street. (202) 282-1063. Open Wednesday through Saturday 10 A.M. to 5 P.M., Sunday noon to 5 P.M. Closed Monday, Tuesday, and federal holidays. Tours are given Wednesday, Thursday, and

Friday at 10 A.M, 1 P.M., and 3:30 P.M.; reservations are suggested. **All ages.**

Local professional artists display their works here in rotating exhibits throughout the year. Art classes are offered on Saturday morning with a different artist-in-residence each month. Artist demonstrations are held on Sunday from 1 P.M. to 3 P.M.

● Peirce Mill

Rock Creek Park, Beach Drive and Tilden Street. (202) 426-6908. Open daily 10 A.M. to 3:30 P.M. Closed federal holidays. **All ages.**

The last of eight nineteenth-century flour mills along Rock Creek, the Peirce Mill is an authentic restoration of an 1820 grist mill. Costumed helpers grind grain into flour, which is then sold for about $2 to $4 per pound. Choices include buckwheat, corn, rye, or other flours, depending upon what's in stock. You can watch demonstrations of butter churning and batter-cake making, tour art exhibits, or participate in a children's activity day. You also may encounter lacemaking, stone carving, dulcimer making, fish-decoy carving, wheat weaving, and basketmaking demonstrations.

● Rock Creek Nature Center

5200 Glover Road. (202) 426-6828. Open daily 9 A.M. to 5 P.M. Closed federal holidays. **All ages.**

The buildings and nature trails here are designed to teach youngsters about the natural world and their relationship to it. An exhibit hall displays examples of local animal life, including a live bee colony, and minerals. The nature walks, led by park rangers and scientists, usually emphasize a single theme—ecology, mushrooms, Indian life. These walks occur on weekdays to accommodate school groups, but weekend tours are also available.

The center includes a planetarium that presents two free shows, at 1 and 4 P.M. on Saturday and Sunday. The early show, "An Introduction to the Night Sky," is for ages 4 and up; the 4 P.M. show is geared to children ages 7 and up and changes monthly. Free tickets are handed out 30 minutes before each show.

● Washington National Cathedral

Massachusetts and Wisconsin Avenues, at Woodley Road. (202) 364-6616 (recording), (202) 537-6200, (202) 537-8982 (herb cottage), (202) 537-6263 (greenhouse). Open daily 10 A.M. to 4:30 P.M., until 9 P.M. in summer. Walk-in tours are given Monday through Saturday 10 A.M. to 4:30 P.M.,

Sunday at 1 P.M. and 2 P.M. Hours subject to change. There is no charge, but a donation of $2 for adults and $1 for children is suggested. Special-interest tours and a Tuesday tour that includes a tea break ($15 charge) are available; call (202) 537-6207. Observation Gallery is open Monday through Saturday 10 A.M. to 3:15 P.M., Sunday 12:30 P.M. to 3:45 P.M. Membership available. Gift shop. Snack bar. Tourmobile stop. **Ages 6 and up.**

Officially the Cathedral Church of St. Peter and St. Paul, after 83 years of on-again, off-again construction (an amazingly short time for an undertaking of this size), this Gothic cathedral had its last stone set and was formally consecrated in September 1990.

For a self-guided tour of the cathedral, pick up the turquoise-colored brochure near the entrance. A free 30-minute tour starts by the Space Window, a stained-glass creation dedicated to the Apollo 11 moon landing. In the center of the window is a piece of moon rock. At this point, any child who is old enough to think a cathedral tour might be really dull snaps to attention.

The Children's Chapel, built to a child's scale, is interesting, as is the War Memorial Chapel with its image of the raising of the flag at Iwo Jima worked into the lower left-hand corner of the stained-glass window. There's also a Maryland window, and several pieces of glass form prisms that cast rainbows of colors onto the floor and onto the people passing under their rays. Flags of the 50 states are located along the nave, and a prayer is said for one state each week.

The Observation Gallery (push the 7th floor button in the elevator) has a short film about the construction and history of the cathedral and offers some pretty spectacular views from the 70 windows overlooking all of the Potomac Valley, including Tysons Corner in Virginia and the far-away Blue Ridge Mountains. Other views from the gallery include the cathedral's buttresses, towers, and a limited look at some of the gargoyles. You can see the 103 gargoyles and grotesques in more detail if you bring field glasses (it's said that only God and the pigeons see the tops of the gargoyles). The construction display shows a couple of miniature examples, including a grotesque shaped like a television cameraman in honor of the numerous Christmas masses and other services broadcast from the cathedral. The gargoyles and grotesques are used in the rain drainage system; the gargoyles have water spouts but the grotesques do not.

Another pretty good view of Washington is from the south lawn, where the Peace Cross stands.

Although the cathedral is 676 feet above sea level, the bell tower itself is only 301 feet tall. Thus, the Washington Monument is a taller building even though the cathedral is 60 feet higher. The 53-bell carillon weighing 60 tons is played weekdays from 12:15 to 12:45 P.M. A 10-bell ring, the only one of its kind in the world, is rung following the 11 A.M. service every Sunday. The carillon is played on Saturdays at 5 P.M. (12:30 P.M. in winter). Visitors are not permitted at the top of the bell tower.

The cathedral has a medieval workshop that is a hands-on activity center where families can learn something about the craft of building a Gothic cathedral. You can piece together a stained-glass window, build stone arches as a mason (learning a little physics lesson along the way), lay a flagstone patio, try your skill as a stone carver, discover the artistry of the blacksmith, create a piece of needlework, and design your own gargoyle or grotesque. *National Geographic World* magazine sponsored a design contest for children and the winning entries, on display here, were carved by the cathedral's mason and then mounted. Among them is one called the Sagacious Grotesque, who holds an umbrella up to protect itself from the rain. The workshop is open Saturdays from 11 A.M. to 2 P.M. and there's no charge. Admission is on a first-come, first-served basis, but try to tour the cathedral first. The workshop is closed during August. Call (202) 637-2930 for information.

Other attractions are the herb cottage (you can purchase dried herbs for flavor or scent), a greenhouse, and a gift shop. State guest books are available for you to sign in as a visitor of the cathedral. During the school year, organ demonstrations are held on Wednesdays at 12:15 P.M., and the walls virtually shake when the 11,500-pipe organ is played. Sunday afternoon organ recitals following evensong are scheduled, performed by visiting organists.

● The Washington News Observer

811 Florida Avenue. (202) 232-3060. **Ages 6 and up.**

Free tours by appointment weekdays from noon to 3 P.M. for ages 6 and older in groups of 15 or fewer. On the tour you see the day-to-day operation of a small, minority-owned newspaper including question-and-answer sessions with reporters and photographers.

GEORGETOWN

Georgetown, named in honor of King George II, started as an Indian trading center in the 1600s and was a busy tobacco port by the later half of the eighteenth century. Now it's an eclectic mix of smart boutiques, intriguing bookstores, pricey restaurants, and outdoor cafes (weather permitting). It's a great place for "cruising" to see the local sights and personalities and for "cruising" along the canal. Some eateries have been here for decades; others seem to appear and disappear overnight. Fast food also is available.

Parking can be difficult and your pocket can be picked, so watch the parking prohibition signs (particularly on weekends and on neighborhood streets) and be careful when you're walking and shopping.

● C&O Canal Barge Rides

Foundry Mall, 1055 Thomas Jefferson Street (ticket office). (301) 299-2026 (recording), (301) 299-3613. Hours and days vary; summer barge trips depart Wednesday through Sunday at 10:30 A.M.,1 P.M., and 3 P.M.; reduced schedule in effect in spring and fall. Reservations are suggested. Adults, $5; senior citizens (ages 62 and over), $3.50; children ages 12 and under, $3.50. http://www.nps.gov/choh. **All ages.**

You can explore the area via mule-drawn canal rides, at Georgetown in Washington and at Great Falls in Potomac, Maryland, from about mid-April through mid-October. Conducted by the Georgetown C&O Canal National Historical Park, the rides re-create what life was like on the barges more than a century ago.

The 50- to 60-minute round trip aboard the *Georgetown* takes you through the historic part of town. Guides wear period costumes and answer questions about life along the canal prior to 1876. The ride along the canal, which operated from about 1830 to 1924, is a drastic change from the current lifestyle and pace of today's Georgetown. The 90-foot boat is moved through a lock process that visually explains how boats are lifted and lowered from one water level to another.

One-hour day trips and two-hour evening trips can be booked by groups, at special rates. Bring your favorite musical instrument along for an old-fashioned sing-along.

● Dumbarton Oaks

1703 32nd Street. (202) 339-6400 or (202) 339-6401. Museum is open Tuesday through Sunday 2 to 5 P.M. Museum is closed Monday and federal holidays. Free admission, but a $1 contribution is suggested. Group tours of the museum are given Tuesday, Wednesday, Thursday, and Saturday; reservations are required. Ten acres of formal gardens are open daily 2 to 6 P.M. from April 1 to October 30, 2 to 5 P.M. from November 1 to March 31. Gardens are closed on federal holidays. Admission to the gardens is adults, $3; children under 12 and seniors, $2. **Ages 8 and up.**

The museum contains two impressive collections, one of pre-Columbian art and one of Byzantine art that includes a library of more than 80,000 volumes. Younger children (ages 8 and older) should enjoy the pre-Columbian displays of sculpture and gold, but most of the museum's exhibits are more appropriate for older children. Many garden enthusiasts consider these gardens among the most enchanting in the country.

● Francis Scott Key Park, the Star-Spangled Banner Monument near Key Bridge

3414 Prospect Street, NW. (202) 965-3131. **All ages.**

Consider seeing this park, dedicated on September 14, 1993 (the 179th anniversary of Key's writing the famed poem), in conjunction with Fort McHenry in Baltimore. It's located adjacent to where Key lived for most of his life and particularly at the time of the writing of "The Star-Spangled Banner." It overlooks the Potomac River and Virginia, at the Washington end of Key Bridge.

The Centerpiece is a plaza and pergola (a round arbor with plantings), an ornate trellis, and limestone columns. A bronze bust of Key by Georgetown artist Betty Mailhouse Dunston is the focus. A 60-foot lighted flagpole flies the 15-star, 15-stripe flag 24 hours a day. Interpretive plaques describe Key's life, his poem, and the events leading to its composition.

In conjunction with the park's dedication in 1993, the National Geographic Society released a 232-page large-format book, *Star-Spangled Banner: Our Nation and Its Flag,* by Margaret Sedeen. The book is full of facts and anecdotes, is illustrated with 249 photographs and paintings, and traces the evolution of the flag from those flown by early settlers to the largest one ever made—the size of three football fields and unfurled by the Humphrys Flag Company in Pottstown, Pennsylvania, in 1992.

● Old Stone House

3051 M Street. (202) 619-7222. Open Wednesday through Sunday 8 A.M. to 4:30 P.M. Closed Monday, Tuesday, and federal holidays. Limited wheelchair accessibility. **Ages 8 and up.**

This is one of the first dwellings built in Washington and the oldest in Georgetown. It was constructed in 1765 and is considered an excellent example of pre-revolutionary architecture. Colonial-costumed guides take visitors through the house and demonstrate early American cookery, spinning, weaving, candle dipping, and pomander making. Children particularly enjoy the craft demonstrations, and special children's days are scheduled periodically, with the entire day focused on family activities. The National Park Service has restored this house and maintains its colorful gardens.

● Tudor Place

1644 31st Street. (202) 965-0400. Open for tours Tuesday through Friday at 10 P.M., 1 P.M., and 2:30 P.M., and on Saturday every hour on the hour from 10 A.M. to 4 P.M. with the last tour starting at 3 P.M. Reservations are recommended. The suggested donation is $5, which includes a self-guided tour of the gardens. The gardens are open Monday through Saturday from 10 A.M. to 4 P.M. A $2 donation is encouraged for the gardens. **Ages 8 and up.**

Tudor Place is a historic house and garden. For two centuries the neoclassical mansion, filled with family collections, was occupied by the Custis-Peters, descendants of Martha Washington. A children's program is in the works.

● Made By You

1826 Wisconsin Avenue. (202) 337-3180. Sunday through Tuesday 11 A.M. to 6 P.M.; Wednesday through Friday 10 A.M. to 9 P.M.; Saturday 10 A.M. to 6 P.M. Prices ranges from $4 to $65. **Ages 4 and up.**

Throwing clay can be fun and delightfully messy and creative. There's even some instant gratification involved. But for a finished product in considerably less time, stop by Made By You. You choose from 150 ready-made ceramic pieces, design and paint your selection, and the shop will glaze and fire it for you. A kids' club meets every afternoon, with an interesting project for children: Monday through Friday, from 4 to 5 P.M.

● Garrett's

3003 M Street. (202) 333-1033. Monday through Saturday 11:30 A.M. to 10:30 P.M.; Sunday 4 P.M. to 10:30 P.M. **All ages.**

After some time examining full-size railroad apparatuses, it might be fun to head toward a "museum" of railroading memorabilia while you're enjoying a meal at Garrett's. This historic Georgetown colonial house was built by Thomas Sim Lee, second governor of Maryland and a member of the famed Lee family of Virginia. There's a sunny (weather cooperating) glass-enclosed rooftop terrace eating area on the second floor. A resident ghost named Martha is said to visit periodically. Daily specials, a kid's menu, booster seats, high chairs, crayons, and a youthful staff. As of this printing, the children's menu is $3.50.

● **Hamburger Hamlet**

3125 M Street. (202) 965-6970. Open Sunday through Thursday 11 A.M.
to midnight, Friday and Saturday until 1 A.M.

Besides offering a nice hamburger and a quick lunch, HH has
crayons tableside and white drawing paper on the tabletops to encourage
big and little artists to color their own placemats. The good ones go up
on the wall, and you'll find masterpieces from the famous and the not-yet-
famous. In the back room, on the right, is a framed Conehead drawing by
Dan Aykroyd.

Southwest Washington

● Arena Stage

Sixth Street and Maine Avenue. (202) 554-9066 (administrative office), (202) 488-3300 (box office), (202) 484-0247 TTY. Waterfront subway station. **Ages 5 and up.**

Arena, Washington's most prestigious resident theater company (started in 1950 by Zelda Fichandler), actually houses three theaters, the 827-seat Arena (a theater in the round), the smaller 500-seat Kreeger, and the intimate 180-seat Old Vat Room. Almost any play presented here will be appropriate for children as far as language is concerned, but the subject matter of some plays may be suitable only for older children. Check with the administrative office if you have any concerns.

Audio description is available on selected Thursday evenings. Sign interpreted performances are available.

On select Saturday mornings, the Arena has a Kids Play program, a creative series for children and their parents. The adults see an Arena Stage production while the children are engaged with community folk artists, storytellers, Arena staff, and members of the Living Stage Theatre Company. The program is available for children ages 5 to 12.

● Maine Avenue Fish Market

Maine Avenue and Eighth Street. Open daylight hours. Waterfront subway station. **All ages.**

Tucked along the waterfront and under the expressway flyovers, you'll find seafood markets stocking fresh fish, local and imported, as well as seasonal produce. If you've never seen bushel baskets mountained over with live Chesapeake Bay blue crabs, or huge displays of squid, stone crab claws, octopuses, shrimp, salmon, perch, trout, catfish, or any number of other fish types, this is the place to visit. It's also the place to buy fresh produce.

The boats, which double as stores, are in the water; you stand on the land and the transactions are handled over ice shavings and all that fresh fish. If you're squeamish about cleaning the fish, take them into Ben Edwards's fish-cleaning house and watch the guys adroitly use electric scalers and a variety of knives to set the fish in proper order. They'll clean your fish for a small fee.

● Voice of America

330 Independence Avenue. Visitors must join a guided tour. Tour entrance is between Third and Fourth Streets on C Street, in the middle of the building, marked with a blue-and-white sign reading VOA. Tours, lasting about 35 minutes, are by appointment only Monday through Friday at 8:40, 9:40, and 10:40 A.M., and at 1:40 and 2:40 P.M. Call Barbara Jaffie at (202) 619-3919 for tour information. Closed weekends and on federal holidays. Federal Center SW subway station. **Ages 6 and up.**

Because so many television sports and news programs have a camera in a control room, or a newsroom, most children already know what a working television or radio station looks like. What makes the Voice of America (VOA) different is its mission, which is to broadcast 1,200 hours of news, music, and commentary every week to more than 100 countries with a weekly audience of 130 million people. Yes, there are only 168 hours in a week, but VOA broadcasts in 42 languages and the 1,200 hours include all the time when someone is broadcasting.

Starting in the lobby, you view a short videotape on the history of VOA, which has been in operation since 1942, and how it works. Then it's a visit past the control room, the newsroom (which has a bunch of desks, computer terminals, and people rushing around), the studios, and the "bubble." Outside the studio, you can twist a button to hear the language of the radio show being aired, which might be anything from Russian to Romanian. The "bubble" is where telephoned reports from all the correspondents overseas are received. These will be translated or aired as they are. On the walls are exhibits about the history of VOA, and there is an old master control room from before the days of computers.

Southeast Washington

● Frederick Douglass National Historic Site

1411 W Street. (202) 426-5960. Open daily 9 A.M. to 5 P.M. from April to October; 9 A.M. until 4 P.M. the rest of the year. Closed December 25 and New Year's Day. Admission is $6 for adults; $3 for seniors; free for children 5 and under, and school groups. Candlelight tours, starting about dusk and with guides in period costumes, are available periodically (call for dates); reservations are required for a group of 10 or more. Tourmobile stop. **All ages.**

Ideally, your visit to the Frederick Douglass home will start at the visitor center, where you can watch a film about his life. There are two movies; one is 17 minutes long and usually shown to students. The other is 33 minutes long. These are not award-winning flicks and suffer in comparison to the high-tech, laser-light, rap-song entertainments children are exposed to daily. The movies explain Douglass's life and define the context in which he, Harriet Tubman, and John Brown lived and worked. The movie is scheduled to start every hour on the hour.

If you arrive just prior to the half hour, you'll be taken on a tour of the house first (it's a locked-door tour and the entire group of no more than 22 people must stay together) to see the sitting rooms, bedrooms, kitchen, and other areas.

Most of the objects in the house are original to Douglass, the famed nineteenth-century abolitionist, editor, and African-American leader, and a visit is a great way to introduce children to someone they read about in history books. Douglass was born the son of a slave and was self-educated. He became a commanding influence in America's battle for equal rights. He provides a good lesson in how important it is to learn to read and write. For those who have seen the movie *Glory,* Douglass had two sons fight in the storming of Fort Wagner, and a picture of the black military unit hangs on the wall. The large home is typical of upper-middle-class white and African-American homes in the late nineteenth century. When school groups tour, the National Park Service guides provide more of a treasure-hunt format, such as seeing if students can find the wheelchair, the chamber pots, and so on. You can call for a schedule of upcoming class tours and join one of them.

From the west lawn, about halfway up the steps, you can see a pretty good view of Washington, including the Capitol, the John F. Kennedy Center for the Performing Arts, and the Shrine of the Immaculate Conception. The view is better when the trees are naked, however.

The visitor center is fully accessible to the handicapped, and there is a driveway up to the house that can be used as a ramp. The house itself has steps and is not wheelchair accessible. A gift area, with plenty of books by and on Douglass and related matters, is located in the center.

● Anacostia Neighborhood Museum

1901 Fort Place. (202) 287-3369. Open daily 10 A.M. to 5 P.M. Closed December 25. Guided tours of 45 to 60 minutes are given Monday through Friday at 10 A.M., 11 A.M., and 1 P.M. **All ages.**

African-American culture and history is featured in changing exhibits with a program of lectures, workshops, films, and performing arts related to each exhibit. The museum is closed for as much as a month or more between exhibits, so be sure to call before visiting.

● Anacostia Park

1900 Anacostia Drive. (202) 433-1152. Open daily 6 A.M. to dusk. Closed December 25. **All ages.**

This 750-acre park straddles both sides of the Anacostia River. In addition to the parkland, there's a swimming pool operated by the city's Recreation Department, basketball courts, and a roller-skating rink that is open from 1 P.M. to dusk, Monday through Friday. Free skates are available for children under 13. The park affords plenty of room for a picnic, and a mini playground lies adjacent to the picnic area.

● Congressional Cemetery

Eighteenth and E Streets. (202) 543-0539. Open daily dawn to dusk. Free admission, but contributions are accepted (in the form of cash or your time and energy) for tours, **ages 8 and up;** *for picnics and other activities,* **all ages.**

The oldest national cemetery in the United States is open for a visit, a picnic, dog walking, jogging, or a tour. You can even hold a wedding, baptism, or party in the recently restored stone chapel. John Hanley, of the Association for the Preservation of the Historic Congressional Cemetery, usually is at the cemetery from 6 A.M. to 10 P.M. to help you find your way around the place. Hanley will give a tour, or give you a brochure that lists who is buried where. He is a notorious jokester. His favorite outing, it seems, is at Halloween time, when on a Saturday afternoon a haunted vault is opened up, ghost stories are told, and there are games, band music, and a barbecue. Come in costume, if you wish.

The cemetery contains the graves of 78 members of the House of Representatives and 19 Senators, military officers, Indians, mass-accident victims, several criminals, and a variety of ordinary and not-so-ordinary citizens, including Belva Lockwood (the first female candidate for president to receive votes), composer John Philip Sousa, Civil War photographer Mathew Brady, and J. Edgar Hoover.

Also buried here is Leonard Matlovich, who died in 1988. His grave is neatly covered with white gravel and flags wave briskly in the breeze above it. To refresh your memory, the following is etched on his gravestone: "They gave me a medal for killing two men, and a discharge for loving one."

● The Washington Informer

3117 Martin Luther King Avenue. (202) 561-4100. Free tours are offered weekdays by appointment from 9 A.M. to 5 P.M. Anacostia subway station; then take the 35-cent shuttle bus. **Ages 6 and up.**

This five-person newspaper specializes in African-American news in the metropolitan area. Children learn how the paper is put together from beginning to end. They see photographers and reporters in action and can visit the darkroom to see how a photograph is developed.

● Washington Navy Yard

Ninth and M Streets. (202) 433-2218. Navy Museum, Building 76, (202) 433-2651 (recording), (202) 433-4882. Marine Corps Museum, Building 58, (202) 433-3534. Navy and Marine Corps museums are open Monday, Wednesday through Friday 9 A.M. to 5 P.M.; Saturday, Sunday, and federal holidays 10 A.M. to 5 P.M.; open late on Wednesday night in summer when the Navy Band is presenting "The American Sailor" concert. Closed Tuesday. Guided tours are available. The U.S.S. Barry, (202) 433-3377, is open daily for self-guided tours 10 A.M. to 5 P.M. The U.S. Navy Combat Art Center, Building 67, Washington Navy Yard, (202) 433-3815, is open daily 8 A.M. to 4 P.M. Closed federal holidays. No guided tours. Washington Navy Yard subway station. **All ages.**

Several options are available in this historic yard: the Navy Museum, the U.S.S. *Barry* Museum, the U.S. Navy Combat Art Center, and the Marine Corps Museum.

Of all the 4,000 Navy-related historic objects in the Navy Museum—paintings, photographs, ship models, and weapons, ranging from cannons to a casing for the first atomic bomb—what seems to fascinate big and little children most at the yard are the three operating periscopes through which they can view the outside world. The second most popular activity appears to be sitting on antiaircraft guns and pretending to destroy the enemy, or at least to save us all from annihilation and destruction.

Another favorite stop at the yard is the U.S.S. *Barry,* providing adventure and playground all in one. The *Barry* (DD 933) is a decommissioned Navy destroyer now on permanent duty at the Navy Yard. Children can poke their noses into just about every corner of the ship, exploring the mess, galleys, officers quarters, engine rooms, and guns. They can even sit in the captain's chair. Imaginations soar at the homing torpedo attached to a rocket motor.

Artists have recorded the story of United States naval and marine units at sea and ashore, in war and in peace, since before World War II. Military action, launchings, explorations, and sailings have often been captured on canvas. Artworks on these subjects are exhibited at the U.S. Navy Combat Art Center, and each year the collection increases by approximately 150 canvases. Changing exhibits are on display all year.

An hour-long concert, "The American Sailor," is presented in the amphitheater by the Navy Band at 9 P.M. every Wednesday throughout the summer. For free concert reservations, call (202) 433-2218.

The Marine Corps Museum offers a chronological regimental history of the Marine Corps from 1775. Models, dioramas, and various weapons, including cannons from the 1800s, are on display. Older children probably will enjoy this museum more than younger children.

The Navy Museum's annual Seafaring Celebration is scheduled in early November with music, storytelling, and model making, scrimshaw, and hat-making activities.

● Marine Barracks
Eighth and I Streets. (202) 433-6060. Park at Washington Navy Yard and take free shuttle bus service. Washington Navy Yard subway station.
All ages.

Every Friday night from May through August, there's an evening parade, or tattoo. Admission is free, but advance seating reservations are a must. Call for reservations between 8 A.M. and 11 A.M. and 1 P.M. and 3 P.M. Monday through Thursday, preferably three weeks ahead of your desired date.

The gates are opened at 8:30 P.M. After all reservation holders have been admitted, those without reservations who are waiting outside the main gate are offered any remaining seats. An 8:45 P.M. concert opens the event and it is followed by the drills, a 75-minute performance of music by the U.S. Marine Drum and Bugle Corps and precision marching by the Marine Corps Silent Drill Platoon. Bring a camera with fast film if you want to catch this stirring sight.

Northeast Washington

● Kenilworth Aquatic Gardens

1900 Anacostia Avenue at Douglas Street. (202) 426-6905 (recording). Gardens are open daily 7 A.M. to dusk; visitor center open from 8:30 A.M. to 4 P.M. Guided tours are given daily from Memorial Day to Labor Day at 9 A.M., 11 A.M., and 1 P.M. Tours last 60 to 90 minutes, depending upon your interests and the questions asked. **All ages.**

This is the only national park dedicated entirely to water-loving plants. If you arrive in the morning you can see the night-blooming water lilies before they close and the day lilies as they open. It seems as if every water lily and plant in existence is here, including the imposing South American Victoria amazonica. Its leaves, which are like platters with upturned edges, can extend to 6 feet in diameter, large and strong enough to hold a 90-pound child. The wetlands are not only home to plants, but also to animals: turtles, snakes, fingernail-sized frogs, bull-frogs, insects, mosquito fish, muskrats, migratory birds, ducks, and red-winged blackbirds.

About mid-June you may see as many as 70 varieties of day-blooming water lilies; in late July and early August, the day- and night-blooming tropical water lilies are at their peak. Special environmental education programs are offered. There is a small art gallery featuring the plants and blooms of the gardens. Bring your camera and plenty of film. Picnic tables provide a good place to stop for lunch.

The visitor center is wheelchair accessible and displays photographs and related artworks about the gardens.

● United States National Arboretum

3501 New York Avenue. (202) 245-2726. Open daily 8 A.M. to 5 P.M.; Closed December 25. Tours by appointment. National Bonsai Collection is open daily 10 A.M. to 3:30 P.M. Gift shop. Picnic areas. http://www.ars-grin.gov/ars/Beltsville/na. **All ages.**

Occupying 444 acres, the arboretum has nine miles of paved roadway that lead visitors to the various plant collections and gardens. Of particular note to little ones is the National Bonsai Collection, which features trees more to their size. Children also like to see the aquatic gardens (close to the parking lot), home to numerous lilies and some 400 Nishiki koi (the large, colorful carp). Pick up the little brochure that details all manner of trivia, such as the fact that the fish ate 2,600 pounds of food in 1989. The fish are fed from the back terrace at 12:30 P.M. from April to November. Do not bring food from home (it isn't good for them). Children will be given food to feed the fish.

Peak flowering season at the arboretum is in late April and May, when the azaleas (among the most extensive collection in the nation), flowering dogwoods, crabapples, mountain laurels, peonies, elephant-ear magnolias, and old roses present their fashion show. In the fall, tulip poplars and hickories present rich yellow leaves and gums and dogwoods turn red and bronze, creating a beautiful fall foliage display.

The herb garden is interesting because the plants on display demonstrate the significance of herbs in people's everyday lives. In the specialty garden, for instance, you can see which plants are used for dyes, medicine, cooking, fuel, oil, pesticides, fibers, fragrances, and beverages.

The Capitol Columns, removed from the Capitol building in the 1950s as part of the east portico expansion, are another arboretum focal point. They date to the early 1800s, and each weighs 5 tons and stands 34 feet tall. After 28 years of storage, they were moved to the arboretum grounds in the mid-1980s.

On Saturday and Sunday during the spring, summer, and fall, visitors can board a 48-seat tram for a guided 40-minute sightseeing tour of the Arboretum. It passes such attractions as Asian Valley, the Gotelli Dwarf Conifer collection, the azalea collection, the Capitol columns, and other scattered attractions. Tickets are $4.

Views of the Anacostia River and other Washington sites are available at the Kingman Lake and Hickey Hill overlooks. Picnicking is permitted in the arboretum in designated areas.

● United States Post Office

900 Brentwood Road. (202) 636-1208. One-hour walk-in tours are given Tuesday through Friday 9:30 A.M. to 7 P.M.; 24-hour notice is advised, particularly for groups. **Ages 6 and up.**

Mail no more comes from a post office than milk comes from a grocery store, yet it is gathered, sorted, and sent upon its way here. More than 5 million pieces a day are sent off to mail boxes around the world from this operation alone.

The tour, which can be noisy because of all the machinery, first takes you past the collected mail arriving at the loading docks. Here the mail is transferred from trucks to robot-driven bins. The machines separate packages and thick envelopes from thin envelopes, or "flats." Conveyer belts keep the mail flowing, up and down, in and out, turning, dropping, through funnels and slots, until it arrives at the cancellation machines. You can follow packages or mail or both at that fork.

Even with the knowledge of what computers and machinery should be able to do today, it's still amazing that machines can read the address of a letter, check its ZIP code and destination, cancel the stamp, and send it on its way to the tune of 9 letters a second, 54 letters a minute, 3,240 letters an hour, 194,400 letters a day.

● National Shrine of the Immaculate Conception

Michigan Avenue and Fourth Street. (202) 526-8300. Open daily 7 A.M. to 7 P.M. April 1 through October 31; 7 A.M. to 6 P.M. November 1 through March 31. Guided tours (about 45 minutes long) are given every half hour from 9 to 11 A.M. and 1 to 3 P.M. Monday through Saturday; 1:30 to 4 P.M. Sunday. The gift shop is open daily, and the cafeteria is open daily for breakfast and lunch. Brookland/Catholic University subway station. http:// www.nationalshrine.com. **Ages 6 and up.**

The shrine, the largest Roman Catholic church in the United States, has 57 chapels, 176 stained-glass windows, and many icons, statues, mosaics (one of the most extensive collections in the world), domes, and vaults. Its architecture represents the Byzantine and Romanesque styles of 1,500 and 1,000 years ago.

● Franciscan Monastery

1400 Quincy Street. (202) 526-6800. Open daily 8 A.M. to 5 P.M. Free admission, but contributions are accepted. Guided tours (about 45 minutes long) are given Monday through Saturday on the hour 9 to 11 A.M. and 1 to 4 P.M.; Sunday 1 to 4 P.M. **Ages 6 and up.**

The tour of the monastery explains the interior of the monastery's Memorial Church and includes the catacombs, which are a reproduction of the Roman catacombs where Christians hid and worshiped in secret to avoid persecution. Depending on which friar leads the tour, you might hear bloodcurdling tales of martyrs. In any case, children particularly like the catacombs, because they find them "spooky," "mysterious," and "neat."

The beautiful grounds come into full living color during the rose season, for the monastery reportedly has one of the largest rose gardens in the country. They even grow roses here that bloom in December. Along the garden walks are the Stations of the Cross, replicas of the Manger at Bethlehem, the Garden of Gethsemane, the Holy Sepulcher, a statue of St. Francis of Assisi, and other Holy Land shrines. The Easter service is said to be very moving and inspirational. You may stroll by yourself, or take a tour led by a brown-robed monk. The monastery built these replica shrines for those who wouldn't be able to travel around the world to see them. These tours are offered at 9, 10, and 11 A.M. Monday through Saturday, and at 1, 2, and 3 P.M. daily.

● Capital Children's Museum

800 Third Street, NE (at H Street). (202) 675-4120. Open daily 10 A.M. to 5 P.M. Closed Easter, Thanksgiving, December 25, and New Year's Day. Admission, $6; senior citizens over 59, $4; children under 2, free. Union Station subway station. http://www.ccm.org. **Ages 2–14; best for ages 5–8.**

This museum, which is primarily aimed at elementary-school children, is a hands-on learning laboratory where children can touch and play with exhibits. There is an interactive exhibit about sound and deafness, and a Mexican village where visitors can make tortillas and paper flowers and necklaces. Children can also climb through mock sewers, work on computers, dial telephones, play in the grocery store, slide down a fire pole, be enclosed in a bubble, tape a television commercial, feed Rosie the goat, take flight with Superman, make a printer's newspaper hat, learn to juggle, and do countless other things that children enjoy doing.

● Union Station

40 Massachusetts and Delaware Avenues. (202) 289-1908. Train station operations are open daily 24 hours. Retail shops are open Monday through Saturday 10 A.M. to 9 P.M.; Sunday noon to 6 P.M. Some station eateries open to serve early Metrorail and Amtrak riders and visitors. Full-service restaurants stay open for late dining. Parking garage. Union Station subway station. http://nationalmuseum.org/station/washdc/htm. **All ages.**

This is the largest waiting room of its kind in the world. Amtrak, MARC (Maryland Rail Commuters train system, 800-325-RAIL, 325-7245), light-rail commuter services from Fredericksburg and Manassas

VRE (Virginia Railway Express, 703-524-3322), Metrorail, and Old Town Trolley all stop here, and a couple of automobile rental agencies have offices in the station.

Virginia and Maryland officials hope to create "seamless" service for those riding between the District and the surrounding jurisdictions. At best, you wouldn't have to change trains. At worst, you would only need to buy one ticket. Although Amtrak does this already, it is more expensive and geared more toward long-distance travel. Also, Amtrak and VRE already have crossover ticketing.

It's difficult to believe that this grand station, which opened in 1907 and basically closed in 1981, was allowed to deteriorate so much that rain damage caused part of the roof to collapse and toadstools started growing inside. For a while, there was a visitor center that almost no one visited. Now, the station features a large festival marketplace, with 35 eateries (fast-food options from sushi to hot dogs and pizza to hamburgers, from calypso to Japanese to Indian), a few full-service restaurants (including the America Restaurant, which welcomes children; http://dc.diningweb.com), boutiques, and nine movie theaters (you can even charge your movie ticket). Look for the large clock in the Main Hall, just over the entrance to the East Hall. It uses "IIII" at the point where most Roman numeral clocks would use "IV." That's the way it was when the station opened, and that's the way the restorers kept it.

Activities are scheduled at the station throughout the year. During the holiday season a miniature train setup, measuring a huge 16 by 32 feet, is erected. Four half-inch-scale trains roll through a quaint village with people, trees, trolley cars, and bridges; an industrial site; a small town; and a rural area with model farming equipment. The setup, which includes period automobiles, sits beneath snow-capped mountains in a scene reminiscent of Currier and Ives. The model trains are executed with standard LGB body styling finished in slate black and red, yellow, blue, and green.

A five-story, 1,400-car garage with long-term parking spots rises behind the station. Parking is free for two hours to shop customers and three hours for moviegoers. Prepare to show your movie stub or stamped ticket when you exit the garage.

● National Postal Museum (Smithsonian Institution)

At the corner of First Street and Massachusetts Avenue, in the lower level of the former Washington City Post Office Building. (202) 357-2700 (Smithsonian information). Open daily from 10 A.M. to 5:30 P.M. except

on December 25. Times and topics for tours, demonstrations, films and other programs are posted at the museum information desk. Gift shops. Special tours for school and camp groups are available by calling (202) 357-2991 or (202) 786-2414 (TTY), Monday through Friday, 10 A.M. to 3 P.M. Union Station subway station (First Street exit). http://www.si.edu/newstart.htm.
All ages.

There's a new exhibit at the Postal Museum that brings the attraction into the current decade, with holography, 3-D movies, laser images, and interactive computers. No wonder it's the most popular exhibit, for much of the rest of the museum is relatively quiet. You'll discover the world of direct mail (junk mail, that is), which represents 85 percent of the mail you receive. Sponsored by a grant from Pitney-Bowes (who else?) of postage-meter fame, a display shows the genesis of mail-order catalogs from Montgomery Ward, Tiffany's, L.L. Bean, and Burpee seeds. Play with a digital camera and a coded plastic card, answer a few questions about yourself and your friends, and you'll see how precisely targeted most of your direct mail is. You can design a piece of direct mail with underlining, personalized greetings, and splashy envelopes.

The rest of the museum portrays the history of the mail service beginning in pre-revolutionary America. There are six major galleries, including a changing exhibit gallery. Another interesting, but more static, display is the railroad postal car, with its film about sorting the mail on the trains, as they moved from city to city and town to town.

Another highlight is a very brief excursion through the woods as though you were on a Pony Express route. That's probably appropriate because the Pony Express lasted barely 18 months, much less time than books, movies, and legends would have us believe. In bringing us to the computer age, several machines will address a postcard for you. You enter the ZIP code and it tells you what city it's going to, then you type in the street address and name of the recipient. A display shows which plane it will fly out on and when it should arrive. Another machine takes your change, cancels your card, and sends it on its way.

Special programs might include a paper conservation workshop, instructions on starting a stamp collection, or a show-and-tell with other children sharing their stamp collections. Call or check the *Washington Post* Weekend section for current offerings.

It's no accident that the City Post Office was located next to Union Station. By the beginning of the twentieth century, the Postal Department mandated that each post office be located as near as possible to the main railroad station. This makes the National Postal Museum a very convenient place to visit from the Union Station subway stop.

● Lincoln Park

East Capitol Street, between Eleventh and Thirteenth Streets. **All ages.**

In the middle of this park is a bronze statue of Abraham Lincoln and a newly freed slave, just rising from his knees and grasping a broken chain. It celebrates the abolition of slavery in the District of Columbia, and the statue was paid for with contributions from hundreds of former slaves who wanted to pay tribute to the man who proclaimed their freedom in 1863. The freedman was Archer Alexander, a Virginia-born slave, and his rescuer was the Rev. William Greenleaf Eliot, grandfather of poet and playwright T. S. Eliot.

A statue of Mary McLeod Bethune was placed in Lincoln Park in 1974, making it the first one honoring a woman in a public park in Washington, D.C.

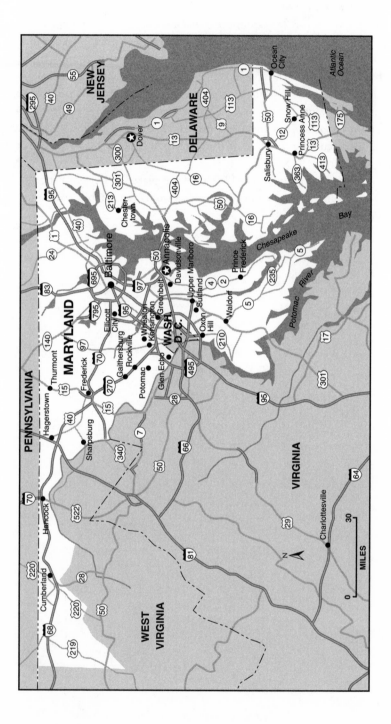

Maryland

CHOOSE FROM ZOOS, MUSEUMS AND galleries, professional sports, space programs, farms, ethnic festivals, boating, and the ocean. Maryland offers a little bit of everything. The following are some favorite things for children, listed alphabetically by city.

ANNAPOLIS

● The *Capital* Newspaper

2000 Capital Drive. (410) 268-5000. Free tours are given by appointment on weekdays at noon and Wednesday at 6 P.M. Groups of 25 or fewer, no strollers or babies in arms. **Ages 8 and up.**

The Capital Gazette company is the oldest newspaper publisher in the United States. The tour shows how a newspaper is written and produced, and compares a 1775 edition of the paper with the current version. The tour includes talks with reporters, editors, and plate-camera workers as well as a tour of the press area.

● Annapolis Gardening School

A summer gardening school (indoor and outdoor) for children ages 5 and up is located in the historic Annapolis district. Half-day, full-day, and month-long sessions are available, with a box lunch provided for those enrolled in the full-day program. Annapolis Gardening School, Box 4577, Annapolis, Maryland 21403. (410) 263-6041. Memorial Day through Labor Day. http:// member.aol.com/boattours/cmt.html. **Ages 5 and up.**

● On the Bay Eco Tour

Recourse Conservancy, Inc., Box 4577, Annapolis, Maryland 21403. (410) 263-6041. (410) 626-1851 (fax). **All ages.**

Join the licensed captain and trained Chesapeake Bay ecologist on a boat excursion to witness the many wonders of the Bay for $6. The Coast-Guard-certified vessel takes you on a 45-minute cruise on the scenic Severn River where you'll marvel at the marsh life, observe osprey nests up close (there are more breeding pairs of osprey in the Chesapeake Bay than anywhere else in the world), and see how people and nature work together in this lovely marine setting.

BALTIMORE

One interesting way to see Baltimore is via the water taxis, which make 11 stops: Maryland Science Center, Federal Hill, Inner Harbor Marina, Harborview, Museum of Industry, Fells Point, Harris Creek, Canton Waterfront Park, Pier Five (concert pavilion), National Aquarium, and Harborplace. Most of these stops are convenient to tourist spots around the city.

The taxis operate from 11 A.M. to 9 P.M. Sunday through Thursday and 11 A.M. to midnight on Friday, Saturday, and holidays in April, September, and October; and 11 A.M. to 11 P.M. from May through August. Cost is about $3.25 for adults and $2.25 for children ages 10 and under with an adult; the ticket is good the entire day of purchase. Service may be suspended during thunderstorms and lightning.

● Inner Harbor

Inner Harbor, at the corner of Pratt and Light Streets, is the renovated and restored area around the harbor, and features a number of fascinating places to visit. There's the Baltimore Maritime Museum, the Baltimore Public Works Museum and Streetscape, Federal Hill (great for a view of the harbor), Harborplace (a festival marketplace filled with eateries and shops), the Maryland Science Center and Davis Planetarium (see below), the National Aquarium in Baltimore (see below), the U.S. Frigate Constellation (see below), and Top of the World, for another view of the area. **All ages.**

You may notice that the Inner Harbor water is particularly litter-free. No, that's not because visitors are very neat. Rather, a boat machine that looks like a cross between an extraterrestrial explorer vehicle and a Rube Goldberg invention putts along the waterway with a tongue-like conveyor belt, swallowing any trash that's on the water and carrying it along to its trash container. Stand around for a while and you're sure to see it motoring about, tidying things up.

Between the two wings of Harborplace is a performance platform where you're likely to see jugglers, singers, musical combos, and other entertainers at almost any time the shops are open. At night, you may come across a telescope that will let you view a distant planet. There's no charge, but donations to the sponsoring astronomy club are accepted.

● National Aquarium in Baltimore

Pier 3, 501 East Pratt Street. (410) 576-3800. Open daily 10 A.M. to 5 P.M.; Friday until 8 P.M. with reduced Friday night admissions (and fewer people); extended summer hours. Closed December 25 and New Year's Day. Timed tickets required. Adults, $11.95; students, senior citizens, $10.50; children ages 3–11, $7.50. Call TicketMaster (service charges added) for advance tickets (202) 432-7328 or (410) 481-7328. Guided tours are given for groups of 20 or more by prior arrangement. Membership available. Gift shop. **All ages.**

There are two absolute favorite places children like to visit here: the seal pool, where harbor and gray seals play in an outdoor 70,000-gallon rock pool (you don't even have to pay to see the pool or to watch the regular daily feedings at 10 A.M., 1 P.M., and 4 P.M.), and the shark tank in the Open Ocean Exhibit inside. This is no small-sardine shark tank. It holds 220,000 gallons of water, as well as lemon, sand tiger, sandbar, and nurse sharks and large game fish. Visiting the shark tank and the 335,000-gallon Atlantic Coral Reef exhibit, which are behind 13-foot-high windows, is like snorkeling among the most beautiful and dangerous creatures of the deep. Three times a day, divers plunge in to hand-feed hundreds of fish, rays, and a Hawksbill turtle.

The Sea Cliffs exhibit re-creates the cliffs of Heimay, Iceland, and is the only display in the country that features three species of subarctic seabirds. Daily feedings and educational presentations of puffins, murres, and razorbills take place at 11 A.M. and 3:30 P.M. Of particular note is that the glass is one-way, so the birds don't see or hear the people looking in at them.

Little children like to stop by the Children's Cove, where the North American Tidal Pools allow them to touch and hold such little critters as horseshoe crabs, sea urchins, and starfish. The aquarium also has a South American rain forest exhibit with exotic birds and lots and lots of humidity.

During the summer, volunteer guides walk around the aquarium holding things for visitors to touch and feel, such as the saw from a sawtooth shark, the jaw from a shark, and the disk from a whale spine (aquarium officials think it's from the whale skeleton hanging atop the large central tank, which weighed a mere 60 tons when alive).

A Marine Mammal Pavilion showcases the majesty of dolphins and whales. Reached via an enclosed skywalk from the original aquarium, it is the most sophisticated installation of its type in the country and combines family entertainment with educational and participatory exhibits. The centerpiece of the new pavilion is a 1.2 million-gallon pool and the 1,300-seat Lyn P. Meyerhoff Amphitheater, home to three beluga whales and six Atlantic bottlenose dolphins. Surrounding the pool are the world's largest acrylic windows. Electronic Vidiwalls, the first of their kind in any zoo or aquarium, project close-up views of the marine mammals' unique characteristics. A discovery room has hands-on artifacts from shark's teeth and jaws to whale vertebrae.

Numerous special programs are offered at the aquarium throughout the year. Call for details.

● Maryland Science Center

601 Light Street. (410) 685-5225 (recording), (410) 685-2370 (office), (410) 837-IMAX (IMAX information). Open Monday through Friday 10 A.M. to 5 P.M.; Saturday 10 A.M. to 8 P.M.; Sunday 12 noon to 6 P.M.; extended summer hours. Friday and Saturday evenings are special IMAX presentations. Adults, $8.50; children ages 4 to 17, senior citizens, and active-duty military personnel, $6.50; children 3 and under, free; IMAX admission included; Davis Planetarium show included. Membership available. **All ages.**

Three floors of activity here offer wonderful hands-on experiences that present science as a part of Maryland life.

The IMAX theater (40 by 75 feet) shows films on space exploration *(The Dream Is Alive),* boating through the Grand Canyon, surfing in Hawaii, or other adventures that transport you without you ever leaving your seat. I prefer a seat close to the front and near the screen to feel like the surf may actually splash on me; you may prefer sitting higher.

The planetarium is not recommended for very young children, but older ones will enjoy exploring the night skies through its various programs. Unfortunately, there's a lot of light pollution in the Washington-Baltimore area, which obliterates much of the night sky. Fortunately, this is the place to find those hidden stars.

Children particularly like several exhibits. A new one on structures lets them work with various-sized building blocks to create their own architecture and construction projects. A kid's room is designed for children ages 3 through 7 years, who may not understand the more advanced scientific exhibits. Among the treasures here are workshop tools; a nature table with bones, feathers, and skins; a dissecting scope that depicts the different stages of a tadpole changing into a frog; an ant farm; a sound table with noise makers; X-rays on a lighted table; books; and a computer with programs about shapes, counting, and the alphabet.

A television studio is available for children to tape themselves doing the weather or sports and then see how they look. An all-time favorite is the Demonstration Stage, where children are asked to participate in scientific experiments dealing with chemistry, electricity, and other facets of science. Other displays deal with the Chesapeake Bay, energy, and space.

The gift shop has everything from kaleidoscopes to holograms and is nearly as interesting as the museum.

● U.S. Frigate *Constellation*

Pier 1, Pratt Street. (410) 539-1797. Figuratively seconds before the 1854 Constellation sank, it was sent off to be restored and renovated. It is in the Fort McHenry shipyard, receiving about $9 million worth of improvements, and should return to the Inner Harbor some time in 1999 or 2000. Previously, the vessel was open Monday through Saturday 10 A.M. to 6 P.M.; Sunday and holidays noon to 6 P.M. May through Labor Day; Monday through Saturday 10 A.M. to 4 P.M.; Sunday noon to 5 P.M. the rest of the year. Closed Good Friday, December 25, and New Year's Day. Admission: adults, $2; senior citizens, $1.50; children ages 6–15, $1. Guided tours were given daily every other hour on the hour. **All ages.**

This remarkable ship is actually younger than once believed. At one time, experts thought it had been launched in 1797, fought pirates in Tripoli, Libya, in 1802, and saw action in the War of 1812. It was believed to be the oldest surviving fighting vessel of the Civil War. As part of the restoration, the ship was examined with lasers, and compared to a design drawn in 1853 by John Lenthall, then the Navy's chief engineer. It matched perfectly. When it reopens, be sure to see the captain's cabin, the gun emplacements, and the fireplaces (on board a ship? yes!).

● Fort McHenry National Monument and Historic Shrine

East Fort Avenue. (410) 962-4290. Open daily 8 A.M. to 5 P.M.; summer 8 A.M. to 8 P.M. Admission to fort buildings for adults, $1; children ages 16 and under and senior citizens 62 and over, free. Admission to grounds, free. **All ages.**

The fort is known as the place during the War of 1812 where, on the night of September 13, 1912, the flag flew that inspired Francis Scott Key to write "The Star-Spangled Banner." A 16-minute movie about the Battle of Baltimore and the writing of the national anthem is shown every

30 minutes on the hour and half hour. At its conclusion, the national anthem commences and the curtain on the right-hand wall opens to reveal a humongous flag, measuring 30 by 42 feet. Everyone stands, of course, which is great planning because that's when you're supposed to leave the building and go into the center of the fort.

The fort played an important part in history before and after the War of 1812. During the Civil War it was a prison camp, and during World War I it was a large army hospital base. Exhibits explain the fort's uses over the years.

Children particularly love the cannons and the cannonballs. They're never fired, but during the summer people are dressed in replica uniforms from the War of 1812 and go through the drills and duties of garrisoning a fort in those days. Visitors can talk with them and ask questions, as well as see the barracks, the powder magazine, and the flagpole.

The fort grounds are nice for a picnic and a little exercise.

● Pompeian Inc.

4201 Pulaski Highway. (410) 276-6900. Look for the ancient olive press set up in the company parking lot. Free 90-minute tour given on Monday, Wednesday, and Friday morning and afternoon, including the administrative offices, packing room, storage room and warehouse, offered to groups of at least 10; smaller groups can be added to a larger tour. Reserve at least 10 days in advance. **Ages 6 and up.**

Olives grown in Spain, Morocco, and Tunisia are shipped here to be processed. On any one day the plant can process between 30,000 and 50,000 glass bottles of olive oil in 2-, 4-, 8-, 16- and 32-ounce sizes. It can also produce 8,000 to 12,000 gallon drums full of oil a day. The best, of course, is the extra-virgin olive oil, which comes from the first pressing. Free refreshments are offered after the tour. You can buy the olive oil here, but only by the case.

● Dr. Samuel D. Harris National Museum of Dentistry

31 S. Greene Street (at Lombard). (410) 706-0600. Open Wednesday through Saturday from 10 A.M. to 4 P.M.; Sunday from 1 to 4 P.M. Closed Monday, Tuesday, and major holidays. Admission is $4.50 for adults (19–59); $2.50 for children (7–18), senior citizens and students with ID; children ages 6 and under are free. www.dental.umab.edu/dental/museum. **Ages 3 and up.**

This is the fun place to discover the world of teeth, at the only museum of its kind. Catch a look at "32 Terrific Teeth," with a life-size model of an "iron jaw" performer who hangs by his teeth high above the audience. Play a commercial tune on the tooth jukebox (including Bucky Beaver for Ipana, Scope, and Ultra Brite). View George Washington's not-so-wooden teeth. Let children see a video on what a first visit to a dentist is like. There's everything dental here (except an appointment for a cleaning) from molar chairs to a dental tool case designed as a doll house, and more. Local children can participate in a program that marks the loss of their baby teeth with gold stars. Special programs may include "Tooth Tales by the Tooth Fairy," "Straight from the Horse's Mouth," "Branches, Bristle, and Batteries: Toothbrush by Design," and a family festival day of craft-making, story telling, treasure hunts, demonstrations, music, and more.

School programs are available for pre-kindergarten to high school groups. The hour-long programs generally consist of a 10-minute orientation with hands-on objects, followed by a 45-minute tour of the permanent exhibition. All students participating in a school program receive a complimentary toothbrush and tube of toothpaste.

● Walters Art Gallery

600 North Charles Street at Mount Vernon Square. (410) 547-ARTS (recording), (410) 547-9000. Open Tuesday through Friday 11 A.M. to 4 P.M.; Saturday and Sunday 11 A.M. to 5 P.M.; Thursday to 8 P.M. Closed Monday, the Fourth of July, Thanksgiving, December 24 and 25, and New Year's Day. Adults, $6; senior citizens, $4; members, students 18 and older $3; children ages 17 and under, free; free admission on Saturday before 1 P.M.
All ages.

This extraordinary collection ranges over a 5,000-year period, from ancient Egypt to art nouveau, with a hefty helping of decorative arts and illuminated manuscripts. Young warriors will be particularly entranced in the Arms and Armor Gallery, with its ferocious weaponry and gleaming uniforms. Oh, the battles to be fought with a trusty lance and a mighty crossbow!

On the first Saturday of the month there is a preschoolers' program, usually with a short tour, story, and simple art projects, that explores a single theme such as the seasons or animals.

Monthly workshops are held for 6-to-9-year-olds and their parents. Participants may make books, discover architecture, see a variety of endangered animals as depicted by artists through the ages, or work with stained glass. Other workshops and activities are scheduled for older children and family members. Storyteller Rachmiel Tobesman spins tales in various galleries, and the Children's Theatre Association presents plays and sponsors appearances by Umoja Sasa, an African story troupe.

Some activities require advance reservations, and some have a charge or a requested donation.

● B&O Railroad Museum

901 West Pratt Street at Poppleton Street. (410) 752-2490 (information), (410) 752-2461 (administrative office). Open daily from 10 A.M. to 5 P.M. Adults, $6.50; $5.50 for senior citizens; $4 for children ages 3–12; children ages 2 and under are free. Closed Thanksgiving and December 25. Two-mile round-trip rides are given on Saturday and Sunday for $2. **All ages.**

As you walk from your car to the museum entrance, note the railroad tracks under your feet. They were the first long-distance railroad tracks laid in America, in 1830. This was the location of the Mount Clare Station, the oldest continually operating railroad sight in the world and the birthplace of the B&O Railroad. On the grounds and in the 1884 roundhouse are 130 full-sized trains, an extensive and fascinating HO scale-model train, an extraordinary collection of model bridges, ancient fire-engine cars, and the tools that were used to lay the rail network for a modern nation. Among the museum's treasured exhibits is a replica of the famous Tom Thumb steam-powered vehicle built by Peter Cooper in 1829. This vast collection of freight cars, cabooses, locomotives, primitive cars, Conestoga wagons, and other vehicles on wheels delights children of all ages.

● Babe Ruth Birthplace

Baltimore Orioles Museum, 216 Emory Street. (410) 727-1539. Open daily 10 A.M. to 5 P.M. April through October, and until 7 P.M. on days when the Orioles play at Camden Yards. 10 A.M. to 4 P.M. November through March. Closed Easter, December 25, Thanksgiving, and New Year's Day. Adults, $4.50; senior citizens, $3; children ages 5–12, $2; children ages 4 and under, free. Gift shop. **All ages.**

America's second-largest baseball museum (after the Baseball Hall of Fame Museum) is filled with memorabilia of the Babe, the Orioles, and Maryland baseball, although the Orioles part of the museum will move to separate quarters in 1995 in the old Camden Yards train depot, just a few blocks away. A 25-minute film documents Babe's early years and covers his time in baseball from 1914 to April 1948.

Baseball fanatics can get their fill of balls, bats, old uniforms, and trophies. Radios play tapes of the Sultan of Swat hitting the first home run in the newly opened Yankee Stadium in 1923 and his record-breaking 60th home run in 1927. An old-time outfield fence has 714 plaques, one for each of Ruth's home runs, listing the place and date of the run and the pitcher who pitched it.

Children's parties can be held here. If you schedule the party during the baseball season, reserve the space at least two months in advance, and make a contribution to the museum. The Orioles Bird will visit and sign autographs. Call (301) 243-9800 to make arrangements.

● Baltimore Museum of Art

Art Museum Drive. (410) 396-7101, (410) 396-6320 (education office). Open Wednesday, Thursday, and Friday from 10 A.M. to 4 P.M.; Friday and Saturday from 11 A.M. to 6 P.M. Closed Monday, Tuesday, December 25, and New Year's Day. Adults, $5.50; seniors (over 65) and full-time students, $3.50; children ages 7–18, $1.50; free admission on Thursday. Children's tours are given Tuesday through Friday 10 A.M. to 2 P.M. Membership available. Cafe. Gift shop. **All ages.**

One of the highlights, at the largest and most visited museum in Baltimore, is the collection of eighteenth- and nineteenth-century American artists. Children in particular like the historic Cheney Miniatures Rooms (living rooms, silver room, English parlor); the modern collection, because of the generally large scale of the works and their vibrant colors; a Martin Pureyor wooden sculpture that takes up the entire Fox Court; the African collection that's installed close to the ground, at child level; a pre-Columbian collection of little dolls; and the Wurtzburger Sculpture Garden with pieces by Calder, Moore, and Rodin.

● Baltimore Zoo

Druid Hill Park, off exit 7 of Interstate 83. (410) 366-5466 (recording), (410) 396-7102 (administration). Open daily 10 A.M. to 4 P.M.; extended summer hours. Closed December 25. Adults, $6.50; children ages 3 to 15 and senior citizens, $3.50; children ages 2 and under, free; free admission for all children the first Saturday of each month until noon. **All ages.**

The zoo, established in 1876, is the third-oldest in the nation and many of the cages reflect the thinking of zoo procedures of those days, updated a little. You can note some of the updates at the African Watering Hole, a refuge for the endangered white rhinoceros, and habitats for zebras, antelopes, and ostriches.

Of particular interest is the Lyn T. Meyerhoff Maryland Wilderness and Discovery Path, reached through the Children's Zoo, that depicts various Maryland biomes. Children can sit in an oriole's nest, step on giant lily pads, walk under a frolicking otter, poke their heads up through a woodchuck hole, work their way across a swinging bridge, climb a tree to explore its habitat and slide down from the top of the tree's enormous fallen limb, and visit barnyard animals.

The zoo also boasts the most productive colony of African black-footed penguins in the United States; a naturalistic habitat for African elephants; some rare and unusual animals, such as the red panda (arguably part of the panda family, but generally only accepted as part of the species), the sitatunga antelope, lion-tailed macaques, and golden-lion tamarins; and my favorite bird, because of its pretty head feathers, the African crown crane.

Times for the penguin feeding and the African elephant demonstrations are posted. Pony rides are available during the summer at the Children's Zoo; so are the carousel and the Zoo-Choo train.

A tram is available for 25 cents per person to take weary walkers from one part of the zoo to another. Have your hand stamped and ride the tram all day.

DAVIDSONVILLE

● New Ark Petting Farm

15557 Governor's Bridge Road, off Route 424. Open year-round by appointment, and during the summer from 9:30 A.M. to noon, Thursday through Saturday. Family hours on weekends. Admission $6. (410) 798-0206.
All ages.

This is the place to look at exotic animals, and even pet some of them. The collection includes kangaroos, pot-bellied pigs, rabbits, llamas, peacocks, waterfowl, and tigers.

Such special events as a spring picnic catered by Adams' Ribs, a bonfire and hay ride, a tiger's birthday party, and more dot the calendar. And, in the summer there's a day camp where children from 6 to 10 learn to feed and care for animals and do special projects.

ELLICOTT CITY

● B&O Railroad Station Museum

Maryland Avenue and Main Street. (410) 461-1944 (recording). The hours vary according to the exhibit, with the last admission 30 minutes prior to closing. Closed on school holidays and during bad weather emergencies. Adults, $3; children ages 5 to 12, $1; senior citizens, $1; children under 5, free. http://www-rsc.usc.edu/~gkoma/bando.html. Holiday exhibits: **all ages.** *Other exhibits:* **ages 8 and up.**

This was the first passenger terminus of the B&O Railroad. There is a sight-and-sound show with a working HO-scale model rail display of the first 13 miles of the first railroad in America, from Baltimore to Ellicott City; a restored 1927 caboose; and a visitor center. Ellicott City (Route 144) is an old mill town and many original stone buildings and fine examples of early mill workers' homes are still here. Antique and specialty shops are abundant.

FREDERICK

● Rose Hill Manor: Children's Museum and Park

1161 North Market Street. (301) 694-1648, (301) 694-1646. Open Monday through Saturday 10 A.M. to 4 P.M., Sunday 1 to 4 P.M. April through mid-December. Adults, $3; senior citizens, $2; and children ages 16 and under, $1. **All ages.**

Colonial crafts are demonstrated throughout the year, and children are encouraged to touch the exhibits in the many buildings, including the blacksmith shop, carriage museum, farm museum, ice house, log cabin, and manor house. The aim of the museum is to make the nineteenth century come alive for children. And the best place to do this is in the room with the arts and crafts, toys, and costumes to try on. There should be museums and parks like this for adults.

GAITHERSBURG

● *Montgomery County Sentinel*

7 Dalamar Street. (301) 417-1200. Guided tours are given Wednesday through Friday from 11 A.M. to 5 P.M. for **ages 6 and older,** *by appointment, with at least five days notice.*

This newspaper tour includes talks with reporters about how a story is written, a visit to advertising and classified offices, and a visit to the darkroom to see how photographs are developed.

● National Institute of Standards and Technology (formerly the Bureau of Standards)

Quince Orchard and Clopper Road. (301) 975-3585. Guided tours are given Thursday at 9:30 A.M. by appointment only. http://www.nist.gov. **Ages 11 and up.**

The world's largest measurement laboratory is housed in a 21-building complex on 570 acres of land. It provides the basic standards for measuring length, time, mass, and temperature. The laboratory's research and development practices are in the fields of chemistry, engineering, and physics, and it assists in the solving of technological problems. Given that, you'll understand that the tours are very technical and liable to bore easily those who are not scientifically oriented.

The museum is a little more approachable for non-Einstein types and includes displays of scientific apparatus, important memorabilia, exhibits about current research, and historic documents concerning the science of measurement.

● Sportland America

9811 Washington Boulevard. (301) 840-8404. Open Monday through Thursday 11 A.M. to 11 P.M.; Friday 11 A.M. to 1 A.M.; Saturday 10 A.M. to 1 A.M.; and Sunday, 10 A.M. to 11 P.M. No admission charge; various charges for different activities, including roller skating and bumper cars.
All ages.

This is the biggest play area for children on the East Coast, with air hockey, baseball/softball batting cages, billiards, bumper cars, gladiator climbing walls, group parties and functions, miniature golf, orbitron gyro, Par T golf, a party area, roller skating, skee ball, a children's recreation area, and a video arcade.

GLEN ECHO

● Glen Echo Park

7300 MacArthur Boulevard. (301) 492-6282 (recording), (301) 492-6663 (carousel). Open daily from 6 A.M. to 1 A.M. Closed December 25 and New Year's Day. http://www.nps.gov/glec. **All ages.**

What do you want from a park? A half-century-old carousel? A puppet theater? A children's theater? An art gallery of local artists? A Spanish Ballroom with dancing four or more nights a week from spring through late fall? Picnicking? This is the place.

Glen Echo Park used to be an amusement park and anyone who has been around here for more than a few years can tell you about the roller coaster, bumper cars, the fun house, and the miracles that occurred here, like falling in love under a full moon.

Greater miracles have happened. Following years of neglect, the park now belongs to the National Park Service. People have been working hard to restore it so future children can have wonderful memories here, too.

The carousel has been at the park since 1921, and is one of 27 remaining Dentzel-manufactured carousels in the United States and Canada. It has two chariots and 52 hand-carved figures (of which 36 are "jumpers"), including 40 horses, 4 ostriches, 4 rabbits, a deer, a tiger, a lion, and a giraffe. It usually operates April through October on Wednesday and Thursday 10 A.M. to 2 P.M. and Saturday and Sunday 12 noon to 6 P.M. The cost is 50 cents. If the carousel is the only reason you're going to the park, call ahead to confirm that it's running. Children under 8 must be accompanied by an adult. Park rangers have even been known to give a 20-minute carousel tour that explains the history of the ride.

Adventure Theater presents fairy tales and other children's stories every Saturday and Sunday at 1:30 and 3:30 P.M. Admission is $4.50, and reservations are suggested. The Puppet Company performs several times a day, several times a week. Tickets are $4. The Glen Echo Dance Theater is the resident dance company at the park, with regularly scheduled classes and performances.

GREENBELT

● National Aeronautics and Space Administration (NASA)/Goddard Space Flight Center

Visitor Center and Museum, Soil Conservation Road. (301) 286-8981, (301) 286-8103 (TDD). Visitor center is open daily 9 A.M. to 4 P.M. Guided tours available (see below). Sign interpreters can be provided for all events with one week notice. Gift shop. Picnic tables and snack vending machines. Free admission. Http://pao.gsfc.nasa.gov. **Ages 3 and up** *for exhibits;* **ages 9 and up** *for tours.*

Goddard is the hub of NASA tracking activities, the center of the nation's space exploration program. It welcomes visitors to relive old space shots via films, exhibits, and interactive computers.

NASCOM (NASA communications) public tours, for children ages 9 and up and adults, last approximately one hour. They are offered Monday through Saturday at 11:30 A.M. and 2:30 P.M.; first and third Sunday at 11 A.M. A 90-minute van tour of the Testing and Evaluation areas is offered on the second and fourth Sunday at 11 A.M. and 2 P.M. Group tours of 15 to 40 people must reserve at least one month in advance.

Model rocket launches are held on the first and third Sunday of the month at 1 P.M. Goddard is the home of the most rocket launches in the United States. They may be small, but they are plentiful. On Saturday night, from 7 to 9 P.M. between September and April, star-gazers of all experience levels are invited to see the wonders of the night skies (assuming they're clear) and then see films and presentations on astronomical topics. Bring your own telescope or binoculars, or use the Visitor Center equipment.

On the second Sunday of each month, at 1 P.M., all are invited to see a space-themed video in the Hubble Theater.

Younger children, ages 9 and up, are invited to participate in a Kids in Space program on the second Sunday of the month at 2 P.M. Presentations and hands-on activities focus on earth and space science. Reservations are required, and the group is limited to 15 participants.

On the fourth Sunday of each month, at 1 P.M., children ages 15 and up are invited to meet the scientists, project managers, and staff of the Goddard Space Flight Center for an inside view of current activities. A question and answer session follows the presentation.

Outside, in the rocket garden, you can see a Delta launch vehicle, a scale model of a lunar vehicle, and other representatives of outer-space voyages.

Community Day, held in mid-September, admits visitors to areas normally closed to the general public. This special tour stops at both the NASCOM Division Center and the Spacecraft Systems Development and Integration Facility. The latter is one of the largest "clean rooms" in the world, with 86,000 square feet of contamination-free environment for building large payloads. Of particular importance and interest are the various everyday applications derived from research from various space-shots. Model rocket launches, international ham-radio demonstrations, and musical entertainment also are on the program.

KENSINGTON

● Washington Mormon Temple Visitors Center
9900 Stoneybrook Drive. (301) 587-0144. Open daily 10 A.M. to 9:30 P.M.
Ages 10 and up.

Called "one of the world's most technologically advanced religious exhibits," the temple is closed to non-Mormons, but much of the temple's beauty and spirit are to be found in the visitors' center. For several weeks starting in late November, hundreds of thousands of tiny colored lights decorate the trees and bushes around the temple. This is a favorite photographic spot starting shortly before sundown. Carolers perform songs of the season, with concerts beginning nightly at 7:30 P.M.

OCEAN CITY

Maryland's only seaside resort community has a 10-mile stretch of wide, sandy beaches and plenty of fishing (it's known as the White Marlin Capital of the World) and watersports (sailing, jet skiing, water skiing, parasailing, and windsurfing, particularly in the bay waters). On week-ends, the little more than three-hour drive from Washington and Balti-more to Ocean City can become almost hopelessly jammed with traffic, so a midweek visit is best. Also, the weather stays milder longer than in the city, so if you visit before Memorial Day and after Labor Day you'll still find some activity. Numerous festivals are scheduled throughout the year, and there are several amusement parks with rides and water slides.

OXON HILL

● Oxon Hill Children's Farm Park

6411 Oxon Hill Road. (301) 839-1177 (recording). Open daily 8 A.M. to 4:30 P.M. Closed Thanksgiving, December 25, and New Year's Day.
All ages.

This is a turn-of-the century working farm with chickens, cows, pigs, horses, vegetables, and demonstrations of farming practices and seasonal arts and crafts of the early 1900s. You can watch wheat threshing, corn picking, molasses cooking, sorghum-syrup making, and sheep shearing.

Cow milking is done every day at 10:30 A.M. and at 4 P.M. and egg gathering occurs at 2 P.M. Occasional farm chores and activities go on throughout the day. Obviously, some things are seasonal, such as sheep shearing, so call if there's something in particular you want to see.

Guides and farm workers in period costumes are available as escorts, but visitors may walk around on their own and pet the animals, watch the farmers at work, or even help with the harvesting.

POTOMAC

● Great Falls Park

Off MacArthur Boulevard. Open daily from dawn to dusk. Admission for each vehicle is $4 for a 7-day pass and $10 for an annual pass; visitors who enter by motorcycle, bicycle, or on foot, $2; Bookstore. http://www.nps.gov/choh/ index.htm. **All ages.**

This long, linear park features mule-drawn barge rides along the historic Chesapeake & Ohio Canal, kayaking, hiking, and biking. An exhibit center explains the history and importance of the canal and is often the site of local art exhibits. Ranger-led walks, talks, and bike rides are presented throughout the year, but mostly from May through Octo-ber. In addition to walking or hiking or biking the canal towpath, you can hike the Gold Mine trail (which used to lead to a gold-mine, but the mine is now closed off), the River trail, and the nationally known Billy Goat Trail. This four-mile trail between the canal and the river is named for its rough and tough nature, but it also rewards the hiker the best and most scenic views. There is also a handicapped-accessible walkway from the towpath to an overlook of the Great Falls of the Potomac. A concession stand for beverages and light snacks is available.

● **C&O Canal Barge Rides**

11710 MacArthur Boulevard. (301) 299-3613. Rides are available at Georgetown in Washington and here at Great Falls, from about mid-April through mid-October. Hours and days vary; summer barge trips depart Wednesday through Sunday at 10:30 A.M., 1 P.M., and 3 P.M.; reduced schedule in effect in spring and fall. Reservations are suggested. Adults, $4; senior citizens (62 and over) and children 12 and under, $3.50. http:// www.nps.gov/choh/. **All ages.**

Organized by the C&O Canal National Historical Park, the mule-drawn Canal Clipper carries you along a craggy river gorge and through the woods on a ride that recalls canal travel of a century ago. Guides wear period costumes and explain life in the mid-1800s on the canal and in the barges. The 90-foot boat is worked up and down lock 20 during the 50- to 60-minute ride; the process visually explains how boats are lifted and lowered from one water level to another.

One-hour day trips and two-hour evening trips can be booked by groups, at special rates. Bring along a banjo or guitar and have an old-fashioned sing-along.

PRINCE FREDERICK

● **Battle Creek Cypress Swamp Sanctuary**

Grays Road off Route 506. (301) 535-5327. Open Tuesday through Saturday 10 A.M. to 5 P.M., Sunday 1 P.M. to 5 P.M. April through September; until 4:30 P.M. October through March. Closed Thanksgiving, December 25, and New Year's Day. **All ages.**

This is the largest, northernmost stand of bald cypress trees. There's no Spanish moss hanging from the branches, and no southern belles in hoop skirts, but there is a wooden walkway through the swamp. Spring flowers are beautiful here and the nature center has plenty of displays, including an occupied beehive. Special programs are held throughout most of the year.

ROCKVILLE

● Sportrock I

14708 Southlawn Lane, Rockville. (301) 762-5111. Open weekdays from noon to 11 P.M., Saturday from 11 A.M. to 8 P.M., and Sunday from noon to 8 P.M. **Ages 6 and up.**

For an introduction to rock-climbing, Sportrock I (and Sportrock II in Virginia) is well-supervised and highly controlled and fun. There's a children's night every Friday evening for children ages 6 through 14, with one instructor for every four children, and a 12-child limit to the class. Children should wear sneakers to the climbing class, and Sportrock will provide each child with a helmet and a harness. With a variety of increasing steepness to the 30-foot walls, children progress at their own speed. Once they establish some confidence, they're even allowed to climb blindfolded, which helps develop the use of senses other than sight. Parents may stay and watch, if they wish, or leave for awhile.

● Imagine That

1616 East Jefferson Street, Congressional Plaza (in rear). (301) 468-2101. Kids Club membership, visit four times and receive fifth visit free. **All ages.**

This is where learning comes into play, according to the Imagine That people. There's a real ambulance, a fire truck (with clothes the children can don), an airplane, a sports car, a grocery store, a TV room (complete with a news desk for reading the news), a painting room, a ballet and tap room, a computer room, a sand box, a room equipped with a light you turn on and then off and your shadow appears, a pirate ship, a room with large Lego blocks, and a place to eat. Best of all, mom and dad don't have to clean up after the children are done playing.

● Schaeffer's Piano Company

419 East Gude Drive. (301) 589-3039. Open Monday through Friday 10 A.M. to 8 P.M.; Saturday 10 A.M. to 6 P.M. **Ages 10 and up.**

This piano company has been building fine instruments for about 90 years. At this warehouse and refurbishing area you can see what goes into restoring a piano, including storage (grand piano lids are stored separately), working with keys and strings, stripping, brass polishing, tuning, and anything else that may be involved.

There is also a nickelodeon that the staff will turn on for you so you can watch the drums drum and the keys tinkle and the cymbals clang.

● White Flint Discovery Zone FunCenter

White Flint Mall, 11301 Rockville Pike, third floor between the movie theaters and Borders Books. (301) 231-0505. Open Monday through Thursday, 9 A.M. to 9:30 P.M.; Friday and Saturday 9 A.M. to 10 P.M.; Sunday 10 A.M. to 8 P.M. Admission for children is $6.99 for up to two hours; adults play for free. Annual Discovery Zone family memberships are available. **All ages.**

This center is a creative learning environment designed to foster children's physical and social development. Free-play or unstructured activities are available as well as specially designed equipment promoting child and parent activities that help develop children's motor skills, strength, confidence, and self-esteem. Among the options are: a "Mega Zone," with a series of tubes, ball baths, slides, trampolines, moon walks, trapezes, and an obstacle course designed for children over 40 inches tall; a "Micro Zone," with a smaller version of some of the abovementioned, for those under 40 inches tall; and a "Starter Zone," with toys and activities suited to youngsters who are crawling or just learning to walk.

Other activity areas are available, including a quiet zone and, of course, a place to purchase branded wearing apparel and equipment. Parents may accompany children, but children must accompany parents. Socks-on-feet only; no shoes. Kids Coaches are stationed throughout the FunCenter. Birthday parties can be easily accommodated.

SHARPSBURG

● Antietam National Battlefield

Maryland Route 65, 5831 Dunker Church Road. (301) 432-5124. Open 8:30 A.M. to 5 P.M. in winter; 8 A.M. to 6 P.M. in summer. Tours of the battlefield are given in summer if there is sufficient staffing. Admission is $2 per person; $4 per car load. Children ages 17 and under are free. http:// www.nps.gov/ncro/. **All ages.**

Start your tour in the visitor center with the 26-minute film shown every hour on the hour. This is not a rehash of the battle, but is complementary to the driving tour. The political issues of the day are covered and the film includes Lincoln's visit here after the battle. A small museum shows a uniform, medical tools, and items that a soldier would have carried with him. An observation room displays three paintings done by Captain James Hope during the battle; a fourth painting is in the lobby. You can see about two-thirds of the battlefield from the visitor center.

Antietam, which resulted in the largest number of deaths in any single day of any battle fought by American soldiers, marked Robert E.

Lee's unsuccessful attempt to invade the North. The site offers plenty of gun embankments and fields of battle on which to imagine this major event of the Civil War. A driving tour is laid out just as the battle was fought, from morning through the cornfields, into the afternoon at Bloody Lane, and later at Burnside Bridge. A cassette describing the battle can be rented at the visitor center for $4, or purchased for $7.

Children who have studied this period of history will benefit most from a visit and probably find it more interesting than young children.

SUITLAND

● Paul E. Garber Facility (Smithsonian Institution)

1000 Old Silver Hill Road. (202) 357-1400. Open for free three-hour guided tours daily at 10 A.M. except December 25, and weekends at 1 P.M. Reservations should be made two weeks in advance by calling the above number or by writing Tour Scheduler, National Air and Space Museum, Smithsonian Institution, Washington, D.C. 20960. Visitors without reservations may be accepted on a space-available basis. **Ages 6 and up.**

This suburban facility of the Smithsonian's Air and Space Museum is where restoration and preservation of classic and historic planes take place. During your tour, you will see more than 100 aircraft. In Building 10, you will see restoration work in progress on a Nieuport 28, a Hawker Hurricane, an Aichi Seiran, and a Pitts Special, *Little Stinker*. Buildings 20 and 23 contain several rare aircraft; many are one-of-a-kind. Paul E. Garber joined the Smithsonian Institution in 1920 and is responsible for a great number of acquisitions, including Lindbergh's *Spirit of St. Louis*.

An open house usually is held in even numbered years (1996, 1998, etc.) during the last weekend in April, with aerospace-related demonstrations and activities, free concerts, and intergalactic views through telescopes.

The buildings are not heated or air-conditioned and you should wear comfortable shoes. There are no bathroom facilities available during the tour (although there are for the open house). Young children certainly find the tour interesting, but because of its length it may be better to bring them to the open house, if you have that option.

THURMONT

● Catoctin Mountain Zoological Park

Off U.S. 15. (301) 271-7488, (301) 662-2579. Open daily from 9 A.M. to 5 P.M. Adults, $6.50 and children 2 to 12, $4.75. **All ages.**

More than 400 native rare and endangered mammals, birds, and reptiles live here and participate in daily shows. Phase one of the North American Exhibit, which was opened in 1990, is a hands-on operation where visitors can touch the animals. If there is an education person or a volunteer in the teaching building, then the animals are outside the exhibit. If not, they're inside, particularly in the off-season. Children can also make arts and crafts.

UPPER MARLBORO

● Watkins Regional Park
301 Watkins Park Drive. (301) 249-6202 (nature center). Open daily 7 A.M. to dusk. Closed Thanksgiving, December 25, and New Year's Day. **All ages.**

Plenty of facilities are available in the park, including a nature center, a miniature-train ride, picnic grounds, a campground, a playground, an old-fashioned farm, an antique carousel, and, in December, the annual Festival of Lights (no charge, but donations of food or money are accepted).

The nature center has regularly scheduled activities for all age groups, from studying animals and insects to hiking and basket making. Another strong draw is the pride and joy of the park, the hand-carved, hand-painted, 80-year-old carousel, which, along with the train ride, operates only in fair weather.

During the summer there's a $5-per-car camping charge for people who do not live in Prince George's County or Montgomery County, Maryland.

WALDORF

● *Maryland Independent* Newspaper
7 Industrial Park. (301) 843-9600. **Ages 6 and up.**

Free tours are given by appointment on Monday, Wednesday, and Friday from 8:30 A.M. to 5 P.M. for ages 6 and older. The visit starts with a video on how the newspaper is produced and then proceeds to each department where visitors have a chance to question editors, reporters, and photographers and follow up with a view of the printing press.

WHEATON

● Wheaton Regional Park
2000 Shorefield Road. (301) 946-7035. Open daily dawn to dusk. Closed Thanksgiving, December 25, and New Year's Day. **All ages.**

In and around this area you will find a playground, a picnic area, ballfields, a carousel, miniature train, a nature center, an ice rink, and a garden center.

The Herschell-Spillman carousel was manufactured between 1909 and 1915 and supposedly was designed to travel, because it could be assembled and disassembled in one day. It has 33 horses, 3 zebras, 2 chariots, and all the animals are "jumpers." The carousel is open during the warm season only; rides are 60 cents and parents who stand alongside seated children are admitted free.

On the playground children will find a navy jet fighter to climb atop and slide down the other side, the Wheaton Stage Coach, pony rides, and a two-mile trip on a replica of a colorful 1865 steam-engine train.

● Brookside Nature Center

1400 Glenallan Avenue. (301) 946-9071. Open Tuesday through Saturday 9 A.M. to 5 P.M.; Sunday 1 to 5 P.M. Guided tours by appointment only.
All ages.

This center focuses on the natural history of metropolitan Washington, with attractions that include aquariums, an indoor turtle pool, an occupied beehive, slide shows, and movies.

● Brookside Gardens

1500 Glenallan Avenue. (301) 949-8230 (recording). Grounds are open 9 A.M. to dusk; the two conservatories are open daily 9 A.M. to 5 P.M. Closed December 25. **All ages.**

Within this 25-acre parkland are two conservatories filled with plants and flowers, including some exotic and foreign specimens. Outside are a number of public display gardens, including the following types: raised, azalea, formal (perennial, yew, rose), fragrance, trial, Japanese-style with teahouse, winter, aquatic, and butterfly.

At times you may see a blooming coffee tree, bananas, and chrysanthemums, or the annual Christmas flower show with such traditional seasonal plants as the Jerusalem cherry, cyclamen, and kalanchoe. Easter lilies, azaleas, hydrangeas, fuchsias, and dogwood are the stars of the spring flower show.

● National Capital Trolley Museum

Bonifant Road between Layhill Road and New Hampshire Avenue. (301) 384-6088 (recording). Open Saturday, Sunday, Memorial Day, Fourth of July, and Labor Day noon to 5 P.M.; until 9 P.M. Saturday and Sunday in December for Holly Trolley Fest; Wednesday during July and August 11 A.M. to 3 P.M. Closed December 25 and New Year's Day. Free admission; trolley

*rides are $2.50 for adults, $2 for children ages 3–17, free for children ages
2 and under. The last trolley ride leaves 30 minutes before closing time. Gift
shop.* **All ages.**

From presidents Lincoln to Kennedy, Washington, D.C., had street-
car trolleys. The tracks were dug up or paved over by 1962.

For those who've never seen a trolley, or for those who miss them, this
is a collection of American and European trolleys. It includes an 1889
Sweeper 07 used until 1962 to help maintain the Washington-area trolley
system during snowy weather. An American deck-roof trolley of 1918 and
vehicles from Vienna and Graz built in the early 1900s are in the collection. There's also a four-wheeled car of the Gay Nineties and a shiny
streamliner.

A visitor center built to resemble an old-time railroad station is the
boarding point for the trolley rides. Film programs are offered, and you
can purchase trolley-related items in the gift shop.

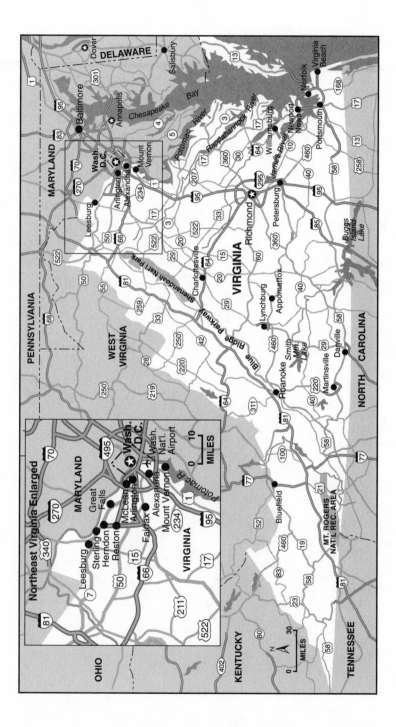

Virginia

ACCORDING TO THE SLOGAN coined by Virginia's tourism promoters, Virginia is for lovers. By that they mean lovers of the outdoors, history, arts, science, sports, or whatever it is that you love to do. You'll find plenty of things to love in this area. This section is organized alphabetically by city.

ALEXANDRIA

● River Farm, American Horticultural Society

7931 E. Boulevard Drive. (703) 768-5700. Open weekdays from 8:30 A.M. to 5 P.M. No admission charge. **All ages.**

Children can explore specific-purpose gardens at River Farm, including one that attracts bats (great for eating insects and garden pests) and another that attracts butterflies, bees, and birds. The stone garden has child- and adult-sized stones for sitting, and the pizza garden has such herbs as basil, oregano, parsley, and thyme, to show children they can grow their own pizza spices. A bat cave is great for children ages 5 and under to play hide-and-seek, follow-the-leader, and other games of the imagination. Its fort-like structure has a window and a skylight, and it is covered with fragrant plants and vines.

● Torpedo Factory

105 North Union Street. (703) 838-4565, (703) 683-0693 (tours). Open daily 10 A.M. to 5 P.M. Guided tours by appointment only. **All ages.**

The Torpedo Factory (for that's what it used to be) is home to 150 artists dealing in prints, pottery, sculpture, glass, paint, and musical-instrument production. Children love the place because they can see work in progress and talk with the artists. No question is asked too often or left unanswered.

Three free sheets explain self-guided tours directed toward children, one for children ages 8 to 11, one for those ages 11 to 14, and a third for ages 14 to 18. An outside tour brochure (small charge) is designed for children ages 6 to 12.

The indoor tour for the youngest children is based on a mystery theme. Children are challenged with questions about shapes, colors, smells, and senses. The tour for the next oldest group, which involves journalistic techniques, encourages children to write an article about their observations and interviews. The high-school-level tour treats art as an avocation or an occupation. It suggests that teens select a medium and visit five artists to learn what they can about the art business.

Free hour-long, docent-led tours that relate the history of the building and focus on some of the artists can be arranged in advance and are suitable for children.

● Sportrock II

5308 Eisenhower Avenue. (703) 212-7625. Open weekdays from noon to 11 P.M.; Saturday from 11 A.M. to 8 P.M. and Sunday from noon to 8 P.M.
Ages 6 and up.

Sportrock II, as with its sister operation in Rockville, offers an introduction to rock-climbing. See page 125 for details.

● West End Dinner Theatre

4615 Duke Street. (703) 370-2500 (box office). (800) 368-3799 (group sales). (703) 823-9061 (business office). **Ages 3 and up.**

West End offers a Children's Theatre series on Saturday afternoon with such productions as a musical adaptation of the classic Lewis Carroll tale *Alice in Wonderland, Cinderella,* and *Babes in Toyland.* There is no meal service, as there is with the adult performances in the evening (these are different than the children's theater selections), but refreshments can be purchased.

West End offers a summer performing arts camp for children ages 8 through 14, from beginners to advanced. Daily classes include acting, music and voice, and theater dance with a showcase at the end of the camp session.

West End features such family theater fare as *Singing in the Rain, Annie Get Your Gun, South Pacific,* and *Hello Dolly!,* all shows suitable for family viewing. There is a reduced price for children (ages 12 and under) for the Tuesday through Friday and Sunday evening performances, and Wednesday and Sunday matinees. Subscription prices also are available.

● Alexandria *Gazette Packet*

1610 King Street. (703) 549-7185. Free tours by appointment between 9 A.M. and 5 P.M. Monday for groups of 15 or fewer. **Ages 6 and up.**

Children will see reporters at work as they file stories into their computers and watch as paginators design the paper. They will also tour the photo laboratory and composing room.

● Washington National Airport

Take Fourteenth Street Bridge from Washington, D.C., to George Washington Parkway toward Alexandria to airport. Or take the subway to the National Airport subway station. http://www.metwashairports.com. **Ages 6 and up.**

The airport opened on June 16, 1941, with dire predictions that it would never be used to capacity. It was expanded, renovated, and modified over the years. A beautiful, modern, new terminal opened in 1997, with a five-story-tall glass wall (1.5 acres of glass) offering a sweeping view of airplanes taking off and landing, the Potomac River, and a spectacular view of Washington, D.C., the Mall, and the monuments. The best view is from Gate 43. The new concourse has 24 food and beverage outlets and 38 retail shops, and numerous carts offering souvenirs and other retail sale items. Picnic areas are outside, ideal for eating al fresco in nice weather. A meditation area is at the south end of the terminal.

After the huge window view, visitors can see the many artworks on display, including paintings, mosaics, murals, and sculptures by 30 different artists, from Lisa Scheer to Frank Stella.

The new terminal is much more accessible by subway than before, via covered moveable walkways.

Washington National Airport offers tours every Thursday (reservations required). Groups, from 10 (or fewer) to 50 in number are taken through the terminal, onto a plane at the gate, through the airport police station, and to a visit with Sgt. McGruff, the famed canine crime-fighter. School groups arriving by bus also can tour the airport fire station. A special gift package is given to all visitors. Call (703) 417-8003 for information and reservations.

ARLINGTON

● Arlington National Cemetery

Off Memorial Drive. (703) 607-8052 (cemetery). Parking lot is $1 per hour for the first three hours, $2 per hour or portion thereof after that. Gift shop. Tourmobile stop. Arlington Cemetery subway station. **All ages.**

You are allowed to drive through the cemetery if you are attending a funeral or visiting a specific gravesite. In either case you have to obtain a special driving pass at the visitor center. To visit the cemetery otherwise, enter through the visitor center and pay $4 for adults and $2 for children to take the narrated 40-minute Tourmobile ride (of which at least 15 minutes is spent boarding and unboarding at three stops along the route). Alternatively, you can walk. It's an uphill trek, but plenty of people do it. The Tourmobile stops at the Kennedy gravesites, the Changing of the Guard, and at Arlington House (see following entry).

At the Kennedy gravesites, you'll see the graves of John F. Kennedy, Jacqueline Kennedy Onassis, two of their children, and Robert F. Kennedy.

Also buried at Arlington are President and Chief Justice William Howard Taft; Supreme Court justices Earl Warren, Oliver Wendell Holmes, and William O. Douglas; Grand Canyon explorer John Wesley Powell; astronauts Dick Scobee and Michael Smith; sports figures Joe Louis and Abner Doubleday; and actor Lee Marvin.

At the Tomb of the Unknowns (with servicemen from World War I and II and the Korean and Vietnam conflicts), soldiers from the Third U.S. Infantry ("The Old Guard") stand guard 24 hours a day. The Changing of the Guard takes place every hour, on the hour, 8 A.M. to 5 P.M. from October 1 to March 31, and every half hour 8 A.M. to 7 P.M. from April 1 to September 30. At night the guard is changed every two hours. The guards take 21 steps before turning and facing the tomb for 21 seconds, corresponding to the 21-gun salute. The guards have taps, or "cheaters," on their shoe bottoms and on the insides of their shoe heels, which make the snap of their salute sound so sharp. Their gloves are soaked in water to help the guards keep a better grip on their custom-made wood-handled M-14 rifles, which are fastened with a pair of "keeps" that circle the wrist like sweatbands.

Each year three major events are held in the 5,500-seat Memorial Amphitheater behind the Unknowns: Easter Sunrise, Memorial Day, and Veterans Day services. Additionally, numerous veteran and civic groups hold memorial services throughout the year.

Nearby is the mast of the U.S.S. *Maine,* and memorials honoring the crew from the space shuttle *Challenger* (two of whom are buried here), and the eight men who died in the 1980 Iran hostage rescue attempt.

● Arlington House

On the grounds of Arlington National Cemetery. (703) 557-0613. (703) 557-0614 (TDD). Open daily 9:30 A.M. to 6 P.M. April through September,

9:30 A.M. to 4:30 P.M. October through March. Closed December 25 and New Year's Day. Self-guided tours during regular hours. Guided tours are offered October through March by appointment only. Candlelight tours are offered in the fall; special tours for the visually or hearing impaired by appointment only. Special observances are held on January 19, Lee's birthday, and on June 30, his wedding anniversary. Gift shop. Tourmobile stop. Arlington Cemetery subway station. **Ages 6 and up.**

This home was the residence of Robert E. Lee for more than 30 years. It fell into northern hands during the Civil War, and now is a tribute to the southern lifestyle that just preceded the war. Many of the items—furniture, artwork, housewares—belonged to the Lee, Washington, and Custis families or are excellent reproductions. From the portico (on the north side), there is a great view of downtown Washington and the memorials and monuments.

Upstairs are five bedrooms and a playroom. Lee's three youngest daughters shared one room and his three sons shared a second room; his oldest daughter had her own room. The playroom is filled with diminutive furniture, dolls, and toys of the 1800s.

Around Christmas, the house is decorated as it would have been while Lee lived there. Special events are held to celebrate the season.

● Women in Military Service Memorial

Main gateway, Arlington National Cemetery. Guided tours available by calling (800) 222-2294 or (703) 533-1155. For other information, call (800) I SALUTE (472-5883). Open from 8 A.M. to 7 P.M. April through September; to 5 P.M. October through March. Closed December 25. Enter through the left, or south, pillar. Elevators are available to the upper level, as are four staircases cut into the arches. Gift shop. Arlington Cemetery subway station. http://www.wimsa.org. **All ages.**

The first major national memorial in the country to honor the 1.8 million servicewomen from all eras and services who have defended America throughout history opened in 1997. The memorial includes 14 exhibit alcoves; a 196-seat theater; a hall of honor and a computerized database of U.S. servicewomen. The Women in Military Service Memorial Foundation is seeking the names, addresses, photos, and memorable experiences of women who have served. Descendants and friends of deceased servicewomen are asked to register them (a $25 fee).

This engineering marvel was cut into the ground behind the curved memorial wall that is at one end of Memorial Drive, symbolically linking the north with the south, from the Lincoln Memorial to Arlington House. Its top is glass to allow plenty of daylight into the memorial, and when the sun is right, the quotations etched into some of the glass panels reflects down into the memorial. At other times, the glass acts as a natural prism, throwing rainbows of light into the lower space.

● Netherlands Carillon

Meade Street and Marshall Drive. Rosslyn subway station. (703) 285-2598. **All ages.**

Above and to the north of the Arlington National Cemetery, this marvelous carillon was donated by the Dutch in gratitude for help from the United States during World War II. Its 127-foot-tall square tower contains 49 bells, and stands as a symbol of friendship between the two countries. The largest and lowest-toned bell, known as the bourdon bell, measures more that 6 feet in diameter. The smallest is 9 inches in diameter and weighs just 37½ pounds. Verses cast on each bell were written by Dutch poet Ben von Eysslesteijn. The large bells represent the adults of the Netherlands; the small ones symbolize the country's youth.

Concerts by such well-known carillonneurs as Frank Della Penna are presented on weekends and holidays, April through August. Call for the schedule.

● United States Marine Corps War Memorial (Iwo Jima)

Arlington Ridge Road, north boundary of Arlington National Cemetery. Rosslyn subway station. (202) 433-6060. **All ages.**

The Marine Sunset Parade is held on Tuesday nights at 7 P.M. from June through August. This is a 75-minute performance of music and marching by the Marine Drum and Bugle Corps and the Marine Corps Silent Drill Platoon. Parking is available at the Arlington National Cemetery ($1 per hour for the first three hours), and a free shuttle service to the parade grounds is provided by the marines, starting at 6 P.M. No reservations are necessary.

Many television crews set up by this statue to cover Washington's annual Fourth of July fireworks celebration along the Mall. Bring a blanket, picnic, and plenty of friends.

● The Newseum

1101 Wilson Boulevard. (703) 284-3700 or (888) NEWSEUM (639-7386). Open Wednesday through Sunday, 10 A.M. to 5 P.M. Gift shop. Rosslyn subway station. http://www.newseum.org. **Ages 6 and up.**

News junkies and those fascinated by news collection and presentation, whether by print or electronics, flock to this, the world's only interactive museum of news. You'll find a news history gallery, a domed theater (introductory film to the museum), a broadcast studio, News Byte Cafe (which serves a limited menu), and Newseum Store (items for sale that are equally as interesting as those on exhibit). It opened on April 18, 1997, and had already had 100,000 visitors by June 22 of that year.

You and your children can make a videotape doing a weather forecast, covering a breaking news story, or announcing a feature TV segment. The tape is $10. You can view the front pages of 70 newspapers, from the 50 states and from other countries, to see how each covered that day's news. You can go to a computer kiosk and call up your birthdate to see what happened on that day, and buy a hard copy of it. Even the bathrooms are papered with hysterical and historical headlines.

Once a day, visitors to the Newseum get to meet top print and broadcast journalists as part of the "Journalist of the Day" program. This is a great chance to ask newspeople how they began their careers, and how they do their jobs. Most of these "broadcasts" are not aired to the public. There are enough interactive exhibits, including lessons on how and why editorial decisions are made, to keep almost any child happy, but the more your child can read, the more he or she will enjoy this museum.

Adjacent to the Newseum is Freedom Park, a three-block walkway framed by plantings and grassy terraces, that was once an aborted high-way. The park features various icons of freedom: segments of the Berlin Wall, stones from the Warsaw Ghetto, a bronze casting of Martin Luther King, Jr.'s jail-cell door, a bronze casting of a South African ballot box, women's suffrage banners, a Native American circle of stones, a memorial to journalists who have died while on the job, and more. A "Walk with Freedom" brochure for children and adults is available from the Newseum to help explain the various statues, signs, stones, and symbols. The brochure asks questions about each item that helps start conversations about freedom. The memorial to journalists features transparent panels upon which the names of the slain journalists have been etched, and the panels work as prisms creating interesting and constantly changing light colors. This area also is a sensational place to take pictures of the downtown Washington monuments.

FAIRFAX

● *Northern Virginia Sun*

2710-C Prosperity Avenue. (703) 204-2800. Free tours are given by appointment on Wednesday morning for groups of 30 or fewer. **Ages 8 and up.**

Children see a quick demonstration of how a story is written and put together, and watch the press running.

● Fairfax Station Railroad Museum

11200 Fairfax Station Road. (703) 425-9225. Open the third Sunday of each month, from 1 to 5 P.M. No admission fee, but a suggested donation is $2 for adults and $1 for children. Gift shop. http://www.fairfax-station.org.
Ages 5 and up.

Model railroad fanciers are invited to visit with members of the Northern Virginia NTRAK as they set up their N-scale trains for your enjoyment. The display is at adult waist level, so be sure your children are tall enough to see the trains, or be prepared to pick them up.

GREAT FALLS

● Great Falls National Park

9200 Old Dominion Drive. (703) 285-2966. Open daily 7 A.M. to dusk. Entrance fee per vehicle, $4. **All ages.**

Within the 800 square acres of this park you'll have the opportunity to enjoy nature and learn some of the area's history. Tours are given at least once a day of the Patowmack Canal, the only civil-engineering project ever worked on by George Washington. Along the way you'll stop by the old ghost town of Matildaville, and you'll enjoy a spectacular view of the Potomac River where it takes an exuberant 77-foot drop at Great Falls into Stephen Mather Gorge.

Most East Coast falls do not drop all at one time, as Niagara Falls does. Instead they drop, like this one, in a series of rapids. At times, it's said, more water tumbles over this drop than over Niagara. The Great Falls section of the river can be very hazardous, so heed the signs and the rangers if you're contemplating swimming or boating.

● Riverbend Park and Nature Center

8814 Jeffrey Road. (703) 759-3211. Park is open daily dawn to dusk. Entrance fee per car, $4 for non-county residents; free to county residents. The nature center is open Wednesday through Monday noon to 5 P.M. Closed Tuesday and on weekdays in January and February. **All ages.**

Part of the park, located next to Great Falls National Park, is a nature center with plenty of organized and unorganized activities, particularly for little youngsters. One of the favorites is the hike along a quarter-mile stroller-friendly route with eight stops to look for natural treasures. Reserve a discovery bag with a squirrel puppet, sniff boxes (sassafras and other aromatic things), and pictures to take along this Duff (stuff that accumulates on the forest floor) 'n' Stuff (and the stuff that goes with it) trail. Inside the center, a museum with changing exhibits might include live snakes, fish, silkworm cocoons and eggs, birds and bird seed, or whatever else is in season.

The Paw Paw Passage is a winding, 1¼-mile-long trail that covers bridges, hills, and dales. Older children can search for tree fungi, mushrooms, and even a deer's jawbone along this path. While walking along the Potomac, you can watch kayakers shoot the rapids at Great Falls.

● Roosevelt Island

George Washington Memorial Parkway (accessible only from northbound lane, coming from Washington). (703) 285-2598. Open daily 7 A.M. to dusk. Guided tours for children and school groups by appointment only. http:// www.nps.gov/ncro/. **All ages.**

Accessible only by footbridge (there's a parking lot), the island is the site of a memorial to Theodore Roosevelt. An uphill, unpaved trail leads to the memorial, which includes a bronze statue of the former president and large granite stones with some of his thoughts etched on them. There is a moat and plenty of sitting space. Trails (Swamp Trail and Highland Trail) lead all the way around the island, which is home to a variety of birds, animals, and plants. Although approached from Virginia, the island is in Washington, and adults hoping to take advantage of the fishing opportunities will need to purchase a Washington fishing license; children under 16 do not need a license.

During the summer, one-day children's camps for ages 7 to 11 are held on Wednesday from 8:30 A.M. to 3 P.M. You need to reserve a space and to provide an extra pair of really old and grungy sneakers, because the children love to participate in the swamp tromp, where they actually get into the swamp. Children choose from four to eight activities, including arts and crafts and a talk from the park police.

HERNDON

● The Washington and Old Dominion Railroad Regional Park

5400 Ox Road, Fairfax Station (park office address). (703) 352-5900, (703) 437-1910 (trail office). Open 7 A.M. to dusk. **All ages.**

This is the skinniest and one of the longest parks in Virginia, measuring 45 miles long by 100 feet wide. The park stretches through three counties—Fairfax, Arlington, and Loudoun—from Shirlington to Leesburg along the former roadbed of the W&OD Railroad. You can walk it, run it, bike it, or ride it on horseback. Along the way you'll find Parcours fitness stations and trails that lead off in all directions. There are

numerous entrances to the park, and the easiest way to decide what to do
and where to do it is by calling the trail office and requesting a map. The
cost is $4.50 by mail, $3.50 if you pick it up yourself.

Six old railroad stations and an old post office that is now a museum
are located in the park. Located at mile marker 20, the museum has a
statue out front of William Lewis Herndon, a U.S. Navy captain whose
name became attached to the post office in 1859. Inside the museum
you'll find arrowheads, spearheads, turn-of-the-century clothing, toys of
yore, Victorian dollhouse furniture, and a model of the ship that took
Herndon's life in 1857. The museum is open only periodically, usually
one Saturday a month and on special occasions. You can call (703) 437-
5556 to arrange a special tour through the Herndon Chamber of Commerce.

LEESBURG

● Federal Aviation Administration (FAA)

*825 East Market Street. (703) 771-3451. Hour-long tours are given,
Monday through Friday 9 A.M. to 3 P.M. (last tour starts at 2 P.M.);
reservations are requested, but it's possible to be booked on a tour the day you
call. http:/www.faa.gov.* **Ages 8 and up.**

Included on the tour are examples of all the electronic equipment
used to control the traffic flow of 1.3 million aircraft operations each
year. You see what the controller does, watch the radarscopes, check the
weather, and listen to air-to-ground communications. You learn what the
FAA is, what different departments are involved, how quality assurance
operates when there's been an accident, and how air-control specialists
keep traffic moving safely in the skies.

● *Loudoun Times-Mirror*

*9 East Market Street. (703) 777-1111. Free tours by appointment Monday
through Thursday from 8:30 A.M. to 5 P.M. for groups of 24 or fewer.* **Ages 5
and up.**

Children are allowed to see how a newspaper is put together, from the
reporters to the presses.

● The Naturalist Center (Smithsonian Institution)

*741 Miller Drive, Suite G2, Leesburg. (800) 729-7725 or (703) 779-
9712. Open Tuesday through Saturday from 10:30 A.M. to 4 P.M. http://*

www.si.edu/newstart.htm. **All ages,** *but children ages 9 and under are limited to a small area outside the main research room.*

This branch of the National Museum of Natural History is in this temporary setting until its regular home in Washington is remodeled, sometime in the year 2001. Explorers will be in their element discovering and uncovering the 30,000 items stored in large, well-marked drawers, or enjoying those on exhibit. Look for butterflies, hummingbird nests, a bison hairball, and skunks, and plan on a fun hands-on experience. The Center works on projects from the major scientific disciplines: anthropology, botany, mineral sciences, paleobiology, and zoology.

MCLEAN

● Claude Moore Colonial Farm

6310 Georgetown Pike. (703) 442-7557. Open Wednesday through Sunday 10 A.M. to 4:30 P.M. April through December. Closed during inclement weather and on Thanksgiving and December 25. Adults, $2; children ages 3–12, $1. Membership available. **All ages.**

This small-scale farm is worked with the same tools and methods used by farmers in the eighteenth century, just prior to the Revolution. The busy family here will answer your questions, as long as they don't relate to material after the 1770s. Among the animals present are bronzeback turkeys (they eat the green tobacco hornworms that attack tobacco leaves), razorback and Ossabaw Island hogs, quarter horses, cattle, bees, and Dung Hill Fowl chickens.

Market fairs are held on the third full weekends of May, July, and September. Other seasonal celebrations are held on the third full weekends of June, August, and October.

MERRIFIELD

● *Journal Express* Newspapers

2720 Prosperity Avenue. (703) 846-8395. Free tours by appointment weekdays from 9 A.M. to 3 P.M. for children ages 8 and older, in groups of 10 or fewer. (Availability is limited; you may have to wait a short time until the next tour is organized.) **Ages 8 and up.**

Children learn how reporters gather and write the news and hear an explanation of how the editorial, advertising, and circulation departments interact.

MOUNT VERNON

● Mount Vernon Plantation

George Washington Memorial Parkway. (703) 780-2000. (703) 799-8121 (TDD). Open daily 8 A.M. to 5 P.M. April through August; starting at 9 A.M. in March, September, and October; closing at 4 P.M. the rest of the year. Adults, $8; senior citizens, $7.50; children ages 6 through 11 when accompanied by an adult, $4; free admission on the national celebration of Washington's birthday, the third Monday in February. Self-guided tours, with guides available in the various rooms to talk about the room and answer questions; allow at least two hours to view the mansion, dependencies, and grounds. Tourmobile stop (summer only). Gift shops. Food service. http:// www.mountvernon.org. **All ages.**

School students all over the country study George Washington and his Mount Vernon home, but seeing this grand estate and how the Washington family lived in the 1800s is completely different from reading about it in a book. The mansion, which overlooks the mile-wide Potomac River, has been fastidiously restored with many original furnishings, including the bed in which Washington died.

Washington was a general and our first president, but he was also a surveyor (there are almost as many places in Virginia that boast "George Washington surveyed this property" as say "George Washington slept here") and a farmer. Some 3,000 acres of the estate's 8,000 acres were used for producing items for the home and for sale at such places as the old Alexandria Farmer's Market.

In addition to the columned plantation house, 12 dependencies, such as the coach house, greenhouse, smokehouse, stable, storehouse, spinning house, and slave quarters are on view. Children particularly like the kitchen (it was too much of a fire risk to have the kitchen in the house) because they can see how food was prepared and served (no fast food or grocery stores in those days). There normally are no craft demonstrations, but visitors can see how laundry was done, how shoes were made, and the types of vehicles people traveled in. For four weeks after Washington's birthday, there are demonstrations of crafts of the colonial period and ceremonies at Washington's tomb and the Slave Memorial. These events are scheduled weekdays from 9:30 A.M. to 12:30 P.M.

Boy scouts, girl scouts, and campfire girls can walk along the historic trail and answer questions that will allow them to buy a Mount Vernon patch.

Mount Vernon has one of the better gift shops of any visitor attraction, with the expected T-shirts and books about Washington, but also a nice selection of eighteenth-century games. On your visit to Mount Vernon you may also catch sight of an old tradition: all ships of the U.S. Navy and visiting navies offer a salute as they pass the estate.

RESTON

● United States Geological Survey (USGS)

12201 Sunrise Valley Drive. (703) 648-4748. Open Monday through Friday from 1 to 4 P.M. An introductory slide show runs at 1 P.M. The hands-on room is open from 1 to 4 P.M. At 3:30 P.M. a different movie of the week runs about 20 minutes. Tours are given Monday afternoon 1:30 to 4 P.M.; Tuesday and Thursday 9:30 A.M. to 4 P.M.; reservations are requested. Depending on the age group, tours can be geared for anyone from pre-kindergartners on up, or you may be able to join a previously booked group. The information center is open Monday through Friday 8 A.M. to 4 P.M. A cafeteria is open for breakfast and lunch; picnic tables are scattered throughout the grounds. **Ages 5 and up.**

A wide range of geology-related activities occur here, and the hour-long group tours can be tailored to specific interests. In general, scout and school groups see and learn about igneous and sedimentary rock formations, rock quarries, and dinosaurs.

Almost everything has a hands-on approach, from standing in the toe prints of a multimillion-year-old dinosaur to learning how to work a compass. You can even watch the presses printing some of the 1 million maps turned out here every year. Hikers, land planners, park service employees, the people involved in the decennial U.S. Census (the USGS maps the streets for the door-to-door surveys), and many others use USGS-produced maps, which range in scale from 1:24,000 to 1:250,000.

Outside, in the forest north of the building, the Woodlands Walk is a marked trail with labeled trees. Guided or self-guided tours of the grounds are available, plus there's an orienteering program and a nature trail.

The Earth Science Information Center carries maps, books, and pamphlets.

STERLING

● Weather Bureau

Off Route 606. (703) 260-0107. Guided tours of 15 to 60 minutes are given Monday through Friday by appointment only (scout troops may make special arrangements for weekend tours); children below fourth grade will find the information too advanced. You can just walk in, but you take your chances on guide availability; severe weather will also affect tour possibilities. http:// www.nws.noaa.gov/er/lwx/. **Ages 10 and up.**

When you watch the radar map on your local weather channel, it comes from the weather bureau. The Sterling section provides the forecast for the Washington area cable channel carrying the weather.

A tour of this building, one of the newest and most modern weather offices in the country (occupied in March 1990), takes you into the operations area, where three or four meteorologists issue forecasts for the mid-Atlantic states. (Yes, they operate on a 24-hour day.) They have a Doppler radar screen, which is more high-tech, detailed (they can see inside a storm), and colorful than older radar screens.

The first stop is the public desk, where the forecast you hear over the radio is formulated. A second area produces information for pilots and the FAA on the immediate geographic area and more-distant points. Marine forecasting takes place at the third desk, covering about 20 miles to the Chesapeake Bay and the coastal waters of Delaware, Maryland, and Virginia. There is also some offshore forecasting, reaching from central New Jersey to South Carolina and Bermuda. The fourth desk is a public-service operation that answers questions and takes reports from private contractors.

Still another area of the bureau has hydrologists monitoring the rise and fall of major rivers to be able to warn residents and businesses, particularly along the riverbanks, of impending increases or decreases in water height.

VIENNA

● Reston Animal Park

1228 Hunter Mill Road. (703) 759-3636 (general information recording), (703) 759-6761 (recording of weekend events). Open Monday through Friday 10 A.M. to 4 P.M.; weekends 10 A.M. to 5 P.M. April through mid-November; extended weekday hours in summer. Adults, $5.50; children and senior citizens, $4.50; children under 2 are free; add $1 in each category on weekends; season passes, $25. **All ages.**

Children have a chance to pet and feed cuddly baby animals, watch an egg hatch, whoop with a gibbon (that's not limited to children), ride a giant tortoise (50-pound limit) or a small African elephant named Sukara (300-pound limit), take a hayride or ride a pony, and see a buffalo, eland, elk, and Watusi bull. The children also can look at the tiny South American squirrel monkeys on Monkey Island, but they can't pet them because the creatures bite. Fairfax County regulations prohibit keeping some types of adult animals, so many of the babies here will be transferred to other facilities as they grow older. Cups of pet food are sold in the barn for 50 cents, so please do not bring food from home.

The farm regularly schedules special events, such as craft making, puppet shows, story hours, and animal shows. Once-a-year activities include sheep shearing and scarecrow making. Picnic tables and a playground are available.

● Wolf Trap Farm Park for the Performing Arts

Trap Road exit off Dulles Access Road. (703) 255-1900 (general information), (703) 225-1860 (recording), (703) 642-0862 (International Festival for Children). Open daily dawn to dusk. http://www.wolf-trap.org.
All ages.

This 100-acre park is the first and only national park in the country dedicated to the performing arts. There are no playgrounds, creeks, or other natural attractions, other than simply pretty grounds.

A full schedule of internationally renowned artists, including rock stars, orchestras, jazz groups, and traveling Broadway shows, is presented just about every night during the summer. Seats in the open-air theater and on the lawn are available. Shows are also given in the Barns, which makes productions possible during the winter.

A number of activities geared primarily toward children are held from June to September. Among these are puppet shows, starring live actors who play the role of the characters, and the Children's Theater in the Woods program, a joyous, performance-filled, activity-intensive International Festival for Children held every Labor Day weekend. The festival, directed toward children ages 4 to 8, features dancers, acrobats, face painting, singing, hula hoops, clowns, and crafts. This arts extravaganza finds 35,000 children and adults viewing performing artists from all over the world and participating in arts workshops.

Hotels

HOTELS IN THE WASHINGTON AREA range from relatively inexpensive to very costly. Weekend rates are generally lower than midweek rates, although special events such as a presidential inauguration may place premium prices on every night or even initiate a minimum-stay requirement. Winter rates are less expensive than spring and summer rates. Hotels in the suburbs tend to be less expensive than downtown properties.

For a list of hotels and motels, check the American Automobile Association (AAA) tour guide or write to the tourism bureau(s) where you would like to stay. Look in the Before You Visit section of this book for addresses.

Some hotels provide special services and attractions for children. When evaluating a place, check for free or special accommodation rates and children's menus that not only offer smaller portions of an adult order, but such items as pizza and hamburgers that children like to eat.

Ask hotels about regularly planned activities, what they cost, the hours of operation, and if there is a mandatory reservation time (such as by 3 P.M. the day of the service).

The following hotels have children's programs (such as Camp Hyatt), discounted or free lodging for children, a great view of the city, a children's menu, or an indoor pool (important when you're looking for something to do before or after a day of sightseeing and you don't feel like sitting in your room watching television). This is not a definitive list, but an alphabetical sampling of what's available. All of the hotels are located in Washington, unless otherwise indicated.

● Doubletree Hotel

2899 Jefferson Davis Highway, Crystal City, Arlington, Virginia. (800) 426-6774.

Children ages 12 and under stay free with their parents in the same room. A heated indoor pool, roaring fireplace, library with big-screen television, breakfast buffet, and evening peanut butter sandwiches are all included at the Doubletree.

● Doubletree Hotel

300 Army Navy Drive, Arlington, Virginia. (703) 416-4100.

The Skydome is a rooftop lounge that makes its 360 degree revolution every 55 minutes. You can view everything from the Pentagon to the downtown Washington monuments.

● Four Seasons Hotel

2800 Pennsylvania Avenue, NW. (202) 342-0444.

From milk and cookies at bedtime to a host of games and activities, children of all ages enjoy a vacation at the Four Seasons. The V.I.C. (Very Important Children) program includes natural sodas, snacks, balloons, games, and magazines. There's also a personal note from the manager. Water toys and kickboards are available at the pool; and electronic and board games compete with videos and coloring books for attention, all provided free. Children's menus are available at the Seasons and Garden Terrace restaurants. Included in the suite stay is a kid-sized plush terry bathrobe.

Dogs are welcome also, with a large stuffed doggie bed, Evian water, flowers, ceramic water and food bowls, and more. Doggie birthday celebrations can be arranged.

● Henley Park Hotel

926 Massachusetts Avenue, NW. (202) 638-5200.

As of the summer of 1997, the Henley Park offers a buffet luncheon with storytelling, befitting its castle-like Tudor architecture with gargoyles, dragons, and chivalrous knights, for children ages 4 to 7. All children attending the event receive a gargoyle statuette to protect them from evil spirits. The 118 gargoyles perch above the window sills and doorways of the hotel, and each one has a different stance as they watch the comings and goings of people from around the world. Among the gargoyles are the architect and his wife.

● Hilton Hotels

Various locations. (800) HILTONS, 445-8667. http://www.hilton.com/ programs/families/html.

The Hilton Hotels have a summer Hilton Vacation Station program which is available at area Hiltons located in McLean and National Airport, Virginia; Washington Hilton and Towers, Embassy Row Hilton, and Capital Hilton, in Washington; and the Columbia Hilton in Maryland.

The Vacation Station program features free, age-appropriate welcome gifts for children ages 11 and under, free use of popular Hasbro, Playskool, Kenner, Tonka, Nerf, Milton Bradley, and Parker Brothers toys and games at lending desks; and Family Fun Kits with local vacation resources and ideas for your visit. Participating units offer room service Family Pizza Meal with a free in-room movie of your choice.

● Washington Hilton and Towers

1919 Connecticut Avenue at Columbia Road and T Street, NW. (202) 483-3000. Old Town Trolley stop. Dupont Circle subway station (3 blocks).

Children of any age, including adults, stay free with their parents in the same room. There are three lighted tennis courts (users pay a fee) and a heated outdoor pool that's open 7 A.M. to 11 P.M. from late April to late October. The coffee shop has a children's menu and coloring books and crayons.

On the hotel's terrace level is an olivewood carving, "Monuments," by Carl Malouf. It features some of Washington's most noteworthy architecture, places you may visit while in the area. If the reception area is not in use, stop by the sculpture to see if your children recognize the Washington Monument, the Supreme Court of the United States, the Old Post Office Building, and the Library of Congress.

● Hotel Washington

Fifteenth Street and Pennsylvania Avenue, NW. (202) 638-5900. Old Town Trolley stop. Metro Center subway station (two blocks).

Children ages 14 and under stay free with parents in the same room at this centrally located hotel. The Sky Terrace restaurant offers a spectacular view during the summer, particularly in the evening. It is open daily from 11:30 A.M. until 1 A.M. serving meals in the $5 to $15 price range, and drinks. Arrive early, or start table-hopping if you want the best front-row view. Lines form during the evening hours, but move rather quickly.

● Howard Johnson

Various locations. (800) I-GO-HOJO, 446-4656. http://www.hojo.com.

Howard Johnson has a "Kids Go HoJo" promotion at some proper-ties, in partnership with Scholastic's "The Magic School Bus," the most-watched children's program on PBS stations nationwide. FunPacks, filled with toys, games, activities, and coupons, await children, ages 3 to 11. Children stay free with adults at Howard Johnson properties. Numerous locations around the area. The Magic School Bus tours various properties; call for the schedule.

● Hyatt Hotels

Three in downtown Washington; also one each in Bethesda, Crystal City, Dulles, Reston, Arlington, Fair Lakes. (800) 233-1234.

The nine Hyatt hotels in the Washington area offer some form of the Camp Hyatt program, which provides board games, videos, books, and arts and crafts for children ages 3 to 15. Each hotel program has different hours, charges, and days of operation. These activity-oriented babysitting programs are generally open from 5 or 6 P.M. to 10 or 11 P.M. on Friday, Saturday, and sometimes Sunday evenings; they cost $4 to $5 per hour each for the first and sometimes second child, with lower prices for the third or more children.

Hyatt meals include a children's breakfast in the very affordable range of less than $3 and lunch and dinner for less than $5. At all Hyatts the second room is half the cost of the first room, so children can stay in a separate room, if available.

Seven Hyatts have swimming pools; six of them indoors (Grand Hyatt Washington, Hyatt Regency Washington on Capitol Hill, Park Hyatt Hotel, Hyatt Regency Bethesda, Hyatt Regency Reston at Town Center, Hyatt Fair Lakes), and one outdoors (Hyatt Regency Crystal City). The Reston Hyatt also has an ice-skating rink and skate rentals. The Hyatt Regency and the Grand Hyatt are Old Town Trolley stops.

● Key Bridge Marriott

1401 Lee Highway, Arlington, Virginia. (703) 524-6400. Rosslyn subway station. (Van pick-up every 20 minutes.)

On the banks of the Potomac River, this Marriott houses the View Restaurant, a terrific spot from which to look out on the city at nighttime and on Sunday at brunch. Brunch prices are adults, $23.95; children ages 14 to 20, $18.95; children ages 6 to 13, $14.95; and children ages 5 and under, free. All children under age 18 stay free with their parents in the same room.

● Lansdowne Resort

44050 Woodridge Parkway, Lansdowne, Virginia. (703) 729-8400.

Lansdowne is the only full resort in the Washington, D.C., area. From pool to golf to spa to tennis, there are plenty of activities for the entire family. During the summer there's a Resort Rascals program, which includes a cooking class on Saturday mornings.

● Loews L'Enfant Plaza

480 L'Enfant Plaza, SW. (202) 484-1000. Old Town Trolley stop. L'Enfant Plaza subway station.

Located on top of the L'Enfant Plaza subway station, an amusement arcade, and a shopping mall, the Loews features special getaway weekends with many benefits included in a stay. Children under age 14 stay free with parents in the same room. There is an outdoor pool and a pretty good view of the city. Book ahead if you'd like to watch the Fourth of July fireworks from the 14th floor of the hotel.

The hotel recently added a seasonal cover to its rooftop swimming pool to allow for year-round enjoyment. The hotel occupies the 11th through 15th floors of the building, and offers sweeping views of the Potomac River and the waterfront (south side), most of the national monuments (north side), and the Washington Monument (west side).

● New Hampshire Suites

1121 New Hampshire Avenue, NW. (202) 457-0565, (800) 762-3777. Foggy Bottom subway station.

Suites come with kitchenettes, complete with coffee maker (complimentary coffee), mini-refrigerator (stocked with popcorn and pizza, for a fee), microwave oven, fresh flowers, and a note on the next day's weather forecast at nightly turndown. Children ages 11 and under stay free with parents in the same suite. Free breakfast in the club room.

● The Omni Shoreham Hotel

2500 Calvert Street, NW. (202) 234-0700. Woodley/Zoo subway station (half a block away).

The Omni Shoreham Hotel offers an "I'm A.O.K." (I'm an Omni Kid) family weekend package with discounts in hotel and neighborhood shops, children's shows in the hotel's Marquee Lounge, and personal service from "Kid Concierges," local Washington children who advise their visiting peers on where to go and what to do during the summer months. In 1997, the Shoreham renovated its top-floor suite 800G, the one that's reputed to have a ghostly past. This 4,700-square-foot suite, with its

spectacular view of Rock Creek Park, has been unoccupied for the past 37 years, but now the hauntings are a selling point. Supposedly, tinkling piano keys, flickering lights, and other strange occurrences are among the haunted behaviors.

● Red Roof Inn

Nine locations (downtown; Columbia, Hanover, Jessup, Gaithersburg, Lanham, Oxon Hill, and Laurel, Maryland; and Alexandria and Manassas, Virginia) throughout the greater Washington area. (800) THE ROOF, 843-7663.

Children 18 and under stay free with their parents at all locations. The D.C. property has a family suite, and several units have discount tour tickets. Check at the front desk.

● Renaissance Washington, D.C.

999 Ninth Street, NW. (202) 898-9000. Gallery Place subway station (two blocks away).

Near the convention center and the MCI Center, the Renaissance has an indoor pool (children under age 18 must be accompanied by an adult) and an active conservation program. The children's menu is on recycled paper and suggests several ways they can become involved in saving the earth and endangered species.

● Sheraton Carlton

16th and K Streets, NW. (202) 638-2626, (800) 325-3535. Farragut North or McPherson Square subway station (two blocks away).

Children up to age 17 stay free in their parents' room. A Carlton Kid program for children up to age 12 includes unlimited use of a selection of such electronic and game toys as Nintendo, Trivial Pursuit, chess, backgammon, and checkers. Milk and cookies for children arrive with the evening turndown. Cribs for infants come with a complimentary basket of disposable diapers and a gift of a soft and fuzzy stuffed animal.

● The State Plaza Hotel

2117 E Street, NW. (202) 861-8200 or (800) 424-2859. Foggy Bottom subway station (4½ blocks away).

The State Plaza Hotel has first-floor suite accommodations that conform with American Disabilities Act compliance standards.

● The Westin Washington, D.C. City Center

1400 M Street, NW. (202) 429-1700. McPherson Square subway station (3½ blocks away).

Children up to age 10 are invited to join the Westin Kids Club, which includes children's room service, express meal service, preferred restaurant reservations, special laundry pricing for children, high chairs, jogging strollers, and other services. Children receive age-appropriate presents, which might include bath toys, a coloring book, a baseball cap, and a sippy cup. Up to four people stay in a room with no additional charge, so children of all ages stay free in the same room with their parents.

● Willard Inter-Continental

1401 Pennsylvania Avenue, NW. (202) 628-9100. Metro Center subway station. (Thirteenth Street exit, two blocks away.)

Children age under 14 stay free with parents in the same room; for older children, there is an additional $25 charge. Children's items appear on the menu in Cafe Espresso and on the room-service menu. Holidays are a little more special, with cookies in the room and chocolate Santa Clauses. Check the lobby ceiling for seals of the states, and try to locate your home state.

For information about other area hotels and packages, try Washington, D.C. Accommodations, a D.C.-based hotel and tour reservation service. (800) 554-2220.

Things to Do from A to Z

Activities listed here are located in suburban Maryland, northern Virginia, and Washington, D.C., as noted.

Airplanes

MARYLAND
Paul E. Garber Facility. 1000 Old Silver Hill Road, Suitland. (202) 357-1400. (See page 127)
National Aeronautics and Space Administration (NASA)/Goddard Space Flight Center, Visitor Center and Museum. Soil Conservation Road, Greenbelt. (301) 286-8981. (See page 121)

VIRGINIA
The Flying Circus. 1930s Barnstorming Airshow, Route 17, Bealeton. Admission $10 adults; $3 children. (540) 439-8661.

WASHINGTON
The National Air and Space Museum. Independence Avenue between Fourth and Seventh Streets. (202) 357-2700, (202) 357-1686 (recording about Langley Theater presentations). (See page 32)

Airplane Rides

MARYLAND
Freeway Airport. 3900 Church Road, Mitchellville. Freeway Airport Flight School offers rides in a number of small planes. (301) 390-6424. http://www.access.digex.net/~flyw00/.
Lee Airport. Route 2, Edgewater. Annapolis Flying Services offers rides in a Cherokee 180. (410) 956-2114.

Montgomery Air Park. 7940 Airpark Road, Gaithersburg. Congressional Air offers rides in a variety of planes. (301) 840-0880.

Potomac Airfield. 10300 Glen Way, Fort Washington. ATC Flight Training offers rides in a Cessna 172. (301) 248-1480.

Suburban Airport. Brockbridge Road, Laurel. Suburban Air Service offers rides in Piper airplanes. (301) 953-2293.

Washington Executive Hyde Field. Piscataway Road, Clinton. Blue Sky Aviation offers rides in a assortment of small planes. (301) 297-4216.

VIRGINIA

Flying Circus Aerodrome. Route 17, Bealeton. The Flying Circus offers open-cockpit biplane rides on Sunday. (703) 439-8661.

Manassas Regional Airport. Route 28, Manassas. Dulles Aviation offers rides in Cessnas. (703) 361-2171.

Warren County Airport. Stokes Airport Road, Front Royal. CassAviation offers rides in a variety of small planes. (703) 635-3570.

Washington Dulles International Airport. Dulles Airport Road, Reston. Squadron Aviation offers rides in a variety of planes. (703) 581-1600 or (703) 471-4719.

Amusement Parks (see Theme Parks)

Animal Parks (see also Farms)

VIRGINIA

Reston Animal Park. 1228 Hunter Mill Road, Vienna. (703) 759-3636. (See page 146)

Aquariums

MARYLAND

National Aquarium. Pier 3, 501 East Pratt Street, Baltimore. (410) 576-3810. (See page 111)

WASHINGTON

National Aquarium. Department of Commerce, Fourteenth Street and Constitution Avenue. (202) 377-2825. (See page 70)

National Museum of Natural History. Tenth Street between Constitution Avenue and Madison Drive, NW. (202) 357-2700. (See page 42)

Band Concerts (see also Tattoos)

During the summer, military, jazz, country, and big bands offer free outdoor concerts nightly from Memorial Day through Labor Day, beginning at 8 P.M. at the locations mentioned below. Listen to local radio stations for cancellations due to weather.

Questions on band schedules can be answered by calling the following numbers: U.S. Navy Band (202) 433-6090, (703) 524-0830, (800) 821-8892; U.S. Army Band (202) 696-3647; U.S. Marine Corps Band (202) 694-3502; U.S. Air Force Band (202) 767-4310; or for general information on bands, call (202) 475-1281.

Monday: **U.S. Navy Band,** U.S. Capitol, west side.

Tuesday: **U.S. Army Band,** Sylvan Theater on the Washington Monument grounds. **U.S. Air Force Band,** U.S. Capitol, west side.

Wednesday: **U.S. Marine Corps Band,** U.S. Capitol, west side. **Big Band Concerts,** Sylvan Theater on the Washington Monument grounds, (202) 619-7222 or (202) 619-PARK. **U.S. Navy Band,** Washington Navy Yard, 9 P.M. (202) 433-2218, (202) 433-2678 for reservations.

Thursday: **U.S. Navy Band,** U.S. Navy Memorial on Pennsylvania Avenue, (202) 347-6327.

Friday: **U.S. Army Band,** U.S. Capitol, west side. **U.S. Air Force Band,** Sylvan Theater on the Washington Monument grounds.

Saturday: **Alternating military bands** at the U.S. Navy Memorial on Pennsylvania Avenue.

Sunday: **U.S. Marine Corps Band,** Sylvan Theater on the Washington Monument grounds. Alternate Sundays: Concerts on the Canal Foundry Mall, 30th and Thomas Jefferson Streets, 1:30 to 4 P.M. (202) 619-7222.

Barge Rides

MARYLAND
C&O Canal Barge Rides. 11710 MacArthur Boulevard, Potomac. (301) 299-3613. (See page 124)

WASHINGTON
C&O Canal Barge Rides. Foundry Mall, 1055 Thomas Jefferson Street (ticket office), Georgetown. (310) 299-2026 (recording), (202) 653-5844. (See page 89)

■ Battlefields

MARYLAND

Antietam National Battlefield. Maryland Route 65, 5831 Dunker Church Road, Sharpsburg. (301) 432-5124. (See page 126)

■ Bike Rentals

There are numerous gorgeous biking trails around the Washington area, providing shade and refreshing alternatives to Washington's summer heat and humidity. Some of them, however, can be very secluded and although you may be biking through the woods, this is a "big" city with all its potential dangers. Do not bike alone. Take identification with you, including your local hotel name and number if you're visiting from out of town.

The trails take you around lakes, up the C&O Canal, along the Potomac, through Rock Creek Park, and elsewhere. There are several publications for free or purchase at local bookstores and parks departments. Check with the appropriate tourism bureau for additional information.

You may take your bike aboard the subway on weekends and all holidays except the Fourth of July, and on weekdays from 10 A.M. to 2 P.M. and after 7 P.M. You need a photo permit, which costs $15 for three years, and you must take a proctored test on the rules of use. Call (202) 962-1116 for specific information. (See page 13)

You may rent bikes at the following locations:

VIRGINIA

The Bicycle Exchange. 1506 C Belle View Boulevard, Alexandria. (703) 768-3444.

WASHINGTON

Better Bikes Inc. Free delivery and pick-up. A trail map, helmet, and backpack are furnished, and roadside assistance is available. (202) 293-2080.

Fletchers' Boat House. 4940 Canal Road, NW. (202) 244-0461.

Metropolis Bicycles. 709 Eighth Street, SE. (202) 543-8900.

National Sculpture Garden Rink. Ninth Street and Constitution Avenue, NW.

Thompson's Boat Center. 2900 Virginia Avenue, NW. (202) 333-4861.

Bike Tours

WASHINGTON
Bike the Sites, Inc. 3417 Quesada Street, NW. (202) 966-8662.
bikesites@aol.com. (See page 15)

Boat Rentals

You can cool off on a hot Washington summer afternoon by renting
everything from a canoe to a pedal boat (with required life jackets unless
otherwise noted). The most famous crafts are the pedal boats (also called
paddle boats) at the Tidal Basin, but there are other suburban locations.
Generally, the boating season runs from late spring to early fall.

MARYLAND
Allen Pond. 3330 Northview Drive, Bowie. (301) 262-6200. Canoes, row
boats, and paddle boats. Group rates available. Additional charge for
nonresidents.

Clopper Lake. Seneca State Park, 11950 Clopper Road, Gaithersburg.
(301) 963-8788. Rowboats, canoes, and two-person pedal boats. A one-
hour pontoon-boat nature tour of the lake is 75 cents and operates
Saturday and Sunday at 1:30, 3, 4:30, and 7:45 P.M. Reservations required
for Saturday evening. Park admission is $4 for Maryland residents; $5 for
out-of-state residents.

Cosca Lake. Cosca Regional Park, 11000 Thrift Road, Clinton. (301)
868-2397. Rowboats, canoes, and pedal boats.

Lake Needwood. Rock Creek Regional Park, 15700 Needwood Lake
Circle, Rockville. (301) 948-5053. Rowboats, canoes, and pedal boats.

Patuxent River. Patuxent River Park, 16000 Croom Airport Road,
Upper Marlboro. (301) 627-6074. Canoes. Reservations required.

Swains Lock. Great Falls. (301) 299-9006. Canoes and rowboats.

VIRGINIA
Burke Lake Park. 7315 Ox Road, Fairfax Station. (703) 323-6600.
Rowboats.

Lake Fairfax. 1400 Lake Fairfax Drive, Reston. (703) 471-5414. Paddle
boats.

Lake Fountainhead. Fountainhead Regional Park, 10875 Hampton
Road, Fairfax Station. (703) 250-9124. Flat-bottom rowboats. You can
bring your own electric motor, up to 10 horsepower.

WASHINGTON

Fletcher's Boat House. Canal and Reservoir Roads, NW. (202) 244-0461. Canoes and rowboats.

Jack's Boats. 3500 K Street, NW. (202) 337-9642. Rowboats and canoes.

Thompson's Boat Center. Rock Creek Parkway and Virginia Avenue, NW. (202) 333-4861. Rowboats and canoes, shells, double shells, and Sunfish.

Tidal Basin. Fifteenth Street and Maine Avenue, SW. (202) 484-0206. Pedal boats (for two and four people). (See page 49)

Bookstores

Half a dozen children's bookstores are located in the Virginia and Washington area. In addition to having your child's favorite books, they have craft workshops, performances, chalk talks for aspiring authors and autograph collectors, and reading and storytelling sessions. At A Likely Storey, local politicians and administrators have been known to read their favorite stories to an appreciative audience. Cheshire Cat had a window display of monarch butterflies so observers could watch from egg to caterpillar to chrysalis. The Berenstain Bears Brother and Sister Bear characters have visited the Story Book Palace. And Clifford the Red Dog has been to the Book Nook.

MARYLAND

Audubon Book Shop. 8940 Jones Mill Road, Chevy Chase. (301) 652-3606. Stores dealing with the natural sciences are a favorite with children. The Maryland branch of the Audubon Book Shop is particularly good because it's on the grounds of the society's nature preserve, so you can combine a shopping trip with an exploration trip along the nature trail that winds through the spacious grounds.

Drusilla's Books. 817 N. Howard Street, Baltimore. (410) 225-0277. Drusilla@interloc.com. Children's books—old and rare—and many obscure volumes are in stock. Book search service is available for that favorite book from your childhood that you now want your children to read and treasure.

Travelbooks and Language Tapes. 4931 Cordell Avenue, Bethesda. (301) 951-8533. Every book, map, dictionary, and travel necessity you and your children might need for your travels are available at Rochelle Jaffe's store.

VIRGINIA
A Likely Storey. 1555 King Street, Alexandria. (703) 836-2498.
Imagination Station. 4530 Lee Highway, Arlington. (703) 522-2047.

WASHINGTON
Audubon Book Shop. 1620 Wisconsin Avenue, NW, Georgetown. (202) 337-6062.
Cheshire Cat. 5512 Connecticut Avenue, NW. (202) 244-3956.
National Zoo Book Store. Education Building, 3000 Connecticut Avenue, NW. (202) 673-4967.

Camping

MARYLAND
Capitol KOA Kampground. 768 Cecil Avenue, Millersville. (410) 923-2771, (800) 638-2216. There are numerous campgrounds in Northern Virginia and suburban Maryland. This one, however, will let you try camping without having to invest in a lot of rental or purchased equipment. This campground, the closest KOA to Washington, D.C., has 12 Kamping Kabins with beds for four or six people. You have to bring your own sleeping bags or bed linens and cooking utensils if you plan to do your own cooking. A picnic table and barbecue grill are located on each site. The campground has a pool, plenty of recreational activities for adults and children, and a convenience store. A free weekday shuttle to D.C. and Baltimore trains is available, as is a daily sightseeing trip to Washington, for a fee. No pets are permitted.

Carousels

MARYLAND
Baltimore Zoo. Druid Hill Park, off exit 7 of Interstate 83, Baltimore. (410) 366-5466. (See page 117)
Columbia Mall. 10300 Little Patuxent Parkway, Columbia. (410) 730-3300.
Glen Echo Park. MacArthur Boulevard at Goldsboro Road, Glen Echo. (301) 492-6663. (See page 120)
Watkins Regional Park. Enterprise Road, Largo. (301) 249-9220.
Wheaton Regional Park. 2000 Shorefield Road, Wheaton. (301) 622-0056. (See page 128)

VIRGINIA

Burke Lake Park. 7315 Ox Road, Fairfax Station. (703) 323-6600.

Lake Accotink Park. 5660 Heming Avenue, Springfield. (703) 569-3464.

Lake Fairfax. 1400 Lake Fairfax Drive, Reston. (703) 471-5415.

Lee District Park. 6601 Telegraph Road, Alexandria. (703) 922-9841.

WASHINGTON

On the Mall. Constitution Avenue and Tenth Street.

Cemeteries

VIRGINIA

Arlington National Cemetery. Off Memorial Drive, Arlington. (703) 607-8052 (cemetery). (703) 557-0614 (TTY). (See page 135)

WASHINGTON

Congressional Cemetery. Eighteenth and E Streets, SE. (202) 543-0539. (See page 96)

Chess Tables (Outdoors)

WASHINGTON

Dupont Circle, NW. (See page 57)

Lafayette Square, NW. (See page 79)

Churches

WASHINGTON

Franciscan Monastery. 1400 Quincy Street, NE. (202) 526-6800. (See page 103)

National Shrine of the Immaculate Conception. Michigan Avenue and Fourth Street, NE. (202) 526-8300. (See page 103)

Washington National Cathedral. Massachusetts and Wisconsin Avenues, at Woodley Road, NW. (202) 364-6616 (recording), (202) 537-6200. (See page 86)

Dental Museum

MARYLAND

National Museum of Dentistry. 31 S. Greene Street (at Lombard), Baltimore. (410) 706-0600. (See page 114)

■ Drill Teams (See Band Concerts, Tattoos)

■ Equestrian Centers

MARYLAND
Prince George's Equestrian Center. The Showplace Arena, 14900 Pennsylvania Avenue, Upper Marlboro. (301) 952-7900.

■ Farms

MARYLAND
Carroll County Farm Museum. 500 South Center Street, Westminster. (410) 848-7775.
Hardbargain Farm. Alice Ferguson Foundation, 2001 Bryan Point Road, Accokeek. (301) 292-5665.
National Colonial Farm. 3400 Bryan Point Road, Accokeek. (301) 283-2113.
Old MacDonald's Farm. 301 Watkins Park Drive, Upper Marlboro. (301) 249-7077.
Oxon Hill Children's Farm. 6411 Oxon Hill Road, Oxon Hill. (301) 839-1177. (See page 123)

VIRGINIA
Claude Moore Colonial Farm. 6310 Georgetown Pike, McLean. (703) 442-7557.
Reston Animal Park. 1228 Hunter Mill Road, Vienna. (703) 759-3636. (See page 146)

■ Farmers' Markets

Note: Produce and other products are frequently sold out before the posted closing time. For the widest variety, shop early. Markets without dates are open all year, but may have fewer vendors in fall, spring, and winter than during summer months.

MARYLAND
Bethesda Farmers' Market. 900 Wisconsin Avenue (at NIH Parking Lot 41B), Bethesda. (301) 217-2244. Tuesday, 2 to 6 P.M. June to October.
Bowie Farmers' Market. 15200 Annapolis Road (Route 450) at Bowie High School, Bowie. (301) 262-6200. Sunday 9 A.M. to 1 P.M. June to November.

Damascus Farmers' Market. 9701 Main Street (Route 108), Damascus Library, Damascus. (301) 217-2244. Sunday 9 A.M. to 1 P.M. June to October.

Gaithersburg Farmers' Market. 8 South Summit Avenue, Southern States parking lot, Gaithersburg. (301) 217-2244. Thursday 3 to 7 P.M. June to October.

Montgomery County Farm Women's Cooperative Market. 7155 Wisconsin Avenue, Bethesda. (301) 652-2291. Wednesday and Saturday 7 A.M. to 3:30 P.M.

Prince George's County Farmers' Market. 5211 Calvert Road, Ellen Linson pool complex, College Park. (301) 277-3717. Saturday 7 A.M. to noon May to November.

Rockville Farmers' Market. Rockville Town Center, Middle Lane parking lot across from the Rockville subway station, Rockville. (301) 309-3337. Wednesday 1 A.M. to 2 P.M. and Saturday 9 A.M. to 1 P.M. June to October.

Silver Spring Farmers' Market. Wayne Avenue and Fenton Street, Silver Spring Armory, Silver Spring. (301) 217-2244. Saturday 7 A.M. to 1 P.M. June to October.

Southern Maryland Regional Farmers' Market. Route 301, Cheltenham. (301) 372-1066. Tuesday and Thursday 1 to 6 P.M.; Saturday 9 A.M. to 3 P.M. May to November.

Takoma Park Farmers' Market. Laurel Avenue between Carroll and Easter Avenues, Takoma Park. (301) 270-5900, ext. 515. Sunday 10 A.M. to 2 P.M. April to November.

VIRGINIA

Alexandria Farmers' Market. 301 King Street, Market Square at City Hall, Alexandria. (703) 370-8723. Year-round Saturday 5 to 10 P.M.

Arlington Farmer's Market. North Fourteenth Street and North Courthouse Road, near the Courthouse, Arlington. (703) 358-6400. Saturday 7 A.M. to noon April to October. Saturday 8 A.M. to noon November and December.

Burke Centre Farmers' Market. 6000 Burke Commons Road, Burke. (703) 324-5390. Saturday 8 A.M. to noon May to November.

Centreville Farmers' Market. Route 28 and Route 29, Centreville. (703) 324-5390. Thursday 3 to 7 P.M.

Eastern Loudoun Farmers' Market. Route 7 and Countryside Boulevard, Eastern Loudoun County. (703) 478-1850, ext. 0426. Sunday 9 A.M. to 12:30 P.M. May to October.

Fairfax Extension Farmers' Market. 10409 Main Street, City of Fairfax. (703) 324-5390. Tuesday 8 A.M. to 12:30 P.M. May to November.

Falls Church Farmers' Market. 300 Park Avenue, City Hall, City of Falls Church. (703) 241-5027. Saturday 8 A.M. to noon May to October.

Great Falls Farmers' Market. Georgetown Pike at Walker Road, Great Falls. (703) 324-4390. Sunday, 11 A.M. to 2 P.M. May to November.

Herndon Farmers' Market. 730 Elden Street, Herndon Town Hall, Herndon. (703) 324-5390. Thursday 9 A.M. to 1 P.M. June to October.

Leesburg Farmers' Market. 500 East Market Street (Route 7), Leesburg. (703) 478-8476. Saturday 9 A.M. to noon June to October.

Manassas Farmers' Market. Center and West Streets, Old Town Manassas. (703) 361-6599. Thursday 7:30 A.M. to 12:30 P.M. April to October.

McLean Farmers' Market. 1659 Chain Bridge Road, McLean. (703) 324-5390. Friday 9 A.M. to 1 P.M. May to November.

Mt. Vernon Farmers' Market. 2511 Parker Lane, Mt. Vernon Government Center, Mt. Vernon. (703) 324-4390. Tuesday 9 A.M. to 1 P.M. May to November.

Prince William County Farmer's Market. One Dale Boulevard, Dale City Commuter Lot, Dale City. (703) 792-6285. Sunday 9 A.M. to 1 P.M. April to October.

Sterling Farmers' Market. Sterling Boulevard at Sterling Plaza Shopping Center, Sterling. (703) 478-1850. Wednesday 4 to 7 P.M. May to October.

Vienna Farmers' Market. 9601 Court House Road, Vienna. (703) 324-5390. Wednesday 9 A.M. to 1 P.M. May to November.

WASHINGTON

D.C. Farmers' Market. Fifth Street and Neal Place, NE. (202) 577-3142. Tuesday through Thursday 7 A.M. to 6 P.M., Saturday 7 A.M. to 7 P.M., and Sunday 7 A.M. to 2 P.M.

D.C. Open Air Farmers' Market. Oklahoma Avenue and Benning Road, NE (in Redskin Stadium Parking Lot six). (202) 678-2800. Thursday and Saturday 7 A.M. to 5 P.M. all year. Also Tuesday 7 A.M. to 5 P.M. July to September.

Eastern Market. Seventh Street and North Carolina Avenue, SE. (202) 543-7293. Saturday 7 A.M. to 6 P.M.

Fencing Lessons

For beginners and more advanced fencers, individual sessions or a series of lessons. **Ages 10 and up.**

MARYLAND

Chevy Chase Community Center. Connecticut Avenue and McKinley Street, NW, Chevy Chase. (301) 774-7777.

Fencing Academy of Silver Spring. 8241 Georgia Avenue, Silver Spring. (301) 565-0665.
Montgomery Recreation. 11315 Falls Road, Potomac. (301) 217-6797.

VIRGINIA
Fairfax Fencers. Various locations. (703) 352-2642.

WASHINGTON
Capitol Hill Fencers. Various locations. (202) 543-7434.
D.C. Fencers. 3815 Nebraska Avenue, NW, Alice Deal Junior High School. (301) 961-5335.

 ## Fishing

Check with the businesses below for directions, licensing requirements, rules and regulations, what's being caught, and suggestions for a successful fishing day.

MARYLAND
Rocky Gorge and Tridelphia Reservoirs. 2 Brighton Dam Road, Brookeville. (301) 774-9124.

VIRGINIA
Occoquan Reservoir. 9751 Ox Road. (703) 690-2121.

WASHINGTON
Fletcher's Landing. Canal and Reservoir Roads. (202) 244-0461.

 ## Fish Markets

WASHINGTON
Maine Avenue Fish Market. Maine Avenue and Eighth Street, SW. (See page 93)

Forts

MARYLAND
Fort McHenry National Monument and Historic Shrine. East Fort Avenue, Baltimore. (301) 962-4290. (See page 113)
Fort Washington. Fort Washington Road, Fort Washington. (301) 763-4600.

VIRGINIA

Fort Ward Museum and Park. 4301 West Braddock Road, Alexandria. (703) 833-4848.

WASHINGTON

Fort Stevens Park. Thirteenth Street and Piney Branch Road, NW.

Disc (Frisbee) Golf

MARYLAND

Calvert Road Community Park. 5202 Old Calvert Road, College Park. (301) 277-3717.

Seneca Creek State Park. 11950 Clopper Road, Gaithersburg. (301) 963-8788.

VIRGINIA

Bluemont Park. North Manchester Street and Wilson Boulevard, Arlington. (703) 554-8643.

Bull Run Regional Park. 7700 Bull Run Drive, Centreville. (703) 631-0550.

Burke Lake Park. 7315 Ox Road, Fairfax Station. (703) 323-6601.

McLean Central Park. 1468 Dolley Madison Boulevard, McLean.

Pohick Bay Regional Park. 10651 Gunston Road, Lorton. (703) 339-6104.

Galleries

MARYLAND

Walters Art Gallery. 600 North Charles Street, at Mount Vernon Square, Baltimore. (410) 547-ARTS (recording), (410) 547-9000. (See page 115)

VIRGINIA

Torpedo Factory. 105 North Union Street, Alexandria. (703) 838-4565, (703) 683-0693 (tours). (See page 133)

WASHINGTON

Art Barn Gallery. Rock Creek Park, 2401 Tilden Street, NW. (202) 244-2482. (See page 85)

Corcoran Gallery of Art. 17th Street and New York Avenue, NW. (202) 639-1700. (See page 65)

Fondo del Sol Visual Arts Center. 2112 R Street, NW. (202) 483-2777. (See page 59)

Freer Gallery of Art. 12th Street and Jefferson Drive, SW. (202) 357-2700. (See page 38)

National Gallery of Art. Sixth Street at Constitution Avenue, NW. (202) 737-4215. (202) 842-6176 TTY. (See page 40)

National Museum of American Art. Eighth Street between F and G Streets, NW. (202) 357-2700. (See page 74)

National Portrait Gallery. Eighth Street between F and G Streets, NW. (202) 357-2700. (See page 74)

Navy Combat Art Center. Ninth and M Streets, Building 67, SE. (202) 433-3815. (See page 97)

Phillips Collection. 1600 21st Street, NW. (202) 387-0961 (recording), (202) 387-2151. (See page 60)

Arthur M. Sackler Gallery. 1050 Independence Avenue, SW. (202) 357-2700, (202) 357-2041, (202) 357-4886 (education department). (See page 36)

Renwick Gallery. 17th Street and Pennsylvania Avenue, NW. (202) 357-2700. (See page 66)

Washington Project for the Arts. 400 Seventh Street, NW. (202) 347-8304. (See page 55)

Gardens

MARYLAND

Audubon Naturalist Society. 8940 Jones Mill Road, Chevy Chase. (301) 652-5964.

Battle Creek Cypress Swamp Sanctuary. Grays Road off Route 506, Prince Frederick. (301) 535-5327. (See page 124)

Brookside Gardens. 1500 Glenallan Avenue, Wheaton. (301) 949-8230 (recording). (See page 129)

McGrillis Gardens. 6910 Greentree Road, Bethesda. (301) 949-8230.

Meadowside Nature Center. 5100 Meadowside Lane, Rockville. (301) 924-4141.

VIRGINIA

American Horticultural Society, River Farm. 7931 East Boulevard Drive, Alexandria. (703) 768-5700. (See page 133)

Green Spring Gardens Park. 4603 Green Spring Road, Alexandria. (703) 642-5173.

Ellanor C. Lawrence Park. 5040 Walney Road, Walney Visitor Center, Chantilly. (703) 631-0013.
Meadowlark Gardens Regional Park. 9750 Meadowlark Gardens Court, Vienna. (703) 255-3631.

WASHINGTON
Constitution Gardens. Between the Washington Monument and the Lincoln Memorial, NW. (202) 426-6841. (See page 49)
Floral Library. Near the Tidal Basin, between the Washington Monument and Jefferson Memorial, SW. (202) 619-7222. (See page 50)
Enid A. Haupt Garden. Tenth Street and Independence Avenue, SW. (202) 357-1926. (See page 35)
Kenilworth Aquatic Gardens. 1900 Anacostia Avenue at Douglas Street, NE. (202) 426-6905. (See page 101)
Tudor Place. 1644 31st Street, NW. (202) 965-0400. (See page 91)
United States Botanic Garden. Maryland Avenue, near First Street, SW. (202) 225-8333. (See page 31)
United States National Arboretum. 3501 New York Avenue, NE. (202) 475-4815. (See page 101)

Golf Courses

There are many public courses in the Greater Washington area. There are three within Washington, and a few in Maryland that have easy courses, meaning short with few sand traps or water hazards, suitable for the beginner. Greens fees are quite reasonable, about $15 or less. Call for tee times and greens fees. Some do not accept credit cards.

MARYLAND
Needwood Golf Course. 6724 Needwood Road, Derwood. (301) 948-1075. 18- and 9-hole courses.
Sligo Creek Golf Course. 9701 Sligo Creek Parkway, Silver Spring. (301) 585-6006. 9-hole course.

VIRGINIA
Fair Oaks Golf Park. 12908 Lee-Jackson Memorial Highway, Fairfax. (703) 222-6600. 9-hole course.
Jefferson District Golf Course. 7900 Lee Highway, Falls Church. (703) 573-0443. 9-hole course.
Lake Ridge Golf Course. 12350 Cotton Mill Drive, Woodbridge. (703) 494-5564. 9-hole course.

Pinecrest Golf Course. 6600 Little River Turnpike, Annandale. (703) 941-1061. 9-hole course.

WASHINGTON

East Potomac Golf Course. Ohio Drive at Hains Point, East Potomac Park, SW. (202) 554-7660. One 18-hole course and two 9-hole courses.
Langston Golf Course. 26th Street and Benning Road, NE. (202) 397-8638. 18-hole course. Driving range.
Rock Creek Golf Course. Rock Creek Park, 16th and Rittenhouse Streets, NW. (202) 882-7332. 18-hole course. Pitching range.

Horseback Riding

Horseback riding takes advantage of the many scenic wonders in the area. Additionally, several evening rides are offered for those who want something to do after the museums and other sites have closed. Most horses are tacked western, but some operations will tack them English, upon request.

MARYLAND

Clay Hill Stables. 9911 Ardwick-Ardmore Drive, Upper Marlboro. Classes. (301) 322-4514.
Double S-S Stables. 16211 McKendree Road, Brandywine. (301) 372-8921. Weekends. Ride through 80 acres of white-fenced fields and evergreen-edged paths.
Equilibrium Horse Center. 1685 Underwood Road, Gambrills. Lessons. (410) 721-0885.
Meadowbrook Stables. 8200 Meadowbrook Lane, Chevy Chase. Lessons for children and adults. (301) 589-9026.
Merrymount Equestrian Center. 8801 Frank Tippett Road, Upper Marlboro. Lessons for children and adults. (301) 868-2109.
Piscataway Horse Farm. 10775 Piscataway Road, Clinton. Pony and horse rides. (301) 297-9808.
Potomac Horse Center. 14211 Quince Orchard Road, Gaithersburg. Lessons and trail rides. (301) 208-0200.
Potomac Polo School. Hughes and River Roads, Poolesville. (301) 972-7241.
Rock Bottom Farm Riding School. 21930 New Hampshire Avenue, Brookville. (301) 924-2612.
West Potomac Stables. 15000 River Road, Potomac. (301) 977-3839. Minimum age is 16, but younger children may ride ponies with parents at lead.

Wheaton Regional Park Stables. 1101 Glenallan Avenue, Wheaton. (301) 622-3311. Guided rides. Reservations required. English saddles.

VIRGINIA

Affinity Farm. 42548 Braddock Road, Route 1, Arcola. Lessons and trail rides. (703) 327-2121.

Arrowhead Equestrian Center. 1191 Nokesville Road, Nokesville. Lessons for children and adults. (703) 594-3512.

Blue Fox Farm. 25154 Gum Spring Road, Chantilly. Lessons. (703) 690-7922.

Cedar Ridge Horse Center. 14600 Leilani Drive, Woodbridge. English riding lessons for children (ages 4 and up). (703) 680-1432.

Equestrian Enterprises. 966 Millwood Road, Great Falls. Trail rides and Saturday instructions. (703) 759-2474.

Greenway Stables. Aldie. Unguided trail rides. (703) 327-6117.

Marriott Ranches. 5305 Marriott Lane, Route 1, Hume. (703) 364-2627. Trail rides.

WASHINGTON

Rock Creek Park Horse Center. Military and Glover roads, NW. (202) 362-0118. Classes and rides. Minimum age to ride is 12.

Ice Skating

MARYLAND

Bethesda Metro Center Ice Center. Wisconsin Avenue and Old Georgetown Road, Bethesda. (301) 656-0588 or (301) 656-0589.

Bowie Ice Arena. 3330 Northview Drive, Allen Pond, Bowie. (301) 262-6200, ext 3090.

Cabin John Regional Park. (year-round) 10610 Westlake Drive, Rockville. (301) 365-0585 (recording), (301) 365-2246.

Herbert W. Wells Ice Rink. 5211 Paint Branch Parkway, College Park. (301) 277-0654.

Putt Putt Golf, Games & Ice Rink. 130 Rollins Avenue, Rockville. (301) 881-2019.

Tucker Road Ice Rink. 1771 Tucker Road, Oxon Hill. (301) 248-2508.

Wheaton Regional Park. 11751 Orebaugh Avenue, Wheaton. (301) 649-2250.

VIRGINIA

Fairfax Ice Arena. (year-round) 3379 Pickett Road, Fairfax. (703) 323-1131.

Mount Vernon Recreation Center. (year-round) 2017 Belleview Boulevard, Alexandria. (703) 768-3324.

Reston Ice Forum. (year-round) 1800 Michael Farady Court, Reston. (703) 709-1010.

Reston Skating Pavilion. Reston Town Center, 1830 Discovery Street, Reston. (703) 318-6300.

WASHINGTON

C&O Canal. Georgetown. Free; check with National Park Service first. (202) 485-9666.

Fort Dupont Ice Arena. 3799 Ely Place, SE. (202) 584-5007.

National Sculpture Garden Rink. Ninth Street and Constitution Avenue, NW. (202) 371-5340.

Pershing Park Rink. Fourteenth Street and Pennsylvania Avenue, NW. (202) 737-6938, (202) 347-9041.

Reflecting Pool. Between the Washington Monument and Lincoln Memorial. Free; check with National Park Service first. (202) 485-9666.

IMAX Theaters

MARYLAND

Maryland Science Center. 601 Light Street, Baltimore. (410) 837-IMAX. (See page 112)

WASHINGTON

National Air and Space Museum (Smithsonian Institution). Independence Avenue between Fourth and Seventh Streets. (202) 357-2700. (See page 32)

Jousting

Jousting, the state sport of Maryland, takes place on the grounds of the Washington Monument usually during October. Call (202) 426-6700 for scheduled tournaments. (See page 45)

Kite-Flying

An annual kite-flying competition is held in late March or early April on the Washington Monument grounds. Write to Margo Brown, 6636 Kirkley Avenue, McLean, Virginia 22101, for information. Enclose a self-addressed, stamped envelope with two first-class stamps. (See page 47)

Libraries

Public libraries are a great resource for children's reading and activities programs. Below you'll find the main branch of area county libraries, their phone numbers, and, if available, their Web sites. Call for current program listings, the library nearest you, or ask to be placed on their mailing list.

MARYLAND

Anne Arundel County Public Library. 5 Harry S. Truman Parkway, Annapolis. (410) 222-7371. http://web.aacpl.lib.md.us.

Charles County Public Library. 2 Garrett Avenue, La Plata. (301) 934-9001.

Howard County Public Library. 6600 Cradlerock Way, Columbia. (410) 313-7750. http://www.howa.lib.md.us.

Montgomery County Department of Public Libraries. 9 Maryland Avenue, Rockville. (301) 217-3850. http://www.mont.lib.md.us.

Prince George's County Memorial Library System. 6532 Adelphi Road, Hyattsville. (301) 699-3500. http://www.prge.lib.md.us.

VIRGINIA

Fairfax County Public Library. 13135 Lee Jackson Highway, Fairfax. (703) 222-3155. http://www.co.fairfax.va.us.library.

Loudoun County Public Libraries. 102 Heritage Way, N.E., Suite 103, Leesburg. (703) 777-0368.

Prince William Public Library System. 13083 Chinn Park Drive, Prince William. (703) 792-6100. http://www.co.princewilliam.va.us/library.

WASHINGTON

Library of Congress. 10 First Street, First and East Capitol Streets, SE. (202) 707-5000. http://lcweb.loc.gov. (See page 24)

D.C. Public Library. 901 G Street, NW (202) 727-0321.

Magic Shops

MARYLAND

Barry's Magic Shop. 11234 Georgia Avenue, Wheaton. (301) 933-0373.

WASHINGTON

Al's Magic Shop. 1012 Vermont Avenue, NW. (202) 789-2800.

Mills

VIRGINIA
Colvin Run Mill. 10017 Colvin Run Road, Great Falls. (703) 759-2771.

WASHINGTON
Peirce Mill. Rock Creek Park, Beach Drive and Tilden Street. (202) 426-6908. (See page 86)

Money (Printing and Engraving)

Bureau of Engraving and Printing. Fourteenth and C Streets, SW. (202) 874-3019. http://www.moneyfactory.com. (See page 39)

Monuments and Memorials

MARYLAND
Fort McHenry National Monument and Historic Shrine. East Fort Avenue, Baltimore. (410) 962-4290. (See page 113)

VIRGINIA
Roosevelt Island. George Washington Memorial Parkway, Great Falls. (703) 285-2598. (See page 141)
United States Marine Corps War Memorial (Iwo Jima). Adjacent to Arlington National Cemetery. (202) 433-6060. (See page 138)
Women in Military Service Memorial. Main gateway, Arlington National Cemetery. (800) 222-2294 or (703) 533-1155. (See page 137)

WASHINGTON
Jefferson Memorial. South bank of Tidal Basin, Fourteenth Street and East Basin Drive, East Potomac Park, SE. (202) 426-6822. (See page 50)
Lincoln Memorial. Memorial Circle between Constitution and Independence Avenues. (202) 426-6841. (See page 47)
United States Navy Memorial Visitors Center. Pennsylvania Avenue at Eighth Street, NW. (800) 821-8892. (703) 524-0830. (See page 54)
Vietnam Veterans Memorial. Constitution Avenue between Henry Balm Drive and 21st Street. (202) 485-9666. (See page 48)
Washington Monument. The Mall between Fifteenth and 17th Streets. (202) 426-6839. (See page 45)

Museums (See also Galleries)

MARYLAND

Babe Ruth Birthplace. Babe Ruth Museum, 216 Emory Street, Baltimore. (410) 727-1539. (See page 116)

Baltimore Museum of Art. Art Museum Drive, Baltimore. (410) 396-7101, (410) 396-6320 (education office). (See page 117)

B&O Railroad Museum. 901 West Pratt Street, at Poppleton Street, Baltimore. (410) 752-2490. (See page 116)

B&O Railroad Station Museum. Maryland Avenue and Main Street, Ellicott City. (410) 461-1944. (See page 118)

National Museum of Dentistry. 31 S. Greene Street (at Lombard), Baltimore. (410) 706-0600. (See page 114)

National Aeronautics and Space Administration (NASA)/Goddard Space Flight Center. Visitor Center and Museum. Soil Conservation Road, Greenbelt. (301) 286-8981. (See page 121)

Rose Hill Manor: Children's Museum and Park. 1161 North Market Street, Frederick. (301) 694-1648, (301) 694-1646. (See page 119)

VIRGINIA

The Newseum. 1101 Wilson Boulevard, Arlington. (703) 284-3700. (888) NEWSEUM (639-7386). http://www.newseum.org. (See page 138)

Fairfax Station Railroad Museum. 11200 Fairfax Station Road. (703) 425-9225. (See page 140)

WASHINGTON

Anacostia Neighborhood Museum. 1901 Fort Place, SE. (202) 287-3369. (See page 96)

Anderson House Museum. 2118 Massachusetts Avenue, NW. (202) 785-2040. (See page 58)

Arts and Industries Building. 900 Jefferson Drive. (202) 357-2700, (202) 357-1500 (Discovery Theater reservations, voice or TDD). (See page 35)

Bethune Museum and Archives. 1318 Vermont Avenue, NW. (202) 332-1233. (See page 80)

B'nai B'rith Klutznick Museum and Exhibit Hall. 1640 Rhode Island Avenue, NW. (202) 857-6583, ext. 203. (See page 63)

Capital Children's Museum. 800 Third Street at H Street, NE. (202) 675-4120. (See page 104)

Columbia Historical Society. 1307 New Hampshire Avenue, NW. (202) 785-2068. (See page 58)

Daughters of the American Revolution (DAR) Museum. 1776 D Street, NW. (202) 879-3239 (children's tour and children's program information). (See page 64)

Department of the Interior Museum. Eighteenth and C Streets, SW. (202) 208-4743. (See page 65)

Discovery Creek Environmental Museum. 4954 MacArthur Boulevard, NW. (202) 337-4954.

Dumbarton Oaks. 1703 32nd Street, NW. (202) 339-6400 or (202) 339-6401. (See page 89)

Explorer's Hall. National Geographic Society, 17th and M Streets, NW. (202) 857-7588. (See page 62)

Frederick Douglass National Historic Site. 1411 W Street, SE. (202) 426-5960. (See page 95)

Hillwood. 4155 Linnean Avenue, NW. (202) 686-5807. (See page 83)

Hirshhorn Museum and Sculpture Garden. Eighth Street and Independence Avenue, SW. (202) 357-2700. (See page 34)

Lincoln Museum. 511 Tenth Street, NW. (202) 426-6924. (See page 82)

Marine Corps Museum. Building 58, Ninth and M Streets, SE. (202) 433-3534. (See page 97)

Meridian International Center. 1624 and 1630 Crescent Place, NW. (202) 667-6800. (See page 59)

Museum of Modern Art of Latin America. 201 Eighteenth Street, NW. (202) 458-6019. (See page 63)

Museum of Natural History. Tenth Street between Constitution Avenue and Madison Drive, NW. (202) 357-2700. (See page 42)

National Air and Space Museum. Independence Avenue between Fourth and Seventh Streets, (202) 357-2700, (202) 357-1686 (recording about Langley Theater presentations). (See page 32)

National Archives. Constitution Avenue between Seventh and Ninth Streets, NW. (202) 501-5000 (recorded information about special program events). (See page 53)

National Building Museum. Judiciary Square, F Street between Fourth and Fifth Streets, NW. (202) 272-2448. (See page 77)

National Museum of African Art. 950 Independence Avenue. (202) 357-2700, (202) 357-4860 (education department). (See page 37)

National Museum of American History. Fourteenth Street between Constitution Avenue and Madison Drive. (202) 357-2700. (See page 43)

National Museum of American Jewish Military History. 1811 R Street, NW. (202) 265-6280. (See page 62)

National Museum of Health and Medicine. Walter Reed Army Medical Center campus. (202) 782-2200.

National Museum of Women in the Arts. 1250 New York Avenue, NW. (202) 783-5000. (See page 81)
Navy Museum. Ninth and M Streets, SE. (202) 433-2651. (See page 97)
Old Stone House. 3051 M Street, NW. (202) 426-6851. (See page 90)
Petersen House. 526 Tenth Street, NW. (202) 426-6830. (See page 83)
Textile Museum. 2320 S Street, NW. (202) 667-0441. (See page 61)
Tudor Place. 1644 31st Street, NW. (202) 965-0400. (See page 91)
United States Holocaust Memorial Museum. 100 Raoul Wallenberg Place, SW. (202) 488-0400. (800) 400-9373 (ProTix). (See page 39)
The U.S.S. *Barry.* Ninth and M Streets, SE. (202) 433-3377. (See page 97)
Washington Dolls' House and Toy Museum. 5236 44th Street, NW. (202) 244-0024. (See page 73)
Woodrow Wilson House. 2340 S Street, NW. (202) 673-4034. (See page 61)

Nature Centers

Nature centers feature numerous family activities, generally geared to specific age groups. Such events as watching a lunar eclipse, canoeing, taking a field trip to other centers, woodland walks, animal interviews, butterfly hunts, boat rides, beaver searches, amphibious adventures, seeing nocturnal animals, and countless more are possibilities. Check local papers for schedules, or call the nearest center for events.

MARYLAND
Audubon Naturalist Society. 8940 Jones Mill Road, Chevy Chase. (301) 652-9188, ext 3006.
Black Hills Regional Park. 10926 Lake Ridge Drive, Boyds. (301) 972-3476.
Brookside Nature Center. Wheaton Regional Park, 1400 Glenallan Avenue, Wheaton. (301) 946-9071. (See page 129)
Chesapeake Wildlife Sanctuary. 17308 Queen Anne Bridge Road, Bowie. (301) 390-7010.
Clearwater Nature Center. 1100 Thrift Road, Clinton. (301) 297-4575.
Hawk's Reach Nature Center. Little Bennett Regional Park, 23701 Frederick Road, Clarksburg. (301) 972-9458.
Little Bennett. 23701 Frederick Road, Clarksburg. (301) 972-9458.
Locust Grove Nature Center. 7777 Democracy Boulevard, Bethesda. (301) 299-1990.
Maydale Nature Center. 1638 Maydale Drive, Silver Spring. (301) 384-9447.

FUN PLACES TO GO WITH CHILDREN IN WASHINGTON, D.C.

Meadowside Nature Center. 5100 Meadowside Lane, Rockville. (301) 924-4141.

Meadowside Nature Center, Lathrop E. Smith Environmental Education Center. 5110 Meadowside Lane, Rockville. (301) 924-4141.

Merkle Wildlife Sanctuary Visitor Center. 11704 Fenno Road, Upper Marlboro. (301) 888-1410.

Oregon Ridge Nature Center. 13555 Beaver Dam Road, Cockeysville. (301) 887-1815.

Piney Run Park. 30 Martz Road, Sykesville. (301) 795-3274.

30th Street Nature Center. 4210 30th Street, Mount Rainier. (301) 927-2163.

Watkins Park Nature Center. 301 Watkins Park Drive, Upper Marlboro. (301) 249-6202. (See page 128)

VIRGINIA

Hidden Oaks Nature Center. Annandale Community Park, 4020 Hummer Road, Annandale. (703) 941-1065.

Ramsay Nature Center. 5700 Sanger Avenue, West Alexandria. (703) 838-4829.

Riverbend Park and Nature Center. 8814 Jeffrey Road, Great Falls. (703) 759-3211. (See page 140)

WASHINGTON

Rock Creek Nature Center. 5200 Glover Road. (202) 426-6828. (See page 86)

Nature Walks (see also Walking Tours)

MARYLAND

Backyard Naturalist. 17910 Georgia Avenue, Olney. (301) 924-0024.

WASHINGTON

C&O Canal Nature Walks. Great Falls Tavern Visitor Center, 10 A.M. on the first and last Wednesday and Saturday of each month. Free, but there is a park admission fee. (301) 299-3613. (See page 124)

Newspapers

MARYLAND

The *Capital*. 2000 Capital Drive, Annapolis. (410) 268-5000. (See page 109)

Maryland Independent. 7 Industrial Park, Waldorf. (301) 843-9600. (See page 128)

Montgomery County *Sentinel.* 7 Dalamar Street, Gaithersburg. (301) 417-1200. (See page 119)

VIRGINIA

Alexandria *Gazette Packet.* 717 N. St. Asaph Street, Alexandria. (703) 549-7185. (See page 135)

Journal Express **Newspapers.** 2720 Prosperity Avenue, Merrifield. (703) 846-8395. (See page 143)

Loudoun Times-Mirror. 9 East Market Street, Leesburg. (703) 777-1111. (See page 142)

Northern Virginia Sun. 2710-C Prosperity Avenue, Fairfax. (703) 204-2800. (See page 139)

WASHINGTON

The Washington Informer. 3117 Martin Luther King Avenue, SE. (202) 561-4100. (See page 97)

The Washington News Observer. 811 Florida Avenue, NW. (202) 232-3060. (See page 88)

Observatories

MARYLAND

University of Maryland Observatory. Metzerott Road at University Boulevard, College Park. (301) 454-3001.

WASHINGTON

United States Naval Observatory. Massachusetts Avenue at 34th Street. (202) 762-1467. (See page 84)

Parks (See also Regional Parks)

MARYLAND

Glen Echo Park. 7300 MacArthur Boulevard, Glen Echo. (301) 492-6282. (See page 120)

Great Falls Park. Off MacArthur Boulevard, Potomac. (See page 123)

Rose Hill Manor: Children's Museum and Park. 1161 North Market Street, Frederick. (301) 694-1648, (301) 694-1646. (See page 119)

VIRGINIA
Great Falls National Park. 9200 Old Dominion Drive, Great Falls. (703) 285-2966. (See page 140)

WASHINGTON
Anacostia Park. 1900 Anacostia Drive, SE. (202) 433-1152. (See page 96)
Hains Point, or East Potomac Park. Peninsula between the Washington Channel and the Potomac River. (See page 51)
Lincoln Park. East Capitol Street, between Eleventh and Thirteenth Streets, NE. (See page 107)
Rock Creek Park. Tilden Street and Beach Drive. (202) 426-6832. (See page 85)

Pets

If you and your children can resist the lure of a stray pet longing to be adopted, or if you're interested in adopting a pet, then a visit to an animal shelter can be informative and comforting. Hour-long tours include information about the responsibilities of pet ownership and such animal issues as overpopulation, neglect, and abuse. The Humane Society provides pet-care coloring books, stickers and honorary Human Society identification cards. Call for an appointment. **Ages 6 and up.**

MARYLAND
Montgomery County Humane Society. 14645 Rothgeb Drive, Rockville. (301) 279-1823.
Howard County Animal Control. 8576 Davis Road, Columbia. (410) 313-2780.
Prince George's County Animal Control Facility. 8311 D'Arcy Road, Forestville. (301) 499-8323.

VIRGINIA
Animal Welfare League of Alexandria. 910 S. Payne Street, Alexandria. (703) 838-5042.
Animal Welfare League of Arlington. 2650 S. Arlington Mill Drive, Arlington. (703) 931-9241.
Fairfax County Department of Animal Control. 4500 West Ox Road, Fairfax. (703) 830-1100.
Prince William County Animal Shelter. 14807 Dumfries Road, Manassas. (703) 792-6465.

Petting Zoos

MARYLAND
New Ark Petting Farm. 15557 Governor's Bridge Road, off Route 424, Davidsonville. (410) 798-0206. (See page 118)

VIRGINIA
Reston Animal Park. 1228 Hunter Mill Road, Vienna. (703) 759-3636. (See page 146)

Pick-Your-Own Fruit

As children select and pick their own fruit, they'll learn that strawberries and peaches don't come from the grocery store. Call for what's ripe, and operating times.

MARYLAND
Becraft's Farm. 14722 New Hamsphire Avenue, Silver Spring. (301) 236-4545.
Cherry Hill Farm. 2300 Gallahan Road, Clinton. (301) 292-1928 or (301) 292-4642.
Darrow Berry Farm. Bell Station Road, Glenn Dale. (301) 390-6611 or (301) 390-6191.
Johnson's Berry Farm. 17000 Swanson Road, Upper Marlboro. (301) 627-8316.
Miller Farms. 10140 Piscataway Road, Clinton. (301) 297-5878 or (301) 297-9370.
Parker Farms. 12720 Parker Lane, Clinton. (301) 292-3940.

VIRGINIA
Luckett's Berry Farm. 14114 Griffin Farm Lane, Leesburg. (703) 771-8732.
Potomac Vegetable Farms. 9627 Leesburg Pike, Tysons Corner. (703) 759-2119.
Vager's Blueberries. 12337 Lawyers Road, Herndon. (703) 860-3272.

Planetariums

MARYLAND
Davis Planetarium, Maryland Science Center. 601 Light Street, Baltimore. (410) 685-5225 (recording), (410) 685-2370 (office). (See page 112)

WASHINGTON

Albert Einstein Planetarium, National Air and Space Museum.
Independence Avenue between Fourth and Seventh Streets, SW. (202)
357-2700. (See page 32)

Rock Creek Nature Center. 5200 Glover Road, NW. (202) 426-6828.
(See page 86)

Playgrounds

VIRGINIA

Abingdon Elementary School. 3035 South Abingdon Street, behind
Abingdon School, Arlington. (703) 845-7664. There are plenty of
playgrounds in the area, but this one is unusual; it is in the shape of the
United States. An alligator is Florida; the high climbers are the Rockies.

Polo

MARYLAND

Potomac Polo Club. 10250 River Road, Potomac. (301) 881-5040.
Sunday at 4 P.M.

WASHINGTON

West Potomac Park. Near the Lincoln Memorial, SW. (202) 485-9666.
Sunday at 2 P.M. (See page 47)

Pottery

Generally, there's a fee for the piece of pottery you're painting and an
hourly fee that includes all supplies (usually non-toxic), assistance, glazes,
and firing. Birthday parties can be scheduled. **Ages 4 and up.**

MARYLAND

Made By You. Annapolis Harbour Center, Annapolis. (410) 571-0171.
Made by You. 4923 Elm Street, Bethesda. (301) 654-3206.

VIRGINIA

Kiln' Time. 111 S. Alfred Street, Alexandria. (703) 299-8989.
Made By You. 2319 Wilson Boulevard, Arlington. (703) 841-3533.
The Mud Factory. 2772 S. Arlington Mill Drive, Arlington. (703) 998-
6880.

Paint Your Own Pottery. 10417 Main Street, Fairfax. (703) 218-2881.
Paint 'n Place. Springfield Mall. (703) 719-9732.

WASHINGTON
Made By You. 1826 Wisconsin Avenue, Georgetown. (202) 337-3180.
(See page 91)
Made By You. 3413 Connecticut Avenue, NW. (202) 363-9590.

 Post Office Tours

WASHINGTON
United States Post Office. 900 Brentwood Road, NE. (202) 636-1208.
(See page 102)

Regional Parks (See also Parks)

MARYLAND
Black Hill Regional Park. 13440 West Old Baltimore Road, Boyds.
(301) 972-9397.
Cabin John Regional Park. 7400 Tuckerman Lane, Rockville. (301)
299-4555.
Fairland Regional Park. 14110 Old Gunpowder Road, Laurel. (301)
953-0294.
Little Bennett Regional Park. 23701 Frederick Road, Clarksburg. (301)
972-6581.
Louise Cosca Regional Park. 11000 Thrift Road, Clinton. (301)
868-1397.
Patuxent River Park. 16000 Croom Airport Road, Box 3380, Upper
Marlboro. (301) 627-6074.
Rock Creek Regional Park. 6700 Needlewood Road, Rockville. (301)
948-5053. (See page 85)
Watkins Regional Park. 301 Watkins Park Drive, Upper Marlboro.
(301) 249-9220. (See page 128)
Wheaton Regional Park. 2000 Shorefield Road, Wheaton. (301)
622-0056. (See page 128)

VIRGINIA
Cameron Run Regional Park. 4001 Eisenhower Avenue, Alexandria.
(703) 960-0767.
Meadowlark Gardens Regional Park. 9750 Meadowlark Gardens Court,
Vienna. (703) 255-3631.

Washington and Old Dominion Railroad Regional Park. 5400 Ox
Road, Fairfax Station (park office address). (703) 352-5900, (703) 437-
1910 (trail office). (See page 141)

■ Restaurants

Several restaurants are described within the specific geographic areas;
California Pizza Kitchen and Sgt. Pepper's each have a number of locations in the region and they're listed here rather than repeating the
information in each geographic section.

California Pizza Kitchen, with its wood-fired pizza, pasta, salads and
desserts, has restaurants in Tyson's Corner, Virginia; Annapolis, Bethesda,
and Towson, Maryland; and in Chevy Chase in Washington, D.C. They're
open Monday through Thursday, from 10 A.M. to 10 P.M.; Friday and
Saturday from 10 A.M. to 11 P.M.; and Sunday from noon to 9 P.M.

Sgt. Pepper's is a cafeteria restaurant that's open for lunch and dinner
(11 A.M. to 9 P.M. Sunday through Thursday; until 10 P.M. on Friday and
Saturday), with plenty of salads, soups, pastas, pizzas, and desserts.
Located in Fairfax, Shirlington, Reston, and Pentagon City in Virginia;
and Columbia, by the lake so you can watch the boating and other lake
activities, in Maryland, the menu varies from week to week. Lunch for
children is $3.99 (ages 6-10) and for adults is $5.99. Dinner is $4.99 and
$7.99. Sunday brunch is $4.99 and $8.49. Children 5 and under are free.

■ Road Rallies

Road rallying is a popular activity in the Washington, D.C., area and
during nice weather you can find a rally almost every Sunday. Call or
write the Washington Rally Club, 7705 Beach Tree Road, Bethesda,
Maryland 20817. (202) 822-2876.

■ Rock Climbing Centers

MARYLAND
Sportrock 1. 14708 Southlawn Lane, Rockville. (301) 762-5111. (See
page 125)

VIRGINIA
Sportrock II. 5308 Eisenhower Avenue, Alexandria. (703) 212-7625. (See
page 134)

Roller Hockey

MARYLAND
Columbia Ice Rink. 5876 Thunder Hill Road, Columbia. (410) 730-0321 (recording).

Sailing

Lessons for children, adults (including women-only sessions), and disabled persons are available for the beginner, intermediate, and advanced sailor. Other options: learning to sail larger boats; preparing to charter a boat on your own; and crewing in regular races and regattas. Some boating centers offer weekend courses, and some provide multiweek courses. Call for schedules and fees.

MARYLAND
Annapolis Bay Charters. 7310 Edgewood Road, Annapolis. (800) 292-1119.

Annapolis Sailing School. 601 Sixth Street, Annapolis. (800) 638-9192.

Ays Charters and Sailing School. 416 Edgewood Road, Annapolis. (410) 267-8181.

Chesapeake Region Accessible Boating (CRAB). Sandy Point State Park, Annapolis. Offers sailing lessons to able-bodied, disabled, and developmentally challenged students. (410) 974-2628.

Chesapeake Sailing School. 7074 Bembe Beach Road, Annapolis. (301) 261-2810 (Washington area); (410) 269-1594 (Baltimore or Annapolis area); (800) 966-0032 (out of state).

Harborview Marina. 500 Harbor View Drive, Baltimore. (410) 727-2884.

J/World. 213 Eastern Avenue, Annapolis. (800) 966-2038.

Solomons Sailing School. 1444 Gregg Drive, Lusby. (410) 326-1444.

Womanship. The Boathouse, 410 Severn Avenue, Annapolis. (800) 342-9295.

VIRGINIA
Potomac River Sailing Club. Washington Sailing Marina, George Washington Parkway, Alexandria. (703) 560-6863.

Science Centers

MARYLAND

Columbus Center Hall of Exploration (Marine sciences). 701 E. Pratt Street, Baltimore. (410) 576-5700. http://www.columbuscenter.org. **Maryland Science Center.** 601 Light Street, Baltimore. (410) 685-5225 (recording), (410) 685-2370 (office), (410) 837-IMAX (IMAX information). (See page 112)

Sewing

Classes available for one session or a series, for children from ages 6 and up, preteen, or older, and for beginners or more advanced sewers. Call for information.

MARYLAND

Capital Quilts. 15926 Luanne Drive, Gaithersburg. (301) 527-0598.
G Street Fabrics. 11854 Rockville Pike, Rockville. (301) 231-8982.
Regina's Stitchin' Post. 4530 Natahala Drive, Clinton. (301) 297-7030.
Seams Easy Sewing School. 6401 57th Avenue, Riverdale. (301) 779-3112.

VIRGINIA

Art to Wear. 10455 North Street, Fairfax. (703) 691-9000.
G Street Fabrics. 5077 Westfields Boulevard, Centreville. (703) 818-8090.
Vienna Sewing Machine and Vacuum Center. 322 Maple Avenue, W., Vienna. (703) 281-5225.

WASHINGTON

Ardis School of Fashion Design. 1731 21st Street, NW. (202) 234-6537.

Ships

MARYLAND

U.S. Frigate *Constellation*. Pier 1, Pratt Street, Baltimore. (410) 539-1797. (See page 113)

WASHINGTON

U.S.S. Barry. Ninth and M Streets, SE. (202) 433-3377. (See page 97)

Shooting

MARYLAND

Prince George's Public Shooting Center. 10400 Good Luck Road, Glenn Dale, Maryland. (301) 577-1477.

Skiing (outdoors)

You'll find moderately good ski slopes in western Maryland, Virginia, and Pennsylvania, all about a three-hour drive from Washington. Ski Liberty is only 65 miles away, so you can finish a meeting or a day's sightseeing, hop in your car, ski for a couple of hours, and return for the next day's agenda. Most ski areas have night skiing and snow-making machines. Ski season is generally late November through March and ski areas usually run out of skiers before they run out of snow. That means you can practically have the slopes to yourself in March. Local radio stations give weekend snow-condition reports, or call the numbers listed. Mileages given indicate the distance from the Washington, D.C. area.

PENNSYLVANIA

Blue Knob. R.D. 1, Claysburg. (814) 239-5111. 150 miles. Snow report (800) 458-3403.
Doe Mountain. R.R. 1, Macungie. (215) 682-7109. 155 miles. Snow report (215) 682-7107.
Ski Liberty. Rt 116, Carroll Valley. (717) 642-8282. 65 miles. Snow report (800) 827-4766.

VIRGINIA

Bryce Mountain. 1982 Fairway Drive, Basye. (703) 856-2121. 120 miles. Snow report (703) 856-2151.
Wintergreen. Stoney Creek, Lovington. (804) 325-2200, (800) 325-2200. 145 miles. Snow report (804) 325-7669. Active children's program including instruction, child care, and Kids Night Out for children 4 to 12 while parents enjoy a night of skiing.

Skiing (Indoors)

MARYLAND
Aspen Hill Ski Training Center. 14501 Bel Pre Road, Silver Spring, Maryland. (301) 598-5200.

Swimming Pools

There are a number of public and indoor pools in the area, in addition to hotel pools listed in the Hotels section. The Mongtomery Aquatic Center is an indoor facility that includes a 50-meter pool for lap swimming, instructions, scuba lessons, diving into a diving well, and other water skills. There's also a slide that starts three stories up, runs the length of the 50-meter pool, then dumps riders into a splash pool. Adjacent to the splash pool is a huge family pool that starts at 6 inches deep and goes to a little more than 3 feet deep, with a ramp for wheelchair users. Other facilities in the Maryland suburbs include some of these facets. Some are indoor and some are outdoor.

MARYLAND
Allentown Road Fitness Center. 7210 Allentown Road, Fort Washington. (301) 449-5566.
Bethesda Outdoor Pool. Little Falls Parkway and Hillandale Road, Bethesda. (301) 652-1598.
Ellen E. Linson. 5211 Calvert Road, College Park. (301) 277-0654.
Fairland Aquatic Center. 13820 Old Gunpowder Road, Laurel. (301) 206-2464 (recording); (301) 206 2359.
Glenn Dale Splash Park. 11901 Glenn Dale Boulevard, Glenn Dale. (301) 352-8980.
Long Branch Outdoor Pool. 8700 Piney Branch Road, Silver Spring. (301) 431-5700.
Martin Luther King Jr. Indoor Swim Center. 1201 Jackson Road, Silver Spring. (301) 989-1206.
Montgomery Aquatic Center. 5900 Executive Boulevard, North Bethesda. (301) 468-4211.
Olney Indoor Swim Center. 16601 Georgia Avenue, Olney. (301) 570-1210.
Piney Branch Indoor Pool. 7510 Maple Avenue, Takoma Park. (301) 270-9361.
Robert I. Bickford Natatorium. Prince George's Community College, 301 Largo Road, Largo. (301) 322-0890.

Rollingcrest Splash Park. 6122 Sargent Road, Chillum. (301) 852-9026.

Theresa Banks Memorial Pool. 8615 McLain Avenue, Glenarden. (301) 772-5515.

Upper County Outdoor Pool. 8211 Emory Grove Road, Gaithersburg. (301) 840-2446.

Wheaton-Glenmont Outdoor Pool. Wheaton High School, off Randolph Road between Connecticut and Georgia Avenues. (301) 929-5460.

VIRGINIA

Cameron Run Water Park. Cameron Run Regional Park, 4001 Eisenhower Avenue, Alexandria. (703) 960-0767.

Herndon Community Center. 814 Ferndale Avenue, Herndon. (703) 787-7300.

Splash Down Waterpark. 7500 Ben Lomond Park Drive, Manassas. (703) 361-4451.

Water Mine Family Swimmin' Hole. 1400 Lake Fairfax Drive, Lake Fairfax Park, Reston. (703) 471-5415.

Water Works Waterpark. 5301 Dale Boulevard, Dale City. (703) 680-7137.

WASHINGTON

Capitol East Natatorium. 635 North Carolina Avenue, SE. (202) 724-4495.

Hains Point Pool. 1100 Ohio Drive, East Potomac Park. (202) 727-6523.

Tattoos (See also Band Concerts)

During the summer the U.S. Army and the U.S. Marine Corps offer a series of exciting tattoos. These demonstrations of precision marching, rifle tossing, and silent drills, which involve spinning rifles, circling, and crisscrossing through an ornate maze of half steps, are, to choose a child's word, awesome.

VIRGINIA

Tuesday: **U.S. Marine Drum and Bugle Corps and Silent Drill Platoon,** Iwo Jima Memorial (June through August). 7:30 P.M.

WASHINGTON

Wednesday: **Third U.S. Infantry and the U.S. Army Band,** Ellipse grounds (June through August). 7 P.M.

Wednesday: **Torchlight Tattoo,** Jefferson Memorial (June through August). 8 P.M.

Friday: **Marine Barracks,** Eighth and I Streets (May through August). 8:45 P.M. (202) 433-6060.

Tennis

MARYLAND

Cosca Tennis Bubble. 11000 Thrift Road, Clinton. (301) 868-6462.

Watkins Regional Park. 301 Watkins Park Drive, Upper Marlboro. (301) 249-9325.

WASHINGTON

Drilling Tennis & Golf. 1040 17th Street, NW. (202) 737-1100.

East Potomac Tennis Center. 1090 Ohio Drive, SW. (202) 554-5962.

Rock Creek Tennis Center. Sixteenth and Kennedy Streets, NW. (202) 722-5949.

Theaters

VIRGINIA

Wolf Trap Farm Park for the Performing Arts. Trap Road exit off Dulles Access Road, Vienna. (703) 255-1900 (general information), (703) 642-0862 (International Festival for Children). (See page 147)

WASHINGTON

Arena Stage. Sixth Street and Maine Avenue, SW. (202) 488-3300 (box office). (See page 93)

Constitution Hall. 1776 D Street, NW. (202) 638-2661. (See page 64)

Ford's Theatre. 511 Tenth Street, NW. (202) 638-2941. (See page 82)

John F. Kennedy Center for the Performing Arts. New Hampshire Avenue at Rock Creek Parkway, NW. (202) 467-4600, (800) 444-1324 (recording about shows and ticket purchases), (202) 416-8341 (tours). (See page 71)

National Theatre. 1321 Pennsylvania Avenue, NW. (202) 628-6161 (ticket information), (202) 783-3372 (schedule for Saturday morning and Monday night children's programs). (See page 67)

Theme Parks

Six theme parks are within a three-hour drive of Washington. They are all open daily during the summer, and most are open weekends during April, May, September, and October. Each has a special tot area with small-scale rides for youngsters (each has a maximum height restriction). Do take a change of clothes for those parks with wet areas.

MARYLAND

Adventure World. 13710 Central Avenue, Mitchellville. (301) 249-1500. Lots of water-based activities here, including the newest and latest in roller coasters, the Typhoon Sea Coaster, which mates the log flume and the roller coaster. Eight passenger boats climb a 45-foot incline and then spin around to drop riders backward down the "camel hump" chute, through churns and channels, then to floating into pitch-black tunnels until they begin the final ascent. At the top of the "world's tallest descent" riders are again rotated to face forward to the crashing descent down a 60-foot drop and out the mouth of the skull at Skull Island. There's also Crocodile Cal's Outback Beach House where the family can douse each other with water guns, canyons, geysers, and buckets. On a drier note, you'll find entertainment shows, stunt shows, musicals, comedies, a "Day at the Circus" area, and a wooden roller coaster.

NEW JERSEY

Six Flags Great Adventure. Route 537, Jackson. (908) 928-1821.

PENNSYLVANIA

Hersheypark. 100 West Hersheypark Drive, Hershey. (800) HER-SHEY. **Sesame Place.** 100 Sesame Road, Langhorne. (215) 757-1100. This is the only place in the United States based on the award-winning television program, *Sesame Street,* where children can meet and hug that popular, lovable, red, furry Muppet named Elmo, and other *Sesame Street* friends. Open from mid-May through late October. In addition to parades, water fun, and activities, there's a regularly scheduled interactive sleep-over Camp Sesame with workshops geared toward elementary and junior-level scouts. Reservations are required.

VIRGINIA

Busch Gardens. 1 Busch Gardens Boulevard, Williamsburg. (804) 253-3350, (800) 832-5665.

Paramount's Kings Dominion. 1600 Theme Park Way, Doswell. (800) 876-5000. Kings Dominion includes KidZville, with one-of-a-kind rides, activities, shows, and games designed just for children. The Taxi Jam Coaster is designed for child and parent together. There's also a Kidz Construction Company hands-on play area, a participatory Backyard Circus show, and walk-around Hanna-Barbera characters.

Trains and Trolleys

MARYLAND
B&O Museum. 901 West Pratt Street, at Poppleton Street, Baltimore. (410) 752-2490. (See page 116)
B&O Railroad Station Museum. Maryland Avenue and Main Street, Ellicott City. (410) 461-1944. (See page 118)
National Capital Trolley Museum. 1313 Bonifant Road between Lay-hill Road and New Hampshire Avenue, Wheaton. (301) 384-6088. (See page 129)

VIRGINIA
Fairfax Station Railroad Museum. 11200 Fairfax Station Road. (703) 425-9225. (See page 140)

Transportation

WASHINGTON
Metropolitan Area Transit Authority (WMATA). 600 Fifth Street, NW. (202) 637-7000. (See page 11)
Lil Red Trolley (Gold Line/Gray Line Co.). (202) 289-1995, (800) 862-1400. (See page 15)
Old Town Trolley Tours. (202) 832-9800. (See page 15)
Tourmobile. (202) 554-7950 (recording), (202) 554-7020 (information). (See page 14)
Bike the Sites, Inc. 3417 Quesada Street, NW. (202) 966-8662. bikesites@aol.com (See page 15)

Trapeze
Lessons are available for the next trapeze star, or for the dreamer.

VIRGINIA
Circus Arts Workshop. 1153 Bellview Road, Great Falls. (703) 759-9496. Open April through October. Classes are Wednesday and Thursday, 6 to 8 P.M.; Saturday and Sunday from 10 A.M. to noon; 1 to

3 P.M.; and 4 to 6 P.M. Single and series lessons are available. http://
www.circusarts.com. Ages 7 and up. Children and adults who are fascinated by the circus and gymnastics can learn the art of the trapeze with
the help of a net and safety belt. Lessons start with the basic, from a knee
hang to splits, to the advanced, with daring releases and catches. Michael
Bigotti and Laurent Givry, professional trapeze artists, and Chris
Donahue, a trained instructor, teach the lessons. Birthday parties that
include trapeze, juggling, and tightrope lessons can be booked.

Trash Tours

To see what happens to trash or lawn clippings after they're placed on the
curb in plastic bags, visit one of these sites. A recycling center probably
will offer a more fascinating and informative outing, but a landfill,
transfer station, or composting center will be interesting. Some offer
guided tours (others are self-guided) of the recycling and composting
facilities. Some have videotapes, scale models, or games. Call for a
schedule and an appointment (some only accept groups). **Ages 8 and up.**

MARYLAND
Annapolis Junction Transfer Station (groups). 8007 Brockbridge Road,
Jessup. (410) 724-5964.
Anne Arundel County Landfill. 389 Burns Crossing Road, Severn. (410)
222-6108.
Baltimore Resco. 1801 Annapolis Road, Baltimore. (410) 234-0808. A
fish hatchery is here as well.
BFI Recyclery. 7531 Cemetery Lane, Elkridge. (410) 471-4450.
Charles County Sanitary Landfill. 1001 Radio Station Road, La Plata.
(301) 870-2778.
Laidlaw Waste Systems. 9020 Edgeworth Drive, Capitol Heights. (301)
336-5932.
Montgomery County Recycling Center. 16105 Frederick Road,
Derwood. (301) 590-0046.
Montgomery County Transfer Station. 16101 Frederick Road,
Derwood. (301) 840-2370.
Prince George's County Recycling Center. 1000 Ritchie Highway,
Capitol Heights. (301) 883-7164.
Prince George's County Yard Waste Composting Facility. 6601 SE
Crain Highway, Upper Marlboro. (301) 627-6388.

VIRGINIA
Fairfax County I-66 Transfer Station and Recycling Center. 4681 West Ox Road, Fairfax. (703) 631-1179.
I-95 Energy/Resource Recovery Facility. 9898 Furnace Road, Lorton. (703) 690-6860.
Loudoun County Landfill (groups). 20933 Evergreen Mills Road, Leesburg. (703) 777-0187.
Prince William County Sanitary Landfill. 14311 Dumfries Road, Manassas. (703) 791-3660.
Ogden Martin Systems of Alexandria/Arlington. 5301 Eisenhower Avenue, Alexandria. (703) 370-7722.

Walking Tours (See also Nature Walks)

Learn about a number of walking tours offered through various tour services by calling First Class, an alternative, non-credit, adult-education organization, (202) 797-5102. Among the tours available are Capitol Hill, Inside the Capitol, Walking Tour of Arlington Cemetery, Adams-Morgan Walking Tour, and Monumental Washington.

Windsurfing

Several outfits in the area offer windsurfing lessons, but this list concentrates on rentals. Other opportunities can be found in Maryland at Ocean City and Annapolis.

VIRGINIA
Belle Haven Marina. George Washington Memorial Parkway, Alexandria. (703) 768-0018.
Washington Sailing Marina. George Washington Memorial Parkway, Alexandria. (703) 548-9027.

Zoos

MARYLAND
Baltimore Zoo. Druid Hill Park off exit 7 of Interstate 83, Baltimore. (410) 366-5466 (recording), (410) 396-7102 (administration). (See page 117)
Catoctin Mountain Zoological Park. U.S. 15, Thurmont. (301) 271-7488, (301) 662-2579. (See page 127)

Noah's Ark. Cabin John Regional Park, Tuckerman Lane, Bethesda. (301) 299-4555.

WASHINGTON

National Zoological Park. 3000 block of Connecticut Avenue, SW. (202) 357-2700 (Smithsonian information), (202) 673-4717 (direct line to zoo), (202) 357-1729 (TDD), (202) 357-1697 (voice recording). (See page 55)

Index
Index by Age Group

Ages 2 and up

Ages 3 and up

Ages 4 and up

Ages 5 and up

Index of Places